Other Books in This Series

The Management Century

THE MANAGEMENT

A *Strategy & Business* Book
Booz·Allen & Hamilton

CENTURY

A Critical Review of 20th Century Thought and Practice

Stuart Crainer

Foreword by Bruce A. Pasternack

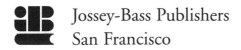

Jossey-Bass Publishers
San Francisco

Jossey-Bass books and products are available through most bookstores. To contact Jossey-Bass directly, call (888) 378–2537, fax to (800) 605–2665, or visit our website at www.josseybass.com.

Substantial discounts on bulk quantities of Jossey-Bass books are available to corporations, professional associations, and other organizations. For details and discount information, contact the special sales department at Jossey-Bass.

Manufactured in the United States of America

Library of Congress Cataloging-in-Publication Data

Crainer, Stuart.
The management century: a critical review of 20th century thought and practice/ Stuart Crainer.
p. cm.—(Jossey-Bass business & management series)
Includes bibliographical references and index.
ISBN 0-7879-5224-9
1. Management. I. Series.
HD31 .C686 2000
658—dc21   99-056006

FIRST EDITION
HB Printing   10 9 8 7 6 5 4 3 2 1

Contents

Foreword

Looking back on a hundred years of gains in organizational theory and productivity, it might seem that now is the time for management students and practitioners to kick back and enjoy—to savor the intellectual achievements and benefits the field of management has both attained and delivered. *The Management Century* argues, quite forcefully, that it is still too early to do that . . . and probably always will be.

Much of the value of Stuart Crainer's survey of management as a historic force stems from his unwillingness to be complacent about the great successes of the past hundred years. Crainer keeps his sights well focused on the equivocal nature of advances in management. Virtually every new concept that corrects the excesses and weaknesses of existing management practice carries the seeds of its own destruction. Typically, it will cause new problems that are the mirror image of the previous ones. Crainer's key message is the simple but always hard-to-take truth: *Nothing fails like success.*

Those who seek to master the discipline of management face a somewhat thankless task. As Crainer states: "Fifty-year-old lawyers can afford to sit back and contemplate their bedrock of knowledge, knowing that updating it will be an occasional chore. Managers have no such luxury. Fifty-year-old managers *can* look back and contemplate their knowledge. If they do so, they will quickly find themselves out of a job.

Management demands change and constant development. There is no hiding place. Updating knowledge is a continuing necessity."

That is a challenging statement, but it shouldn't be seen as defeatist. It is no more pessimistic than to say that the snowblower that served so well in January isn't going to prove helpful in June. Management responsibilities are heavily influenced by an ever-evolving operating environment—by changes in consumer demands, the technological state of the art, workforce expectations, and competitors' actions. As the dynamics of the world economy shift in response to those factors, managers must change the conceptual tools they use to ones that better meet the prevailing demands.

There is no question that managers' constant updating of knowledge occasionally requires wholesale rejection of practices that, only shortly before, had been accepted as *the* standard of excellence. Consider just a few examples Crainer cites (emphasis added throughout):

- "Scientific management [devised by management pioneer Frederick Winslow Taylor] established the job of management as measurement. The manager in Taylor's world was a mere supervisor, a recorder and reporter, gathering information with which to make a decision. What was measured got done. Period. This created an entirely new breed of managers dedicated to supervision, measurement, and observation. They were another layer in the hierarchy. This layer became known as middle management. *The man dedicated to efficiency* [Taylor] *thus created one of the most significant barriers to business efficiency and decision making.*"

- "[Henry] Ford's legacy was, at a macro level, an inspiring one. He was celebrated throughout the world for the sheer scale of his business endeavors and for the creation of a hugely influential product. Aldous Huxley's *Brave New World* (1932) labeled the modern era "A.F."—After Ford. . . . [But] Ford created a corporation built on fear and distrust. The fact that it was hugely successful should not deflect from this. Indeed, *in many ways Ford provides an archetypal lesson in how not to do things.* His management of people was appalling and his management of his company, after initial triumphs, limited. His early innovativeness eventually stagnated. Although his early days were marked by a constant quest for improvement, Ford refused to change the basic Model T technology until it was too late."

- "The multi-divisional form [of corporate structure invented by General Motors President Alfred P. Sloan Jr. during the 1920s] created a trend among large organizations for decentralization. In 1950 around 20 percent of Fortune 500 corporations were decentralized; this had increased to 80 percent by 1970. . . . [Yet, although it was] celebrated as a managerial exemplar . . . the deficiencies of Sloan's model gradually became apparent. The decentralized structure built up by Sloan revolved around a reporting and committee infrastructure that eventually became unwieldy. As time went by, more and more committees were set up. Stringent targets and narrow measures of success stultified initiative. By the end of the 1960s the delicate balance that Sloan had brilliantly maintained between centralization and decentralization was lost—finance emerged as the dominant function—and *GM became paralyzed by what had once made it great.*"

- "The achievements of reengineering, however, were twofold. First, it encouraged managers to consider once again the thorny issue of how best to organize their companies. Second, it promoted organization along process rather than functional lines. This was significant in that it broke free from the organizational rigidity inherent in functional organization. *The trouble was that reengineering replaced one form of organizational rigidity with another.*"

As Crainer notes, "Most management phenomena have a limited shelf life. They disappear from the corporate radar as quickly as misdirected Scud missiles." This is not to say that every management trend reaches an equally swift end. Some trends are linked to larger historic forces that help give them an extended life.

One such sustained trend is the movement toward more humanistic management. Some of management's early, legendary figures could be quite brutal by today's standards. "Now, one of the first requirements for a man who is fit to handle pig iron as a regular occupation is that he shall be so stupid and so phlegmatic that he more nearly resembles in his mental make-up the ox than any other type," Frederick Taylor once wrote. Likewise, Henry Ford stated, "We expect the men to do what they are told. The organization is so highly specialized and one part is so dependent on another that we could not for a moment consider allowing men to have their own way. Without the most rigid discipline we would have the utmost confusion."

Whatever usefulness these attitudes may once have had is long gone. Citing management's best-known thinker, Peter Drucker, Crainer notes that the quest for greater productivity alone—apart from any moral or quality-of-life considerations—will continue to force managers to be more attentive to the needs of individual workers: "Drucker argues that management's great achievement of the century was to increase the productivity of manual workers fiftyfold. While this cannot be underestimated, it is not the great challenge of the next century. This, according to Drucker, is to increase the productivity of knowledge workers— dauntingly, he estimates that *the productivity of some knowledge workers has actually declined over the last seventy years"* (emphasis added).

One of the great ironies of today's world is that although capitalism won big in the arena of politics, Marxism has scored its own victory in the workplace. Crainer has this to say: "Intellectual power is the new route to competitive advantage. This means that Karl Marx's objective of the workers controlling the means of production has been achieved. Our brains rule the corporate world. Capital used to be viewed in purely financial terms; now, it must increasingly be seen in intellectual terms."

Another historical trend sure to continue to shape management thinking and practice is the trend toward globalization. Since *The Management Century* covers a span of time that also has been termed "the American Century," it's not surprising that Americans have often seen themselves as the center of all that is original and truly useful in the field of management. American pride took a blow when "Japan Inc." was at the height of its power, but—amid the protracted stagnation of the Japanese economy and resurgence of American might in industry and services—it has certainly revived.

We can only hope that American management will not be too tempted to return to the chauvinistic attitudes that characterized the high point of American power in the postwar years. To do so would be foolish. The ever-increasing integration of the global economy and management's constant need for new ideas mean that *all* the world's best minds need to be tapped to sustain a steady stream of organizational innovations.

Crainer does a real service in pointing to some of the abundant management insights and advances that were *not* "made in the USA."

For instance, he credits French mining engineer Henri Fayol—whose "contribution . . . to management thinking is now all but ignored"—as being the first to recognize management "as a discipline in its own right" lending itself to systematic study. Turning to more recent times, Crainer also credits the contributions of visionaries such as Einar Thorsrud, founder of Oslo's Arbeidspsykologisk Institut, the driving force behind Scandinavia's experiments in industrial democracy, and Reg Revans, of the United Kingdom's National Coal Board, whose concept of *action learning* later helped trigger an economic renaissance in Belgium.

Crainer essentially argues that there are no final answers in management . . . just lasting questions. "Management continues to defy the theorists who would like to guide it into a corner and nail it down," he affirms. "It continues to escape. It continues to slip though the fingers." Ultimately, the task of trying to isolate what makes some companies world-class successes—such as General Electric, Dell, and Asea Brown Boveri—is as daunting as trying to catch lightning in a bottle. But that very prospect dazzles and entices. At some level, most people have at least an intuitive awareness that management, more than any other force, shapes our day-to-day existence as we enter the twenty-first century. Our nature is never to let so powerful a force remain veiled by mystery. We will continue to probe mighty enterprises and study great leaders, determined to identify what defines managerial excellence once and for all. We will discover that management and leadership are both necessary. Yet we will remain destined, as Crainer tells us, to capture only glimpses of the essence of success.

San Francisco, California
November 1999

Bruce A. Pasternack
Senior Vice President
and Managing Partner
Booz·Allen & Hamilton

Preface

What industrialization was to the 19th century, management is to
the 20th. Almost unrecognized in 1900, management has become
the central activity of our civilization. It employs a high proportion
of our educated men and determines the pace and quality of our
economic progress, the effectiveness of our government services and
the strength of our national defense. The way we "manage," the
way we shape our organizations, affects and reflects what our
society is becoming.
— *FORTUNE, 1966*[1]

The last hundred years have witnessed the dramatic genesis of management. Management has emerged as a profession. Management has
moved from an unspoken, informal, ad hoc activity into one that is routinely analyzed and commented on from every angle possible. Management has emerged from the shadows to be recognized as one of the
driving forces of economic and personal life. Its tentacles spread ever
further. Nothing—no organization, no activity—now appears beyond
the scope or ambition of management.

While management came of age during the twentieth century, it
would be foolish to suggest that it did not exist prior to 1900. Management has been practiced since the very dawn of civilization. But only
during the last one hundred years has it been recognized, analyzed,

monitored, taught, and formalized. The twentieth century was the management century.

Over this period, management has often been narrowly defined as relating to business. As the great management thinker, Peter Drucker, has pointed out, this does management a disservice. Management applies to more than the world of business. Indeed, Drucker argues that the creation of "city managers" early in the 1900s was one of the first occasions in which management, as it is now understood, was applied to a particular job. Management is as appropriate in local government as it is in a corporation. Management is as much at home in politics and government as it is in health care and hospitals. It is as useful in sports—coaching is just one aspect of management—as it is on the factory floor.

Management is all-embracing. Drucker says,

> There are, of course, differences in management between different organizations—mission defines strategy, after all, and strategy defines structure. But the differences between managing a chain of retail stores and managing a Roman Catholic diocese are amazingly fewer than either retail executives or bishops realize. The differences are mainly in application rather than in principles. The executives of all these organizations spend, for instance, about the same amount of their time on people problems—and the people problems are almost always the same.
>
> So whether you are managing a software company, a hospital, a bank or a Boy Scout organization, the differences apply to only about 10 percent of your work. This 10 percent is determined by the organization's specific mission, its specific culture, its specific history and its specific vocabulary. The rest is pretty much interchangeable.[2]

And management is the measure of greatness—both financial and ethical—within organizations. It is no surprise that Berkshire Hathaway chief Warren Buffett invests in well-managed companies. Time and time again, in statements of his investment philosophy, Buffett returns to the issue of sound management. He lauds some of his own managers: "They love their businesses, they think like owners, and they exude integrity and ability."[3] The quintessence of Buffett's investment philosophy is that given the right conditions, good managers produce good companies. Never invest in badly managed companies.

Yet management's recognition as a distinctive discipline has been hard-earned. Despite the executive superstars with their superstar salaries, the power and influence clearly enjoyed by managers, and the fact that a huge percentage of the working population work in managerial jobs, management is rarely regarded as the noblest of callings—or as a calling at all. Management is something people fall into. A job in the customer service department leads to marketing and, before you know it, you are vice president and people are asking you the meaning of management.

Saying "Management is—" leads to quizzical silence and furrowed brows whether you are on a factory floor in Nebraska, a Harvard seminar room, or a trading hall in Hong Kong. Similarly, management's standing in society is elusive. Is it deal making, the distrusted art of salesmanship, decision making, paper-shuffling admin, motivation, the science of analysis, budgeting, or the more distinguished art of leadership? All of them and more. "Corporations and managers suffer from a profound social ambivalence," leading theorists Sumantra Ghoshal, Christopher Bartlett, and Peter Moran have observed. "Hero-worshipped by the few, they are deeply distrusted by the many. In popular mythology, the corporate manager is Gordon Gecko, the financier who preaches the gospel of greed in Hollywood's Wall Street. Corporations are 'job killers.'"[4]

Management has had a bad press. The attraction—and the trouble—is that management is multifaceted. Pinning it down is like nailing Jell-O. It is marketing. It is strategy. It is inspiring people. It is budgeting. It is organizing projects and commitments. It is a complex, highly personal, and now truly global calling.

Given this complexity, it is no surprise that the historical and theoretical strands that go to make up contemporary management are many and varied. The great management thinkers are drawn from a bewildering variety of disciplines and professions—there are economists (such as Harvard Business School's Michael Porter); psychologists (such as Edgar Schein of the Massachusetts Institute of Technology); sociologists (such as Rosabeth Moss Kanter of Harvard Business School);

management consultants (such as Bruce Henderson and Marvin Bower); engineers aplenty (from Frederick Taylor to the civil engineering–trained Tom Peters); even a nuclear physicist, clarinet-playing would-be politician Kenichi Ohmae.

Recent years have seen an explosion of interest in the applicability of lessons from even more fields to management. Orchestra conductors, mariners, football stars, mountaineers, and poets are among those who now routinely address managers. Their message is that their skills, insights, and experience may have a practical use in modern management. (Often, it must be said, they are immune to the opposite argument that the skills, insights, and experience of managers could have a practical use in their occupations.)

The result is an incredibly rich tableau of ideas and best practice. Indeed, what increasingly marks management apart as a profession is its willingness to be driven by ideas. In management, theories make a difference; ideas are put to work and can change the lives of millions of people.

The reverse of this is that if ideas don't work, they are quickly consigned to history. This explains the continual churn of ideas. They come and go with increasing rapidity. Think back over the 1980s and 1990s.

First came what could loosely be termed "excellence," spawned by Tom Peters and Robert Waterman's best-selling *In Search of Excellence* (1982). Excellence led to the quality movement of the eighties. The likes of W. Edwards Deming, Joseph Juran, and Philip Crosby led the corporate world to quality circles, TQM, Just-in-Time and other techniques.

No letup. Then came the concept of the learning organization launched into public consciousness by Peter Senge's best-selling *Fifth Discipline*. The really big idea of the early 1990s, however, was reengineering, eventually followed by knowledge management and intellectual capital.

Theory and practice now appear more closely intertwined. (This has not made it any easier for bright ideas to become best practice—look at reengineering.) The divide between business schools and consulting firms has become blurred—and all but disappeared in some instances. Consulting firms increasingly share the intellectual high ground of thought leadership with the world's leading business schools.

Once anathema, close relationships between top management consulting firms and top business schools now feel entirely natural. They both share a mission to help shape the ideas and practice of business on a global basis, and to educate and nurture future generations of business leaders.

The Management Century aims to gather together many of these gloriously varied strands and provide a concise and insightful guide to the major developments in management thinking and practice during the twentieth century. It provides profiles of the lives and times of some of the great management thinkers and practitioners, as well as of the organizations they created.

To make sense of the maelstrom of bright ideas, hyper-energetic thinkers, and restless managers, the book is organized chronologically by decade. Although this is a generally useful means of organization, it is at times arbitrary. As a result, some events, ideas, and thinkers find themselves constrained by chronology into slightly unexpected surroundings. Each section ends with a timeline of significant events during the period discussed both in the corporate world and in the theoretical.

The end result is, I hope, persuasive and potent proof that management matters and that the twentieth century was truly the management century.

November 1999   Stuart Crainer
                               Twyford, Berkshire, United Kingdom

Acknowledgments

Thanks are chiefly due to Cedric Crocker of Jossey-Bass Publishers, Joel Kurtzman, editor of *Strategy & Business,* and the magazine's publisher, Max Henderson-Begg. The idea for the book was theirs and its genesis from idea to finished product owes a great deal to their insights.

I was assisted in researching *The Management Century* by Stephen Coomber. I hope that his persistence and research shine through the text.

I am grateful to a variety of sources for permission to quote from their work. Quotations from *The Fifth Discipline* by Peter M. Senge are used by permission of Doubleday, a division of Random House. The Brookings Institution allowed me to reproduce a table from A.D.H. Kaplan's *Big Enterprise in a Competitive System,* and Bessie Sparkes Eagles allowed material to be used from Alfred P. Sloan's *Adventures of a White Collar Man.* Time Life granted permission to reproduce excerpts from the Fortune 500 and four tables from TIME Magazine, and Alfred A. Knopf Inc. permitted an extract from Tom Peters's *Liberation Management.*

The Management Century

Chapter 1
1900–1910: Stopwatch Science

> Scientific management does not exist and cannot exist until there
> has been a complete mental revolution on the part of the workmen
> working under it, as to their duties toward themselves and toward
> their employers, and a complete mental revolution in the outlook
> for the employers, toward their duties, toward themselves, and
> toward their workmen.
> —FREDERICK TAYLOR[1]

Bangs and a Feather Duster

Elihu Root (1845–1937) was an exceptional man. Yet the life of this
dandy of the late nineteenth and early twentieth centuries is generally
overlooked amid the pantheon of great statesman and empire-creating
business heroes.

Root was a brilliant lawyer with a ruthless streak and a capacity to
get things done. In one criminal trial, the judge pointedly advised Root
to spend more time with his conscience. Theodore Roosevelt, whom
Root keenly supported, referred to him as "the greatest man that has
arisen on either side of the Atlantic in my lifetime" adding that Root
was "the brutal friend to whom I pay the most attention."[2]

If you wanted brutality with bangs, you called on Root. No less an authority than Gore Vidal described him as "an animated feather-duster." President McKinley called in 1899, asking him to become Secretary of War. This was a surprising appointment. Root was an active New York Republican and lawyer, but was largely unknown and untried. McKinley recognized that Root's brand of intellectual force was what was required in the aftermath of the Spanish-American War.

The war had been won. It had, however, revealed the American military machine to be a complete shambles. The army had problems devising its strategy because it didn't have any maps of the right areas. Soldiers were dispatched to Cuba with winter uniforms. Logistics were chaotic—at one point three hundred railroad cars arrived in Tampa, Florida, without anyone knowing what they contained. After the war's end, the Dodge Commission sought to get to the bottom of the incompetence. It took eight volumes and concluded that "no well regulated . . . corporation could transact business satisfactorily" if organized as the military then was.[3]

The Secretary of War, Russell A. Alger, did the decent thing and resigned, leaving the way open for Elihu Root. What then followed was a complete reorganization of the U.S. Army. The feather duster indulged in a rigorous spot of spring cleaning.

Root identified a lack of coordination among the various parts of the army as a key problem. He wanted to make the various army chiefs accountable and in touch. Too many, Root lamented, "had become entrenched in Washington armchairs."[4] The army's administration was reorganized, a War College established, and—among many other initiatives—a General Staff created. When Root was questioned by Congress on his innovations, one Senator observed that "Washington and Napoleon had no need for strategy boards."

"Well, they are dead; dead as our present system," said Root with commendable brevity.[5]

Elihu Root may occupy a mere footnote in history, but the changes he instigated and made happen in the U.S. Army had wider implications. They were, says Peter Drucker, "the first conscious and systematic application of management principles."[6] Modern management was launched with bangs and a feather duster.

Mining the Theory

While Elihu Root was practicing what we would now call management, he probably would have called it administration—or perhaps, more bluntly, common sense. At the turn of the twentieth century, management lay largely undefined.[7] Or, more accurately, the most convincing attempt at providing a definition for management was little known. This came from a somewhat surprising source, a French mining engineer called Henri Fayol (1841–1925).

The contribution of Fayol to management thinking is now all but ignored. He is granted a passing mention in management textbooks. The fact that he was French is also something of a surprise—perhaps even a handicap in an Anglo-Saxon–dominated discipline. The French have proved remarkably immune to the popularization of the modern management model. Largely indifferent to the wiles of business gurus, skeptical of fashionable theories, they have pursued a doggedly independent course.

Fayol was educated in Lyon, France, and at the National School of Mines in St. Etienne. In 1860 he graduated as a mining engineer and joined the French mining company, Commentry-Fourchamboult-Décazeville. Fayol spent his entire working career with that company. He saved it from the brink of bankruptcy and was managing director between 1888 and 1918.

Along the way, Fayol formulated a distinct managerial philosophy. Fayol's contribution to the management century was threefold.

First, he recognized the universality of management. Management was as applicable to a mining company in France to a hospital or to the French postal office.

Second, Fayol identified management as a discipline in its own right. This hardly appears startling—but until then, "management" as an entity had scarcely existed.

The logical conclusion from this was that it could be rigidly defined. To a hardheaded rationalist like Fayol existence demanded the clarity of definition. What couldn't be defined could hardly be said to exist. If management was a legitimate discipline, what did managers actually do and what did they hope to achieve by doing so?

In response, Fayol developed fourteen "general principles of management." These, he said, were the universal characteristics of management:

- Division of work
- Authority and responsibility
- Discipline
- Unity of command
- Unity of direction
- Subordination of individual interest to general interest
- Remuneration of employees
- Centralization
- The scalar chain
- Order
- Equity
- Stability of personnel
- Initiative
- *Esprit de corps*

Fayol's fourteen principles were what concerned managers—or what should concern managers. To ensure that they were put into effective practice, Fayol said that managers needed to plan, organize, command, coordinate (which has now metamorphosed into lead), and control.

The corollary of Fayol's mapping out of managerial principles was that if something could be defined it could be taught. He provided a starting point for the entire concept—and practice—of management education. Indeed, Fayol lectured at the Ecole Supérieure de la Guerre and, in retirement, set up a Center of Administrative Studies. (In France Fayol's lectures provoked a groundswell of interest in management—by 1925, fifteen thousand copies of his lectures had been printed and a book of his lectures was published.)

And, if management was universal, it was plainly logical that the management skills acquired through education could be universally applied. Nowadays we are used to the concept of the CEO of a software company decamping to a new job at a pharmaceutical company. We believe that the CEO's job does not require detailed knowledge of the exact recipe for a particular drug or of the arcane languages needed by a software programmer. The CEO practices management skills. But, in Fayol's age, work—even in factories—was a matter of specialization. Work restricted. Its parameters were understood. Management opened up new vistas.

Fayol's theory of management—labeled "administrative management"—has proved defiantly and astonishingly robust. While most ambitious theories wither on the vines of time and progress, Fayol's remains largely accurate. Not for nothing is the most prestigious management qualification entitled a Master of Business Administration.

Among the work of all the early thinkers on the subject, Fayol's ideas have probably been the most enduring. At the same time they have been among the most neglected. Fayol's book *Administrative Management* only appeared in English in 1929 (and even then in an obscure edition) and has long disappeared from sight.

Renaissance Man with a Stopwatch

Parallel to Henri Fayol's career was that of Frederick Winslow Taylor (1856–1915). While Fayol wrestled with the broader theoretical question of the nature of management, Taylor was a man of devotedly practical intent, a problem solver. Indeed, Taylor was the ultimate problem solver. In an age that produced more than its fair share of dilettantes, Taylor was a veritable Renaissance man. The breadth of his insights and interests is, even now in an age of hyperbole, astonishing.

Taylor was an inventor. Most notably, working with the metallurgist Maunsel White, he developed the Taylor-White Process for treating tool steel. This revolutionized metal cutting and enabled the development of mass production techniques. Taylor's restless inventiveness spawned over forty patents and made him a fortune. These covered everything from 1909's "Apparatus for Moving Growing Trees and the Like" to a revolutionary "Power Hammer" built for the Midvale Steel Company in the late 1880s, from an apparatus for grinding balls (1900) to a "combined hothouse grapery and greenhouse" (1907).

Taylor was a sportsman. Though apparently not a wonderfully gifted natural athlete, Taylor brought dogged determination and inventiveness to all his endeavors. In 1881 he won the doubles at the U.S. tennis championships. Not content, Taylor then designed his own tennis racket, which resembled a spoon. His patent pageant also included a lawn tennis net (Patent No. 401,082 issued April 9, 1889).

Then Taylor turned his mind to golf. Like many other players through the ages, he encountered problems with his putting. There were no golf gurus to consult, so Taylor attempted to sort out the problem through his own inventiveness. The result was a Y-shaped putter (Patent No. 792,631 issued June 20, 1905)—perhaps the first attempt by anyone to beat the "yips." There is no evidence that this improved his game. Putting obviously took a hold on his imagination because Taylor then looked at putting greens. At his family home in Chestnut Hill, Pennsylvania, he began experimenting with the grass that made up the greens. The trouble was that in the pre-sprinkler age, greens were unpredictable as they relied on rainfall. Taylor believed the problem could be solved by developing a putting green that was not fed by rainfall but by water from below the surface of the soil.[8]

In his quest for solutions, Taylor eschewed notions such as fair play. Greater efficiency was right. Period. It didn't matter if you were talking about hitting a golf ball more accurately or making steel. Inevitably this didn't always go down well. Golf people are not renowned for their willingness to embrace progress. The sight of Fred Taylor strolling down the fairway armed with extra-long clubs with customized heads had members hastily scrambling for their rule books. They might have thrown the rule books away and taken up other sports if they'd seen Taylor's purpose-built harness, which enabled him to drive perfectly every time.

Taylor brought this level of commitment to all of his many and varied activities. He had a passion for order and efficiency—typically, at school he reveled in the neatness of Dewey's classification and subject index for libraries. "He was not the steam roller that some people like to represent him," said one of disciples, Henry Gantt, "but he did believe that a strenuous life was the life worthwhile, and that it not only brought more financial compensation, but that it added to the usefulness and happiness of men."[9]

And Taylor was incredibly persistent. When Taylor presented his paper "On the Art of Cutting Metals" to the American Society of Mechanical Engineers in 1906, it was the result of twenty-six years of experimentation. Taylor's experiments involved cutting over 800,000 pounds of steel and iron into chips with experimental tools. Records were kept of some 30,000 to 50,000 experiments costing the then enormous sum of between $150,000 and $200,000.

An inventor and sportsman he may have been—but, most of all, Taylor was an analytically driven solver of problems.

For this reason, he is often acknowledged as the first management consultant—his business card at one point labeled him a "Consultant to Management." His faith in using the latest analytical tools to provide a solution to a business problem created the template for the modern consultant. Henry Gantt once described Taylor in these terms: "Endowed naturally with untiring energy and a wonderfully analytical mind, he concentrated all the power of that combination on the problem of determining the facts he needed. . . . He was interested in what had been done mainly for the indication it gave of what could be done."[10] (Another disciple of Taylor's, Harrington Emerson, later termed consulting "efficiency engineering."[11])

Looking at Work

The inveterate tinkerer, problem solver, and inventor was born into an affluent Philadelphia family on March 20, 1856. Taylor's father was a lawyer from an old Pennsylvania Quaker family; his mother, Emily Winslow, from an old New England Puritan family. (Her father was a New Bedford whaler.) Emily was a prominent anti-slavery agitator and a campaigner for women's rights.

Taylor was taught in France and Germany, and traveled throughout Europe before eventually returning to the Phillips Exeter Academy. (Taylor retained strong European connections throughout his life. He spent vacations in Brittany and shortly before his death saluted the French and Belgian attempts at repelling the German forces in World War One.)

Despite his well-heeled background, Taylor began his working life at the bottom of the engineering ladder. He initially worked as an apprentice at the William Sellers Company in Philadelphia. In 1878 he left to work at the Midvale Steel Company, near Philadelphia. At Midvale Taylor began as a clerk though he soon moved back down the company's ranks to become a laborer. Taylor's role appeared to change almost monthly. In six years at Midvale he was keeper of tool cribs, then assistant foreman, foreman, master mechanic, director of research, and finally chief engineer of the entire plant. While working he also reactivated his academic career. (He had, as befitted one of his social status, been destined for Harvard before poor eyesight reputedly intervened.) Taylor spent three years (1880–1883) studying engineering at evening classes at the Stevens Institute.[12]

Taylor remained at Midvale until around 1889—he later worked at a variety of places, most notably the Bethlehem Steel Company. At Bethlehem he attempted wide-ranging changes. Not all of these were either successful or popular and Taylor was eventually fired in 1901. While at Midvale Taylor laid the basis for his theories of what became known as *scientific management.*[13] It was scientific management (described by Taylor as "seventy-five percent science and twenty-five percent common sense") that made Taylor one of the most influential figures of the twentieth century. Even today, his influence remains strong on many businesses throughout the world. A 1997 *Fortune* article noted: "Taylor's influence is omnipresent: It's his ideas that determine how many burgers McDonald's expects its flippers to flip or how many callers the phone company expects its operators to assist."[14]

Peter Drucker has cited Taylor's thinking as "the most lasting contribution America has made to Western thought since the Federalist Papers." Wasn't Henry Ford a bigger deal? No, says Drucker. The assembly line was simply a logical extension of scientific management.[15]

The origins of scientific management lay in Taylor's observations of his fellow workers. He noticed that they engaged in what was then called *soldiering.* Instead of working as hard and as fast as they could, they deliberately slowed down. After all, they had no incentive to go faster or to be more productive. It was in their interest, Taylor said, to keep "their employers ignorant of how fast work can be done."[16] "Nineteen out of twenty workmen throughout the civilized world firmly believe that it is for their best interests to go slow instead of to go fast. They firmly believe that it is for their interest to give as little work in return for the money that they get as is practical," Taylor later wrote in *The Principles of Scientific Management*.[17]

The workers had one notable advantage: their superiors had no idea how long a job should take. No one had thought to examine the nature of people's work. Irritated by such brazen inefficiency, Taylor set to. Armed with a stopwatch, he examined in intimate detail exactly what happened and how long it took. Taylor surmised that minute examination of a task would enable the observer to establish the best means of carrying out the job. A single preferred, efficient means of completing the task could then be established and insisted on in the future. Working in the most efficient manner, Taylor calculated, a theoretical pig iron handler called Schmidt could load forty-seven tons a day rather than the more usual twelve and a half tons.

This meant that workers would know exactly what was expected of them and that managers would know exactly how much should be produced. It also meant that more accurate piecework rates could be set with more reliable bonuses and penalties. The introduction of Taylor's ideas at the Watertown Arsenal reduced the labor cost of making certain molds for the pommel of a packsaddle from $1.17 to 54 cents. The labor cost of building a six-inch gun-carriage fell from $10,229 to $6,950. The logic was simple. Measurement increased production as everyone knew what they had to do. Increased production was achieved with lower costs and this led to bigger profits. The gap between the increases in production and pay was increased profit. Typically, Schmidt increased production by 400 percent while receiving 60 percent more pay.

None of this, in itself, looks like a particularly remarkable feat. One man and a stopwatch hardly appear the recipe for a revolution in attitudes. However, Taylor lived in more cavalier times. It is interesting that the pursuit of order should have occupied such minds as those of Dewey and Taylor. Their inspiration was the disorder they saw all around.

Take Taylor's stopwatch. When he produced it with characteristic élan at Midvale, time-consciousness was something of a novelty. In the United States, time zones were only standardized in 1883. Prior to that myriad local time zones existed. Taylor's stopwatch was symptomatic of the change. Time was no longer announced by the rising of the sun or the church clock; it was loudly pronounced by the siren from the factory or the factory clock. Time was measured and announced by managers.

Measured Management

The implications of Taylor's philosophy were felt across the world. Henri Fayol's ideas largely failed to find a mass audience, but scientific management became the first international management theory. It was the TQM or intellectual capital of its day. Taylor's work was known and devoured in Japan. In Russia Lenin was a fan. In France his champion was the metallurgist, Henri Le Chatelier. By the time of Taylor's death, two editions of the French translation of *The Principles of Scientific Management* had been printed and four thousand sold (another three thousand had been, according to Chatelier, "gratuitously distributed").

Taylor's message was timely. The obvious assumption of Taylor's philosophy—and Henry Ford's eventual practice—was that more was good. The need to produce more and in a more efficient way was taken as a first principle. As markets stood waiting to be invented and discovered, this was a fair conclusion. The world was desperate to produce more, to be able to manage its fledgling industries in more efficient ways. If America had abundant land and natural resources, why couldn't it have abundant production capabilities? Taylor's ideas were of their time and for their time.

The pursuit of more—more production, more markets—was the managerial quest of the twentieth century. Taylor provided the means. The ends were assumed and accepted by virtually all who considered them. (Only in the 1990s—with overcapacity in many industries—has this slipped down the level of priorities.) One of the few doubting voices was the novelist John Dos Passos. In his sprawling masterpiece, *USA,* Dos Passos lamented the relentless pursuit of "more steel rails more bicycles more spools of thread more armorplate for battleships more bedpans more barbed wire more needles more lightningrods more ballbearings more dollarbills."[18]

In practice, scientific management often boosted production. In 1910 Harrington Emerson claimed that the U.S. railroads could save $1 million a day if they used scientific management. As working processes had been previously ignored this was not altogether surprising. The immediate result of scientific management, according to Peter Drucker, was a dramatic cut in the cost of manufactured goods. Often costs fell to a fraction—a tenth to a twentieth—of previous levels.[19] This allowed goods to be purchased by more people. Also, scientific management—potentially at least—allowed the raising of wages (even while the cost of the product was dropping).

In terms of management, Taylor's crucial contribution was to invent management as science. Taylor brought analytical vigor to the workplace. Prior to Taylor, no one had scientifically analyzed the nature of work. Taylor brought rigor and discipline to the workplace. He looked at work anew. It is notable, if somewhat bizarre, that the actual tasks undertaken by people in the course of their work have been so little examined. This is particularly true for managerial work. Examinations of what managers actually do are few and far between, even now. The most significant is Henry Mintzberg's study in the early 1970s, which led to his groundbreaking book, *The Nature of Managerial Work* (1973). Mintzberg's conclusions would have shocked and appalled Frederick Taylor—Mintzberg found that managers flitted from task to task, job to job, in a thoroughly inefficient manner.

Taylor's examination of work was significant. Equally so was the fact that scientific management established the job of management as measurement. The manager in Taylor's world was a mere supervisor, a recorder and reporter, gathering information with which to make a decision. What was measured got done. Period.

This created an entirely new breed of managers dedicated to supervision, measurement, and observation. They were another layer in the hierarchy. This layer became known as middle management. The man dedicated to efficiency thus created one of the most significant barriers to business efficiency and decision making.

Taylor's philosophy was not simply related to particular tasks. His introduction to *The Principles of Scientific Management* (1911) pronounced his intention "to show that the fundamental principles of scientific management are applicable to all kinds of human activities, from our simplest individual acts to the work of our great corporations." Scientific management, in Taylor's mind at least, was all encompassing. Once accepted and initiated it covered the entire organization. By measuring each and every task, a company could establish a process of working, a system. Work could be scheduled because the company knew how long each task took and how many people it required. Inventory could be managed and, as a result, finances organized and purchasing systems introduced. One thing led remorselessly to another. Logic could—and would if Frederick Taylor had anything to do with it—take over the world.

There is, perhaps, an air of familiarity to this. Indeed, the logic of processes was the cornerstone of a more recent managerial fashion: reengineering. The basic idea behind reengineering was that organizations needed to identify their key processes and make them as lean and efficient as possible. Peripheral processes (and, therefore, peripheral people) needed to be discarded. The movement's chief theoreticians, James Champy and Michael Hammer, authors of the best-selling *Reengineering the Corporation,* defined reengineering as "the fundamental rethinking and radical redesign of business processes to achieve dramatic improvements in critical measures of performance such as cost, quality, service and speed."

The similarities with Taylor's ideas are clear. So, too, is the hyperbole. Taylor talked of a revolution in thought; Champy and Hammer announced that true reengineering was all-embracing, a recipe for a corporate revolution. "Reengineering calls loudly for action, but its philosophy is prosaic in the extreme. . . . Its focus is on corporate mechanics, not on vision or strategy," observed one critic.[20] Reengineering, as the name suggested, owed more to visions of the corporation as a machine than as a human, or humane, system.

A further comparison with reengineering is that scientific management was often an excuse for crude reductions in employee numbers. Typically, at the Simonds Roller Bearing Company, Taylor's involvement led to headcount being cut from 120 to 35.

The clearest echo of scientific management in reengineering was its concentration on process—business process reengineering was one label attached to the movement. This process-driven model of management can be traced back to Adam Smith's pathbreaking work in the eighteenth century. Maximizing the efficiency of our processes, whether we are widget-makers or McDonald's, has been top of the managerial agenda. Efficient, lean processes with cost-efficient overheads have become regarded as the quickest route to profit heaven.

Contemporary thinkers suggest that good intentions have not been matched by reality. "Overhead in major corporations is not decreasing," note management consultants Charles Lucier and Janet Torsilieri.[21] One contributory factor to this is the rise of the knowledge worker. As Peter Drucker has jokingly lamented, "knowledge workers are abysmally unproductive."

Lucier and Torsilieri suggest that the overriding emphasis on creating processes to divide physical labor—the basic tenet of Taylor's thinking—needs now to be replaced by an emphasis on the division of mental labor. The route to this requires a number of steps. First, routine work—a depressing 80 percent of what we do—needs to be standardized. This means giving people more responsibility, cutting out middlemen. Second, Lucier and Torsilieri suggest that companies "outsource the most complex (often most critical) decisions to the real experts." "Outsourcing the most complex decisions significantly increases both the quality of decisions and level of service," they say. The end result will be lower costs (though only slightly). "Companies will both eliminate expertise-driven overhead and better manage the productivity of knowledge workers," say Lucier and Torsilieri.

Such arguments suggest that the legacy of scientific management may have run its course. Perhaps most persuasively, Peter Drucker argues that management's great achievement of the century was to increase the productivity of manual workers fiftyfold. Although this cannot be underestimated, it is not the great challenge of the next century. This, according to Drucker, is to increase the productivity of knowledge workers—dauntingly, he estimates that the productivity of some knowledge workers has actually declined over the last seventy years.[22]

The Problem with Schmidt

As Drucker's conclusions suggest, although Taylor made the study of work an important discipline and identified the importance of establishing and defining working processes, the downside of Taylor's neat theories was substantial. It is one thing to invent a machine that drives a golf ball two hundred yards down the middle of the fairway in fine weather; quite another to design a machine that can do the same in a strong wind. Life was never as orderly and as controllable as Taylor suggested or hoped.

The first downside of Taylor's thinking was that he put efficiency before ethics. (Again the comparisons with reengineering are strong: it became closely identified with downsizing rather than improving working life and corporate performance.) It is notable that the moral and ethical element behind business was strong throughout the nineteenth century. Many of the great companies that began at this time had a strong ethical element to them. Think of the great British industrialists—people like Robert Owen at the beginning of the nineteenth century, the chocolate manufacturers Bourneville and Cadbury, Lord Lever of Lever Brothers (the precursor of Unilever). Their empires were huge, their fortunes vast—but beneath them stood strong benevolent principles.

Scientific management, however, put efficiency first. Not that Taylor didn't have any thoughts about the wider implications of his ideas. He would have argued that increased efficiency worked for the betterment of all. In this his views were basically in accord with those of socialism. "The principal object of management should be to secure the maximum prosperity for the employer, coupled with the maximum prosperity for each employee," he wrote in *The Principles of Scientific Management.*[23]

Taylor argued that "whenever any labor-saving device of any kind has been introduced into any trade . . . the result has universally been to make work for more men in that trade, not work for less men."[24] The theory was that scientific management increased productivity and lessened costs, enabling lower prices and, as a result, more sales and greater profits. This was all very well until the competition did the same.

At times, Taylor the rationalist struck a naively optimistic tone. "The great good comes from the fact that, under scientific management, they [the workers] look upon their employers as the best friends they have in the world; the suspicious watchfulness which characterizes the old type management, the semi-antagonism, or the complete antagonism between workmen and employers is entirely superseded, and in its place comes genuine friendship between both sides."[25]

Taylor believed that improving the efficiency of production would enhance society. He was not alone. In 1882, Carroll D. Wright, chief of the Massachusetts Bureau of Statistics of Labor, noted, "Better morals, better sanitary conditions, better health, better wages, these are the practical results of the factory system, as compared with what preceded it, and the results of all these have been a keener intelligence."[26] (Admittedly, Taylor says nothing about keener intelligence. This was not what he had in mind.)

Dr. Alexander C. Humphreys, president of the Stevens Institute of Technology, heard one of Taylor's acolytes, Henry Gantt, give a speech on scientific management and observed, "I venture to believe that if this system were generally introduced through the United States, the resulting moral uplift would attract more attention than the increase in dividend-earning capacity."

Scientific management may not have produced a moral uplift, but it was not immoral; it simply subsumed moral considerations under the rationalist drive toward efficiency. People were fodder. Scientific management was built on a lack of trust, a lack of respect for the worth, wit, and intelligence of individuals. In Taylor's mind, management was an ascetic science rather than a humane one. Once again, Taylor was simply reflecting the priorities of his time. Charles Babbage, the English mathematician and creator of the forerunner of the modern computer, wrote one of the first business best-sellers—*On the Economy of Machinery and Manufacturers* (1832). Babbage contended that as machines became more powerful and required less skill to operate them workers with less skills were required. If the machines needed automatons, why employ creative craftsmen?

Little wonder then that Italian Marxist Antonio Gramsci observed in *Americanismo e Fordismo* that "Taylor expresses the real purpose of

American society—replacing in the worker the old psycho-physical nexus of qualified professional work, which demanded active participation, intelligence, fantasy, and initiative, with automatic and mechanical attitudes. This is not a new thing, it is rather the most recent, the most intense, the most brutal phase of a long process that began with industrialism itself. This phase will itself be superseded by the creation of a new psycho-physical nexus, both different from its predecessors and superior. As a consequence, a part of the old working class will be eliminated from the world of work, and perhaps from the world."[27]

Indeed, it was believed that the less thought applied to the task, the more productive the worker was likely to be. Working was not thinking. "Now, one of the first requirements for a man who is fit to handle pig iron as a regular occupation is that he shall be so stupid and so phlegmatic that he more nearly resembles in his mental make-up the ox than any other type," Taylor famously and unfortunately wrote. "He is so stupid that the word 'percentage' has no meaning to him, and he must consequently be trained by a man more intelligent than himself into the habit of working in accordance with the laws of this science before he can be successful."[28]

Similarly, people did not need to be told what was happening elsewhere in the organization. Ignorance was bliss—and good business sense. According to Taylor, there was no need to spread confusion through communication. Employees had to turn their minds off and perform their tasks. Taylor's theories denied people their individuality. And, after initial enthusiasm, people did not like it. Taylor envisaged a world in which industrial conflict was to be replaced by "scientific determination." In *The Principles of Scientific Management,* he wrote of "a determined effort to in some way change the system of management, so that the interests of the workmen and the management should become the same, instead of antagonistic."[29]

There were often few signs of the budding friendships envisaged somewhat wistfully by Taylor when scientific management was implemented. In 1909, over 3,500 unorganized mass production workers revolted against the inhuman working conditions produced by an efficiency drive at U.S. Steel. Proclaiming scientific management as its creed, the company brought in a new production line and a piece rate system that accelerated the production line. Simultaneously, the company reduced take-home pay for the majority of its workers. Controversy dogged the implementation of Taylor's ideas elsewhere.

This was put down to ignorance by Taylor's disciples. The workers did not recognize a good thing when it was foisted upon them. "Taylor was a great scientist. He established certain truths, fundamental in their nature," said Louis Brandeis at a memorial to Taylor at the University of Pennsylvania's Houston Hall, before going on to lament, "We who have had occasion to consider the hostility of labor leaders to the introduction of scientific management, know that the hostility has in large measure been due to misunderstanding. Much of all the waste which Taylor undertook to eliminate has no direct relation to the specific functions of the workingman. It deals with waste in machinery, in supplies, in planning, in adjustment of production and distribution—matters in which changes cannot possibly affect the workman injuriously. And yet we found in many leaders of labor undiscriminating opposition to the whole of the so-called Taylor system."[30]

In 1911 and 1912 Taylor was questioned at length by a special committee of the U.S. House of Representatives. As a result, somewhat comically, laws were passed banning the use of stopwatches by civil servants—restrictions only lifted in 1949.

Taylor was undeterred. The revolution could not be postponed. Looking to the future, Taylor envisaged a world of standardization, of systematic production. He foresaw the emergence of a new breed of tabulators. Men with stopwatches would control the world. Taylor predicted, "The determination of the best method of performing all of our daily acts will, in the future, be the work of experts who first analyze and then accurately time while they watch the various ways of doing each piece of work and who finally know from exact knowledge—and not from anyone's opinion—which method will accomplish the results with the least effort and in the quickest time. The exact facts will have in this way been developed and they will constitute a series of laws which are destined to control the vast multitude of our daily personal acts which, at present, are the subjects of individual opinion."[31]

The nightmarish vision of regularity—explored in literature by Aldous Huxley in *Brave New World* and George Orwell in *1984*—was summed up by Carl Barth, who told the U.S. Commission of Industrial Relations: "My dream is that the time will come when every drill press will be speeded just so, and every planer, every lathe the world over will be harmonized just like musical pitches are the same all over the world . . . so that we can standardize and say that for drilling a 1–inch hole the world over will be done with the same speed. . . . That dream will come true, some time."[32] Some time, perhaps.

The Management Century Timeline

1900

At the turn of the century the average American weekly wage is $9.30—the same as it was in 1870.

Eastman Kodak Company introduces the Brownie box camera.

Bayer's brand of aspirin becomes the first major drug marketed as a convenient tablet—in the United States, 2 billion are now consumed annually.

1901

Walt Disney is born in Chicago.

J.P. Morgan buys Carnegie Steel, which later becomes U.S. Steel.

The Gillette brand starts life on the Boston waterfront as the Gillette Safety Razor Company. The company founder, King Camp Gillette (1855–1932) invested years in developing a product and trying to persuade investors to put their money into the company. Production of its razor sets and blades does not begin until 1903.

The Amos Tuck School of Business at Dartmouth College, the world's first graduate school of management, awards its first degree.

1902

The editors of the *Wall Street Journal* take over management of the Dow Jones Industrial Average after Charles Dow's death.

Franklin C. Mars, aged nineteen, begins selling confectionery.

Pepsi-Cola Company founded.

1903

In Milwaukee a young man called William Harley, and his friend Arthur Davidson, begin experiments on "taking the work out of bicycling." They are joined by Arthur's brothers, Walter and William. They begin production in 1903, build their first business premises at the company's current Juneau Avenue site in 1906, and Harley-Davidson is incorporated in 1907. The total output that year was 150 motorcycles. By the time the famous V-twin went into production two years later the company was cranking out more than 1,100 motorcycles a year.

The Wright brothers make their first flight.

Ford Motor Company founded.

1904

Charles Rolls and Henry Royce found the Rolls-Royce company with the immodest purpose of building "the best car in the world."

First section of the New York City subway opens.

1905

Formation of the Industrial Workers of the World (Wobblies).

1906

William Keith Kellogg establishes the Battle Creek Toasted Corn Flake Company in a wooden shed in Battle Creek, Michigan. The shed didn't last—it was burnt down within a year—Kelloggs the corporation did.

The Dow closes above 100 for the first time on January 12, 1906.

An earthquake followed by a fire destroys the headquarters and two factories of Levi-Strauss & Co. In response, the company extends credit to its wholesale customers so they can get back on their feet and back in business. The company carries on paying its employees and a temporary office and showroom is opened to give them some work to do while a new HQ and factory were being built. Later, during the Great Depression, the then CEO Walter Haas Sr. employed workers laying new floors at the company's Valencia Street plant in San Francisco rather than laying them off.

British Labour Party formed.

Charles Nestlé develops the "permanent" for hair.

1907

Panic in the stock market. More follow.

General Electric is reinstated in the Dow. (It had been removed from the Dow in 1898, returning in the next year only to be removed again in 1901.) After its reinstatement in 1907, it has been in the index ever since.

1908

At the request of President Charles W. Eliot, the Corporation of Harvard University votes to establish a school of business administration. Edwin F. Gay is appointed first dean of Harvard Business School and its first enrollment was of thirty-three regular students and forty-seven special students, taking only certain courses. It awarded its first Master's degree in management in 1910.

William Crapo Durant (1861–1947) founds the General Motors Company of New Jersey.

Ford introduces the Model T.

1909

The year's Sears, Roebuck catalog includes shows at $1.50, a piano (the most expensive) for $138, the best gramophone for $45, and a typewriter for $22.95.

1910

Ford's huge Highland Park plant opens.

Chapter 2
1911–1920: Modern Times

> I have heard it said, in fact I believe it is quite a current thought, that we have taken skill out of work. We have not. We have put in skill. We have put a higher skill into planning, management and tool building, and the results of that skill are enjoyed by the man who is not skilled. . . . The rank and file of men come to us unskilled; and they learn their jobs within a few hours or a few days. If they do not learn within that time they will never be of any use to us.
> —HENRY FORD[1]

The Route to Ford

In 1911 if you had wanted to seek out the future at work, you would have boarded a Chicago-bound train from New York. Once in Chicago, after a long and creaky journey, you would have made your way to one of its more distant suburbs, Highland Park, Michigan. There you would have seen one of the wonders of the industrial world and the first great management wonder of the twentieth century: the Ford factory. The company's Highland Park plant was opened in January 1910 and produced

15 million Model Ts between then and 1927. More than 700,000 were built in 1917 alone. It was the industrial triumph of its time.

The achievements of the Ford company and its founder Henry Ford (1863–1947) are justifiably celebrated. Henry Ford is routinely lauded as the creator of mass production and of the production line. This is, as is usually the way, only partly true. Ford was undoubtedly the first great exponent of mass production, but the roots of the systems he used are long and complex.

In simple production terms, there is little doubt that Ford was at the leading edge. Highland Park was the manufacturing benchmark. Over a hundred years of development had gradually seen the scale and ambition of factories expand. In the late eighteenth century Richard Arkwright (1732–1792) created factories in northwestern England. His management technique was based on the strict division of labor. Throughout the nineteenth century, the evolution of the factory was rapid. There were the armory shops at the U.S. arsenal in Springfield, Massachusetts, early in the nineteenth century and the textile mills of Lowell, Massachusetts. The Singer Company's Elizabethport factory, built in 1873, was reputed to be the largest in the United States making a single product under one roof. By 1900 the world's largest textile manufacturing building was the Amoskeag Mills complex on the Merrimack River in Manchester, New Hampshire—two connected, parallel, four-story buildings half a mile in length. Corporate ambitions—not to mention the huge demand in the marketplace—were helping create manufacturing capabilities on an entirely new scale. In 1864 the Springfield armory produced more than 600,000 rifles—in the preceding seventy years it had managed to produce a grand total only slightly in excess of this figure.

Factories became bigger and bigger as companies sought to meet the expanding needs of markets. Highland Park covered sixty-three acres. Henry Ford's market was the world.

It was not simply the size of these factories that marked them apart as new industrial beasts. They also worked in new ways and organized work in new ways. Ford's other claim to fame is the creation of the system that allowed these increasingly huge factories to match their physical size with production on a massive scale: the moving assembly line.

The assembly line had already been picked up by a variety of industries—though never before on the scale employed by Ford. It was used in the food processing industry in the Midwest United States in the 1870s. Ford himself could have picked up the idea from closer to home. He is reputed to have toured Chicago's meatpacking plants in search of inspiration. The meatpackers had an overhead trolley to speed up production.

Perhaps a more obvious source was Sears, Roebuck's Chicago mail-order plant, which was opened in 1906. It was the largest business building in the world, with 3 million square feet of floor space. Sears had found that size was not necessarily equated with efficiency. Big was not automatically beautiful. The plant was initially sprawling and inefficient. Customers sometimes received five articles when they wanted one or simply none at all. The logistics were a nightmare. Then Sears got its act together. A time schedule was introduced so that once orders were received they were given a time to be dispatched. An array of belts and chutes linked arrivals and departures. It was a moving assembly line of sorts.

Looking further back, the more distant roots of the assembly line can be traced to the concept of producing interchangeable parts. This innovation is most commonly attributed to cotton-gin inventor Eli Whitney (1765–1825).

In 1798 Whitney was asked by the American military to make ten thousand muskets. (Whitney was quite a salesman—at the time he didn't have a factory or even a machine.) In two years he devised a method of production based on the use of jigs. It took him a little longer to actually produce the guns—eight years in fact. His production method used cheaper unskilled laborers to produce sets of interchangeable gun parts. Whitney, ever the showman, delivered the first trial consignment to the government in broken-down form. He then demonstrated the quality of his muskets by selecting components at random and assembling a perfectly functioning musket. In 1812 he received a further order for fifteen thousand muskets. The business potential of this was enormous. Interchangeable parts allowed companies to achieve increased quality through reducing variation.

In fact, Whitney was not the first to explore the concept of inter-changeable parts. Eighteenth-century clockmakers realized the possibilities, and so too did Honoré Blanc, an eighteenth-century French gunsmith.[2] Blanc even arranged a demonstration involving a thousand muskets. Thomas Jefferson, then the American ambassador to France, helpfully reported back from Paris on this development. (It seems that diplomatic bags have been filled with trade secrets since time immemorial.)

Soon Blanc was making a thousand muskets a year for Napoleon. Interchangeable parts meant that he could use unskilled labor. The French government didn't like this. It proclaimed that it simply wasn't practical or sensible for people just to make a bit of a product. Craftsmanship required that individuals made the whole. Blanc's manufacturing methods, the precursor to mass production, were unceremoniously brought to halt.

More successful were the ventures of Marc Isambard Brunel (1769–1849). Brunel was also French, though he was an adopted American (and, at one time, New York's chief engineer). At the same time as Whitney was producing his advanced muskets, Brunel set up in business in England to mass produce a range of standardized ships' blocks. Brunel used specially designed machines that cut down variation and, as a result, cut costs and increased the usefulness of the blocks. For Brunel the standardization of the blocks was a sideshow to his own engineering achievements and those of his son, Isambard.

Clearly, the concept of the assembly line was also closely linked to that of scientific management. Ford's and Taylor's opinions and insights were similar—they ran in parallel rather than having a more direct influence on each other. (Their obsessive natures also suggested a potential common bond.) There were clear echoes of Taylor when Henry Ford talked of "the reduction of the necessity for thought on the part of the worker and the reduction of his movements to a minimum. He does as nearly as possible only one thing with only one movement."[3] When it came to the Model T, production was broken into eighty-four steps.

The assembly line was the ultimate process, a way of keeping jobs strictly separated so that people carried out a single activity in the most efficient way. "The first step forward in assembly came when we began taking the work to the men instead of the men to the work. We now have two general principles in all operations—that a man shall never have to take more than one step, if possibly it can be avoided, and that no man need ever stoop over," said Ford.[4] Simply and unequivocally, the assembly line removed many of the inefficiencies of traditional methods of manufacturing.

Ford himself laid out the principles of work organization in three easy steps:

1. Place the tools and the men in the sequence of the operation so that each component part shall travel the least possible distance in the process of finishing.
2. Use work slides or some other form of carrier so that when a workman completes his operation, he drops the part always in the same place—which place must always be the most convenient place to his hand—and if possible have gravity carry the part to the next workman for his operation.
3. Use sliding assembly lines by which the parts to be assembled are delivered at convenient distances.[5]

The moving assembly line was tried out at Highland Park in April 1913. The initial experiment was on the production of the flywheel magneto. Previously this had been made by a single worker. Working alone, the worker could produce between thirty-five and forty pieces in a nine-hour day, with each magneto taking around twenty minutes. Ford—in Tayloristic fashion—identified twenty-nine separate operations in the assembly process. Introducing an assembly line with each operation being handled by another worker reduced the assembly time to thirteen minutes and ten seconds. Then Ford raised the height of the line eight inches—this was in 1914—and cut the time to seven minutes. Further experimenting with the speed that the work should move at cut the time down to five minutes. "In short, the result is this: by the aid of scientific study one man is now able to do somewhat more than four did only a comparatively few years ago," wrote Ford. "That line established the efficiency of the method and we now use it everywhere. The assembling of the motor, formerly done by one man, is now divided into eighty-four operations—those men do the work that three times their number formerly did."[6]

After a great deal of tinkering from Ford and his engineers, the assembly line began working. Around it Ford created a complex series of production systems that ensured that parts, subassemblies, and assemblies were delivered at the right time to the line. Ford was practicing just-in-time techniques long before they were made popular in the 1980s. (Ford's appreciation that speed offered a competitive advantage also echoes more contemporary management theories of time-based competition.)

The result was substantial improvement in productivity. Labor productivity at Ford increased tenfold according to one estimate.[7] The assembly line worked. The assembly line reduced the time taken to build a motor from nine hours and fifty-four minutes of labor time to five hours and fifty-six minutes. Previously it had taken just over twelve hours for Ford to make a chassis—this method involved parts being carried to a stationary assembly point. The assembly line (actually a none-too-technical rope pulling the chassis past stockpiles of components) reduced the time to a mere hour and thirty-three minutes.

Ford Popular

Of course, as is often the case, the man who made the great leap forward professed little interest in its historical significance. Ford did things and moved on. He did more than most.

Ford's break had come in 1893. The year was highly significant for the Ford family. Henry's only child, Edsel, was born, and a month later Ford was appointed chief engineer of the main Detroit Edison Company plant. The plant had to maintain electricity supply to the city twenty-four hours a day. Ford was constantly on call. The Detroit electricity supply was presumably quite reliable—Ford found plenty of time to play around with his mechanical ideas. By the end of the year, Ford had created his first working gasoline engine. One thing led to another—1896 saw Ford's first horseless carriage, the four-horsepower Quadricycle. This involved a buggy frame precariously mounted on four bicycle wheels.

None of this put Ford ahead of the competition. Indeed, there was a flood of invention and development. The fledgling automobile market was already crowded. People like Charles Edgar and J. Frank Duryea, Elwood Haynes, Hiram Percy Maxim, and Charles Brady King were chasing the great automotive prize.

Ford's strategy was to develop a model and then to sell it. This ensured a steady stream of finance as one bright idea followed another. Backers came and went until, in 1899, a group formed the Detroit Automobile Company. This eventually became the Henry Ford Company when Ford's backers departed, despairing at his constant quest for improvement.

At this time, Ford appeared to be yet another fanatic, up to the armpits in engine oil but with little idea of how to turn a flair for mechanics into a business. Along the way, Ford built several racing cars. These included the "999" racer driven by Barney Oldfield, which set several new speed records.

In 1902 he left the Henry Ford Company, which subsequently reorganized as the Cadillac Motor Car Company. Finally, in 1903, Ford was ready to market an automobile. The Ford Motor Company was incorporated, this time with a less than plentiful $28,000 in cash put up by ordinary citizens. Ford's previous business deals with backers had led him to antagonize the wealthiest men in Detroit. He was never a natural diplomat—as his later attempts at international diplomacy were to prove.

On June 16, 1903, the Ford Motor Company was organized with John S. Gray as president and Henry Ford as vice president. It began assembling cars at a factory at Mack Avenue, Detroit. Its first sale was a two-cylinder Model A Fordmobile. The Model B and the Model C followed.

During its first five years the Ford Motor Company produced eight different models, and by 1908 its output was a hundred cars a day. The stockholders were ecstatic; Ford was dissatisfied and looked toward turning out a thousand a day. The stockholders seriously considered court action to stop him from using profits to expand. Their short-termism could have stopped the Ford Motor Company in its tracks.

Not that Ford was the easiest person to deal with. His approach to business was one of extremes. It was all or nothing. In 1909, to the dismay of some of his stockholders, Ford, who owned 58 percent of the stock, announced that he was only going to make one car in the future, the Model T. The only thing the minority stockholders could do to protect their dividends from his all-consuming imagination was to take him to court, which Horace and John Dodge did in 1916.

Ford got his way. On October 1, 1908, the first Model T was made available to the public. Its price was $850. "I will build a motor car for the great multitude," Ford proclaimed in announcing the Model T's birth. For the next nineteen years the Model T was Ford's sole model. (Ford was also notable for sticking to whatever he said—no matter how ill advised and pigheaded it was.)

Ford's genius in the creation of the Model T lay in what would now be called *vision.* Ford's competitors were fixated on the product. They were mechanics, car fanatics. The usually looked no further than the camshaft. Ford seemed similar. He was a car man, a racer, a car developer. Yet, unlike his competitors, Ford saw the social potential of the car. He saw that it could—and probably would—change the world. Previously car travel had been the preserve of the few. Now it was available to all. Ford's obsessive vision, his big idea, was the company's competitive advantage.

"A Ford will take you everywhere except into society," proclaimed the company. The humble Model T changed the lives of millions of people. Over twenty years, it broke down generations of isolation. Farmers could travel more easily than ever before. Indeed, many traveled for the first time. Vast tracts of agricultural land were switched to new crops as hay for horses was no longer a good market to be in. The car became the heart of major changes in society. For better or worse, vacations, suburbs, highways, urbanization, and many more facets of life were made possible by the car.

The product fitted Ford's vision perfectly. His many years of development, of rejecting ideas others regarded as sufficient, paid off. (Lesson #2: wait until you get the product right.) The Model T (known affectionately as the Tin Lizzie or the Flivver), as we all know, was gloriously simple. It came in black. There were no windshield wipers, no gas gauge, speedometer, battery, or rear view mirror. Farmers didn't want a fancy car. People who lived in the cities wanted a car they could afford; nothing more. (The Model T's very simplicity meant that, as its popularity grew, there were an array of extras available. You could customize your Model T simply by turning to the Sears Catalog, which, by 1920, offered five thousand accessories.)

Ford's vision became reality. More than seventeen thousand Model Ts were sold during its first year, a phenomenal record. Four years earlier, the world's entire automobile industry produced twenty-two thousand cars. In the nineteen years of the Model T's existence, Ford sold 15,500,000 of the cars in the United States, almost 1,000,000 more in Canada, and 250,000 in Great Britain, a production total amounting to half the auto output of the world.

Success brought market domination. The entrepreneurial crowd that had set out to conquer the new market became a select corporate few with Henry Ford at its head. In 1914 the Ford Motor Company with 13,000 employees produced 267,720 cars; the other 299 American auto companies with 66,350 workers produced only 286,770 cars. Ford had 48 percent of the American car market, with $100 million in annual sales. Four years later, at the end of World War I, almost half the cars on earth were Model Ts.

Cost Advantages

The subtext of Ford's desire to create the first people's car was that it had to be affordable for the people. The selling line was "Buy a Ford—Spend the difference." As a result, Ford was involved in a constant and remorseless quest to reduce production costs. He did so simply to reduce the cost of the Model T. Cheaper cars meant more sales. "Every time I reduce the price of the car by one dollar I get one thousand new buyers," said Ford with characteristic brevity. His thinking was similar to that of Frederick Taylor, though they came at the problem from different angles. Taylor started with the task; Ford started with the cost.

Costs fell and Ford reduced the price of the Model T with obsessive zeal. In 1908, Ford produced six thousand Model Ts and sold them at $850; in 1916, he sold six hundred thousand at $360—and in the Model T's final year, the fifteen millionth trundled off the production line to be sold for $290.

In his quest for cheaper production costs, Ford embraced the most advanced production technology. First, in 1910, the company's manufacturing was moved to the Highland Park plant. Then came "Ford's industrial masterpiece" at River Rouge, Michigan. River Rouge opened in 1918 and reached full capacity by the mid-1920s—in 1923 Ford's Model T production peaked at two million.

River Rouge was a mile and a half long, three-quarters of a mile wide. At capacity it employed eighty-one thousand people, covered nearly seven million square feet, and cost the company $267 million to construct. It made Highland Park look positively small. Its creation marked a shift in emphasis. Ford's desire for cost reduction gradually became subsumed under a desire for control. During the First World War, Ford, like other manufacturers, had had to cope with the rationing and control of raw materials. He had also grown impatient with his suppliers. Life as a supplier to Ford was demanding. No matter what, the businesses of the suppliers basically had to keep pace with Ford's heady speed of development and expansion.

One of Ford's suppliers was the Hyatt Roller Bearing Company. Its executives included one Alfred P. Sloan. He later reflected on what life was like as a supplier to the fast-expanding colossus: "The [company] was dependable. We had to be in order to survive in the automobile-parts business. Literally, it was a capital offense to hold up a production line. If any manufacturer engaged in supplying parts failed to make a delivery according to schedule and thus held up an assembly line such as that of Ford, everyone would know it, from Mr. Ford down to the workmen who were made idle. You would not dare go into the plant the next time you were in Detroit!"[8] Sloan may have overstated the threat of death—there is no evidence that it ever got that serious—but his meaning was clear. Sloan went on to run General Motors.

Most of Ford's suppliers of tires, upholstery fabric, and the like were situated in and around Detroit. The trouble was that Ford's increased demands for materials meant that arranging supplies and making deals with suppliers was becoming ever more time-consuming. Coordination was a nightmare, so Ford started stockpiling raw materials and other supplies. This went against his instinct to control costs.[9]

The result was that self-sufficiency became Ford's new mantra. River Rouge was a hungry monster. Raw materials were poured in at one end and, just over a day later, emerged at the other end as Ford cars. It was ambitiously integrated. With a huge pile of cash, Ford could cut out the middlemen. He bought a railroad, sixteen coal mines, and about 700,000 acres (285,000 hectares) of timberland; he built a sawmill, acquired a fleet of Great Lakes freighters to bring ore from his Lake Superior mines, and even bought a glassworks. Ford's power and influence was such that a string of companies lay under his command—from the iron mines of northern Michigan to the jungles of Brazil. And the only gearing was in the cars. Not a cent was borrowed.

Ford became the ultimate in vertical integration. Every day one of the company's freighters would arrive with the day's supply of iron ore that had been extracted from the company's mines. The ore was heated with fuel from the company's coal mines. Then there was wood from the company's forests, rubber from its plantations, and so on.

Vertical integration is one of those ideas that look good on paper but that rarely work. It is the last resort of control freaks. (Ford may have seen how Carnegie Steel followed a similar strategy—by 1900 it had its own ore, coke, limestone, and shipping facilities.) It is perhaps significant that one of the first attempts at vertical integration was attempted by the Cistercians, part of the Benedictine order of monks. Established in 1098, their aim is to escape the excesses of worldliness and to live "remote from the habitation of man." The major disadvantage of this—especially in the eleventh century—was that once you are remote from mankind, you have to fend for yourself. The Cistercians had a mixed record at fending for themselves until Bernard of Clairvaux—later Saint Bernard—arrived in 1112 to take charge. Bernard (1090–1153) decided that the order needed to become efficient and founded more than seventy monasteries. As a result, the order embraced the latest in technology. Monasteries were remote from man but they were near to streams—these were used to provide power (the waterwheel was a relatively recent but vital discovery), running water, and sewage disposal.

River Rouge gave Henry Ford control but it also led to the isolation from reality craved by the Cistercians.

The opening of the River Rouge plant was meant to herald the beginning of another new era. In reality, it was the end of the beginning. Indeed, the early 1920s were the high point for Ford. The company's sales peaked in 1922. Until 1926 Ford's earnings exceeded GM's. But from then until 1986–87, Ford's earnings lagged behind. In 1991 Ford lost $2.3 billion.

A.F.

Ford's legacy was, at a macro level, an inspiring one. He was celebrated throughout the world for the sheer scale of his business endeavors and for the creation of a hugely influential product. Aldous Huxley's *Brave New World* (1932) labeled the modern era "A.F."—After Ford. In 1934 Clyde Barrow, the infamous bank robber, wrote to Ford to express his personal appreciation:

> Dear Sir
>
> While I still have got breath in my lungs I will tell you what a dandy car you make. I have drove Fords exclusively when I could get away with one. For sustained speed and freedom from trouble the Ford has got every other car skinned and even if my business hasent been strickly legal it don't hurt enything to tell you what a fine car you got in the V-8.
>
> Yours truly Clyde Champion Barrow

Ford changed society and was one of the chief creators of the machine age. The production line became the dominant corporate image of the times. But while Ford's overall achievements in turning his vision into reality cannot be doubted, the remainder of his contribution to management practice and thinking is more questionable.

At a management level, Ford is celebrated for one gem of human resource management: the introduction of the $5 daily wage in 1914. This, as was usual with Ford, was an act of brilliant bravado. It was not motivated by benevolence. It was merely great PR and the solution to a business problem: high staff turnover. Ford called it "the smartest cost-cutting move I ever made." In 1913, it was calculated that the Ford company's labor turnover was a staggering 380 percent. At a stroke, the introduction of the $5 day solved the problem.

It appeared remarkably generous. Five dollars for an eight-hour day replaced a rate of $2.34 for a nine-hour day. (The $5 day was introduced for women in 1916.) The reality was that it was a pragmatic solution to the problem of staff turnover. Benevolence was not part of Ford's business strategy. Nor was the $5 day enshrined in stone—in 1929 Ford introduced a $7 day, but with the onset of the Depression in 1932 this was reduced to $4, which was actually less than wages in the rest of the motor industry. (Ford's view of the Great Depression was characteristically unforgiving: "The Depression is good for the country. The only problem is that it might not last long enough in which case people might not learn enough from it.")

While the $5 day grabbed the headlines, more insidious management techniques were at work. If Ford could control the supply of tons of raw materials and sell cars in their millions, he could surely control his own employees. At one level, Ford expressed common sentiments of the time: workers were there to work and to do what they were instructed to do. Simple. "We expect the men to do what they are told. The organization is so highly specialized and one part is so dependent on another that we could not for a moment consider allowing men to have their own way," Ford explained. "Without the most rigid discipline we would have the utmost confusion. I think it should not be otherwise in industry. The men are there to get the greatest possible amount of work done and to receive the highest possible pay. If each man were permitted to act in his own way, production would suffer and therefore pay would suffer. Anyone who does not like to work in our way may always leave."[10]

Ford's "rigid discipline" involved the creation of a "Sociology Department." This basically spied on employees and at one time had fifty investigators. Those who supported unionization were fired. (Ford was fervently opposed to unions. He eventually accepted unionization in 1941—but considered closing the company down before doing so.) Employees with drinking or gambling problems were identified and dismissed. Those with financial problems were similarly dealt with. Ford's intolerance grew in direct relation to his success—"Study the history of almost any criminal, and you will find an inveterate cigarette smoker," he noted; he later blamed Jews for financing the First World War. At the same time, Ford talked of "certain standards of cleanliness and citizenship" that he expected his employees and their families to meet.[11]

"It was expected that in order to receive a bonus married men should live with and take proper care of their families," Ford explained. "We had to break up the evil custom among many of the foreign workers of taking in boarders—regarding a home as something to make money out of rather than a place to live. Boys under eighteen received a bonus if they supported the next of kin. Single men who lived wholesomely shared. The best evidence that the plan was essentially beneficial is the record. When the plan went into effect sixty percent of the workers immediately qualified to share; at the end of six months seventy-eight percent were sharing, at the end of one year eighty-seven percent. Within a year and a half only a fraction of one percent failed to share."[12]

Ford created a corporation built on fear and distrust. The fact that it was hugely successful should not deflect attention from this. Indeed, in many ways Ford provides an archetypal lesson in how not to do things. His management of people was appalling and his management of his company—after initial triumphs—was limited.

His early innovativeness eventually stagnated. Although his early days were marked by a constant quest for improvement, Ford refused to change the basic Model T technology until it was too late. The new Model A was introduced in 1927, but already Ford's competitors had gained ground.[13]

Ford's fundamental error was to believe that his success would allow him unlimited control. He could control his workers. The media criticized him—so, in 1918, he bought the *Dearborn Independent*. He would succeed no matter what. Hubris took over. In 1917, as the First World War raged and U-boats were destroying Allied ships, Ford announced with due solemnity that he could "build 1,000 small submarines . . . a day." (Ford had already made a fool of himself once when he chartered an ocean liner—dubbed the Peace Ship by the newspapers—in November 1915 to travel to Europe to end the war. The *Chicago Tribune* labeled him an "ignorant idealist.")

The Navy was desperate and, notwithstanding his pacifist efforts, brought Ford in to build 200-foot Eagle Boats. Ford, as you would expect, immediately set up a production line. In May 1918, his sub factory came into being; in July it produced its first Eagle. The aim was to produce a boat every day—a rather tame aim considering Ford's previous boast.

The Eagles produced weren't a great deal of use in fighting the Germans. Ford had figured with characteristic arrogance and no little stupidity that making a boat was similar to making a car. This is only partly true. A car doesn't particularly need to be watertight, but a boat does—and Ford's boats leaked. He ignored the best brains on offer at the Navy and plowed on. In the first year, seventeen Eagles were produced. Ford eventually delivered his sixtieth and final Eagle in 1919. By 1939 only eight were still in use.

Having learned his maritime lesson, Ford moved on to produce planes during the Second World War. "If it became necessary, the Ford Motor Company could, with the counsel of men like [Charles] Lindbergh and [Eddie] Rickenbacher, under our own supervision and without meddling by government agencies, swing into the production of a thousand airplanes of standard design a day," pronounced Ford.[14] This time he was more successful. Ford produced 86,865 airplanes, as well as many engines and gliders, tanks, and armored cars during the war.

At a personal level, success cannot be said to have brought out the best in Henry Ford. Money and power, combined with an idiosyncratic and obsessive nature, is a heady and at times unbalanced cocktail.

On the March

Henry Ford and Frederick Taylor were the Siamese twins of early management thought and practice. Their links were strong and clear, but they were two distinct entities with lives and ideas of their own. Their paths were both powerful and difficult to follow. They were both willful, obsessive, and at times objectionable.

Their approaches had an undoubted impact. Indeed, they had an enormous global impact. In manufacturing, the efficiency movement caused an increase in output per unit of labor, between 1907 and 1915, of 33 percent a year—compared to an annual average increase of 9.9 percent between 1900 and 1907.[15]

Taylor's thinking and Ford's practice also spawned a host of acolytes and disciples, imitators and emulators. Among the most productive were the Gilbreths, Frank and Lilian. The Gilbreths carried scientific management forward with the vigor of true converts. Their lives were dedicated to efficiency. Their honeymoon included a stop-off at the St. Louis World's Fair to examine building techniques. They created their own efficiency empire—akin to Stephen Covey's modern corporate empire. They were self-help gurus decades ahead of their time.

The Gilbreths were a combination of Frederick Taylor and *The Waltons.* In *Fatigue Study* (1916), the Gilbreths wrote: "The aim of life is happiness, no matter how we differ as to what happiness means. Fatigue elimination, starting as it does from a desire to conserve human life and to eliminate enormous waste, must increase 'Happiness Minutes,' no matter what else it does, or it has failed in its fundamental aim."[16]

The Gilbreths planned to have twelve children (six of each, naturally) and did so. In between, they studied people at work in much the same way as Frederick Taylor. They labeled this "motion study." Most famously, Frank Gilbreth examined bricklayers at work. They were, somewhat inevitably, inefficient. In response, Gilbreth designed and patented scaffolding that reduced bending and reaching, and increased output by over 100 percent. Gilbreth also invented the process flow diagram and worked with the typewriter maker, Remington, helping develop the more efficient Dvorak keyboard.

Their analysis of motion—aided by photography—led the Gilbreths to conclude there were sixteen units of movement. These units they named "therbligs"—Gilbreth backwards and slightly altered for ease of pronunciation.

When Frank Gilbreth died in 1924, Lilian picked up where he had left off and turned herself into an exemplar of industry. Not only did she bring up their large family, she headed the women's division of President Hoover's Organization on Unemployment Relief (1930–1932), gained various degrees, and along the way became famous. In 1938 Gilbreth was named one of twelve women "capable of holding the office of president of the United States." In 1944 the *California Monthly* said Lilian was "a genius in the art of living."

In fact, after Frank Gilbreth's death, his consulting clients all refused to use Lilian Gilbreth as a consultant simply because she was a woman.

Her response was to use this to her advantage. "If the only way to enter a man's field was through the kitchen door, that's the way she'd enter," wrote Frank Jr. and Ernestine Gilbreth in their book *Belles on Their Toes*. Lilian simply applied efficiency theories to her own and her family's domestic arrangements. The children were brought up using efficiency techniques. Charts recorded if they had brushed their teeth. The children dusted the furniture before being allowed to play. Two stenographers were on hand to record Lilian's insights.

The work of the Gilbreths, Henry Gantt, and a host of others means that management was on the march. And it was moving throughout the world. In Europe, scientific management was eagerly picked on by Lyndall Urwick. The French Minister of War ordered scientific management to be studied and applied. In Japan the new ideas were seized upon. Konosuke Matsushita was one of those inspired by Henry Ford's example. Matsushita's business empire was founded on similar principles: efficient productivity and low costs. Matsushita's theory was that a successful product had to be 30 percent better and 30 percent cheaper than the competition.

The crucial difference between Matsushita and Henry Ford was that Matsushita saw a strong moral and ethical element to business. A company wasn't simply a tool for production but a vehicle for the benefit of society and individuals.

Profit was not enough. "The mission of a manufacturer should be to overcome poverty, to relieve society as a whole from misery, and bring it wealth," said Matsushita. His "basic management objective," originated in 1929, said: "Recognizing our responsibilities as industrialists, we will devote ourselves to the progress and development of society and the well-being of people through our business activities, thereby enhancing the quality of life throughout the world."

Matsushita was not the only one to catch the management bug.

Astonishingly, a talk by Taylor in New York in 1914 attracted a reputed audience of 69,000. Scientific management had an effect throughout the world. (Management was the new rock and roll—but forty years before Elvis.) A Japanese engineer translated *The Principles of Scientific Management* (in Japan it became *Secrets for Eliminating Futile Work and Increasing Production*). In Japan it was a best-seller—a foretaste of the Japanese willingness to embrace the latest Western thinking.

Management: The Movie

Most management phenomena have a limited shelf life. They disappear from the corporate radar as quickly as misdirected Scud missiles. The impact of scientific management, the rise of mass production, and the assembly line can perhaps be measured by the fact that they spawned two movies: Charlie Chaplin's classic *Modern Times* and the less classical but equally interesting *Cheaper by the Dozen*.

Chaplin's film is a brilliant critique of the worst excesses of Fordism. *Cheaper by the Dozen* is a more lightweight (unintentional) parody of the entire efficiency movement and the Gilbreth family. *Cheaper by the Dozen* was based on the 1949 book of the same title by Frank B. Gilbreth Jr. and Ernestine Gilbreth Carey. Lilian was played by Myrna Loy and Frank Gilbreth by Clifton Webb, as an obsessive efficiency expert. The Webb character is so fanatical, he times how long it takes his children to rush into his arms when he returns from business trips.

What Frederick Taylor would have made of all this is impossible to contemplate. As Alan Farnham later noted in *Fortune:* "That Taylor should be remembered through *Cheaper by the Dozen* is as if Christ were to be remembered for having inspired Monty Python's *Life of Brian*."[17]

The Management Century Timeline

1911

Supreme Court breaks up Standard Oil.

Frederick Taylor's *Principles of Scientific Management* published.

1912

Frederick Taylor gives evidence to Congress. Management is suddenly elevated into public consciousness.

Universal Pictures founded; U.S. government passes Radio Act to regulate broadcasting.

1913

Federal Reserve formed.

1914

Edwin Booz leaves Northwestern University with a bachelor's degree in economics and a master's degree in psychology; he goes into business for himself to perform studies and analyses of businesses—a management consulting firm is born. Early clients include the Goodyear Tire & Rubber Company of Akron, Ohio; the Canadian Pacific Railroad; Chicago's Union Stockyards and Transit Company; and the Photographers Association of the United States. In 1936, the company becomes Booz, Fry, Allen, & Hamilton, and subsequently, Booz·Allen & Hamilton.

1915

One millionth Ford car produced.

The Computing Tabulating & Recording Company uses the slogan "Think" for the first time. In the same year Thomas Watson becomes president of C-T-R, which eventually becomes International Business Machines.

Bell Telephone makes first transatlantic voice telephone call.

The Dow's best year. It finishes the year at 99.15, up 81.66 percent.

Coca-Cola runs a design competition to come up with a new design for its bottles. The competition, a smart marketing ploy, is won by the Root Glass Company. Coke's president, Asa Candler, said: "We need a bottle which a person will recognize as Coca-Cola even when he feels it in the dark."

1916

Association of Collegiate Schools of Business founded.

The Dow expands from twelve stocks to twenty. It went to thirty stocks in 1928.

1917

Pacific Aero Products becomes the Boeing Airplane Company.

1918

Konosuke Matsushita founds the Matsushita Electric Housewares Manufacturing Works. Its first product is an attachment plug.

The company that became Hertz starts renting automobiles. The business is started by Walter L. Jacobs, a pioneer of the auto rental sector. Aged twenty-two, Jacobs opens a car-rental operation in Chicago. His original rental fleet is a dozen Model Ts, which he repaired and repainted himself.

Sakichi Toyoda forms a company called the Toyoda Spinning & Weaving Co. It eventually becomes Toyota.

1919

Edsel Ford succeeds Henry as president of the Ford Motor Company.

United Artists formed as the first studio owned and run by actors.

Hilton Hotel Corporation founded.

RCA founded.

1920

America's urban population outnumbers its rural population for the first time.

Chapter 3
1921–1930: Discovering the Organization

A big idea and a big possibility had been given birth. The immediate problem was to weld an unwieldy and incoherent mass into a correlated and co-ordinated whole, by elimination and addition, through an organization based upon the fundamental managerial policy of first determining the facts and then developing the essential plan by capitalizing the group judgement of the most intelligent personnel that could be brought together— always recognizing the importance of an open mind.
> —ALFRED P. SLOAN[1]

Empire Building

At every stage in human evolution, from the Greeks and Romans to modern-day CEOs, people have considered the best ways to organize themselves. Organization has been one of the perennial bugbears of human civilization. Some have been more successful than others. For example, at their peak, the Incas controlled six million people spread over a huge area covering parts of modern Peru, Ecuador, Chile, Bolivia, and Argentina. They spoke many different languages and dialects. How to manage them and their lands was a little bit more problematical than contemplating how to manage a distant subsidiary.

The Incas had the advantage that force was one possibility. But, interestingly, their more peaceful means of persuasion were preludes to later organizational behavior. The Incas decided on a highly standardized system of administration. This was based on units of ten, rather like the modern decimal system. To make sense of their lands they divided them into four quarters—*suyus*—which met at the Inca capital, Cuzco.

The Incas also invested heavily in infrastructure. Their road system eventually covered over twenty-three thousand kilometers. The road system meant that the army could move quickly to sort out trouble and that goods could move equally speedily. And all this was achieved at a time when the Incas had no vehicles with wheels.

The road system was combined with a highly complex logistical network. This was made up of way stations, imperial centers, forts, ceremonial centers, and other meeting and gathering points. Runners were specially trained to pass on messages. The system worked, but briefly: the Inca empire only functioned for a hundred years.

Modern corporations dream of such longevity. But their understanding of the intricacies of organization was not helped by the unwillingness of management pioneers to contemplate organization as a serious issue worthy of their attention. Henry Ford's view of how to organize his industrial giant was one-dimensional—if it existed at all. Ford was a car man with a vision. He chose, therefore, to wrestle with the matters directly connected to delivering his vision into reality—the mechanical intricacies of production, cost control, and the product. Organizational intricacies were ridden over roughshod. Ford's achievement was one of production over management, of ambition rather than organization. He succeeded in building a business empire without management (or so he thought) and without a carefully—or even casually—formulated structure.

Frederick Taylor was similarly purblind to organizational issues. He considered that perfect tasks led to perfect processes that largely provided the structure necessary for a company to thrive.

With Taylor and Ford unhelpfully mute on the subject of the nature of organization, it took a German sociologist, Max Weber (1864–1920), to consider the organizational implications of their theories and practice. Weber looked around and noted the industrial trends, the factories with their supervisors and middle managers, the sheer scale of the new operations. Then Weber envisaged the future of the organization. If these trends were to continue to develop, what would be the best way of organizing a business?

Weber's conclusions did not make for pleasant reading, especially for humanitarians. His vision of the future, encapsulated in *The Theory of Social and Economic Organization* (published four years after Weber's death in 1924) suggested that the depersonalizing effects of industrial growth were inevitable.

While Karl Marx saw industrialization as trampling over the rights to the ownership of labor, Weber offered a more pragmatic view—the subjugation of individuals to organizations was reality; not a stepping-stone to proletarian utopia. Large organizations required that the people involved put the cause of the organization before their own aspirations—and it didn't matter whether the organization was building pyramids, fighting battles, or making widgets. "The capitalistic system has undeniably played a major role in the development of bureaucracy," Weber wrote.[2]

According to Weber, the ultimate form of organization in the newly industrialized world was the bureaucratic system. This, as envisaged by Weber, was impersonal. People got on with their work. It was entirely hierarchical—"The organization of offices follows the principle of hierarchy; that is, each lower office is under the control and supervision of a higher one." It was remorselessly rational, with carefully structured promotions and demarcations. The organization operated as a machine. Each cog in the system—each bureaucrat—fulfilled a clearly defined role.

The machine's aim was to work efficiently. No more; no less. Efficient machines were productive and, therefore, profitable. "The purely bureaucratic type of administrative organization," wrote Weber, "is, from a purely technical point of view, capable of attaining the highest degree of efficiency and is in this sense formally the most rational known means of carrying out imperative control over human beings. It is superior to any other form in precision, in stability, in the stringency of its discipline and in its reliability."[3]

Weber said that the bureaucratic system was characterized by hierarchy, impersonality, written rules of conduct, promotion based on achievement, specialized division of labor, and efficiency. Weber did not advocate the bureaucratic system, he simply described it. As a sociologist, he was interested in scenarios rather than manifestos. The system was the extreme, the eventual outcome if trends observed by Weber continued. In many ways the bureaucratic world mapped out by Weber is similar to Orwell's *1984:* a nightmare scenario rather than a prediction.

Unfortunately, in some respects, the nightmare came to pass. Henry Ford was not alone. Corporations were routinely organized in ways similar to those imagined by Weber. The bureaucratic model built on unquestioning loyalty, subjugation, and stultifying hierarchies became the organizational role model.

It was no coincidence that it took a German to provide definitive insights into the bureaucratic model. The inspiration for Ford's controlled administrative system can be seen as the nineteenth-century Prussian bureaucracy. The Prussians had a flair for organization. Controlled by Heinrich von Stein, Gerhard von Scharnhorst, August von Gneisenau, and Helmuth von Moltke, the Prussian system would have delighted Ford. It was a triumph of control. There were detailed, centralized materials requirements and logistical planning, bountiful rules, rigorously standardized operating procedures, a faith in functional administrative design, and the breaking down of tasks into their simplest components.

The really wonderful thing about the Prussian system was that it was entirely geared toward large organizations. Small businesses could not follow the model. Only very large organizations could take full advantage of the Prussian administrative system. Only they could afford to devote substantial amounts of resources to gathering and processing quantities of data for top management to use to coordinate activities and allocate resources. The logic was simple and conclusive: bigger organizations were better. Small may have been beautiful but it wasn't productive or profitable. Corporate expansion was natural, limitless, and good for business—and, if proof were needed in the 1920s, you could have pointed to Ford, which was carrying the world before it.

The other German inspiration was a military one. During World War One the German military bureaucracy under Erich Ludendorff used sophisticated planning and control systems in order to mobilize Germany's resources. This was called the *Kriegwirtschaftsplan.* It was very similar to Ford's administrative system. Another contemporary impressed by the Germanic approach was Lenin. The centralized planning system, *Gosplan,* used in the Soviet Union to implement its long-term policies and strategic plans simply adapted the *Kriegwirtschaftsplan.* Lenin later defined socialism as the best of every world: "Soviets plus Prussian railway administration plus American industrial organization."

Organizational Thinking

Although the nature of organization failed to spark interest from Taylor and Ford, many other contemporary theorists and practitioners were contemplating organizational issues. Organizational charts had been in use since the building of the railroads and the fledgling executive education world had begun to explore organizational issues more systematically. In 1909 at Harvard Business School Russell Robb gave a series of lectures on organizations. His approach merged military models with the new industrial reality. "All organizations will differ somewhat from each other, because the objects, the results that are sought and the way these results must be attained, are different," said Robb. "There is no royal road, no formula that, once learned, may be applied in all cases with the assurance that the result will be perfect harmony, efficiency, and economy, and a sure path to the main purpose in view."[4]

One of those who may have been in Robb's audience was Chester Barnard (1886–1961). Barnard had won a scholarship to Harvard to study economics. He dutifully and fruitfully attended Harvard from 1906 until 1909 but failed to receive a degree because he lacked a laboratory science. He left and joined the statistical department at AT&T.

Barnard stands out among the theorists and practitioners of management during the twentieth century in that he is one of the few who managed to bridge the divide between theory and practice. He was a highly successful practitioner and an innovative theorist.

As a practitioner, Barnard set the course of his professional career with his move to AT&T. He spent his entire working life with the company, eventually becoming president of New Jersey Bell in 1927. *Fortune* magazine hailed Barnard as "possibly [having] the most capacious intellect of any business executive in the United States." He retired in 1952.

Though he was the archetypal corporate man, Barnard's interests were varied. During World War Two, he worked as special assistant to the Secretary of the Treasury and cowrote a report that formed the basis of U.S. atomic energy policy. Barnard also found time to lecture on the subject of management.

His best-known book, *The Functions of the Executive,* was based on eight of his lectures. The language is dated, the approach ornate but comprehensive. The book continues to attract occasional outbursts of appreciation when discovered by modern thinkers. (It was last resurrected by Peters and Waterman in their 1982 best-seller *In Search of Excellence:* "Its density makes it virtually unreadable; nonetheless it is a monument."[5])

Monumental indeed—much of what Barnard argued strikes a chord with contemporary management thinking. He was the first to elevate rational decision making to the professional heart of management. In addition, he highlighted the need for communication—he believed that everyone needs to know what and where the communications channels are so that every single person can be tied into the organization's objectives. He also advocated lines of communication that were short and direct. "The essential functions are, first, to provide the system of communications; second, to promote the securing of essential efforts; and, third, to formulate and define purpose," he wrote.[6]

To Barnard the chief executive was not a dictatorial figure geared to simple short-term achievements. Instead, part of his responsibility was to nurture the values and goals of the organization. Barnard argued that values and goals need to be translated into action rather than meaningless motivational phraseology. Barnard took what would today be called a holistic approach, arguing that "in a community all acts of individuals and of organizations are directly or indirectly interconnected and interdependent."

Barnard regarded the commercial organization simply as a means of allowing people to achieve what they could not achieve as separate individuals. He defined an organization as a "system of consciously coordinated activities of forces of two or more persons." Not surprisingly given the era in which Barnard lived, there was a hint of Taylor's scientific management in such observations. For all his contemporary-sounding ideas, Barnard was a man of his times—advocating corporate domination of the individual and regarding loyalty to the organization as paramount.

Even so, Barnard proposed a moral dimension to the world of work (one that Taylor certainly did not recognize). "The distinguishing mark of the executive responsibility is that it requires not merely conformance to a complex code of morals but also the creation of moral codes for others," wrote Barnard. In arguing that there was a morality to management, Barnard played an important part in broadening the managerial role from one simply of measurement, control, and supervision to one also concerned with more elusive, abstract notions such as values and organization.

From Billy to Mr. Sloan

As we have seen, Henry Ford wasn't alone in pursuing the automotive dream. One of his early competitors was a Scottish ex-plumber, David Buick (1854–1929). Buick caught the carmaking bug in 1899 and formed the Buick Manufacturing Company in 1902. His company, like many of the others, struggled—despite Buick's putting his plumbing training to innovative use with the first valve-in-head engine and windshields. In desperation, Buick sent one of his engineers to Flint, Michigan, to extract some money from a more successful carriage and wagon maker, the Flint Road Cart Company.

Buick's emissary took one of the company partners out for a ride in the Buick. The other partner was less malleable, refusing all entreaties to have a drive. The Buick engineer wooed him through sheer persistence—driving up and down outside his house and then returning the next day. Eventually, the partner buckled. Only when he was in the car did he realize that he was not being sold a single Buick; he was being offered a share of the company.

The intractable partner was Billy Durant (1861–1947). He liked the Buick so much he bought the company. Durant predicted that one day 500,000 cars a year would be bought. In response, a banker said: "If he has any sense, he'll keep those notions to himself if he ever tries to borrow money."

The banker was right. William Crapo Durant was a novice. But then again everyone was a novice in the car business. At least Durant was in a related field—his successful business made horse-drawn carriages.

Durant took to carmaking. Under Durant, in three years production mushroomed from a mere thirty-seven cars—not bad for a plumber, it should be said—to eight thousand.[7] Business was good. Durant, however, was worried that a one-product company laid itself continually open to failure. His solution was to propose a consortium of carmakers. The consortium, he figured, could reduce risks as well as costs through shared sourcing. (In retrospect, Durant's inspiration is a truly remarkable one. Much the same logic has been used for virtually every industrial merger ever since.) Durant suggested his idea to Henry Ford and Ransom Olds (1864–1950). They weren't interested.

Ford's lack of interest was understandable. He was on the verge of launching the Model T and was hardly a person amenable to cooperative partnerships. Olds's confidence proved misplaced. Oldsmobile was struggling. In 1908 Durant moved in, bought 75 percent of Oldsmobile's shares, and created the General Motors Company by merging Olds and Buick.

Durant was entertainingly reckless and occasionally brilliant. After Oldsmobile had been taken over the company had no new model planned. Then Durant arrived at the Oldsmobile factory in Lansing in a Buick Model 10. He ordered that its body be removed and sawed in half. Durant then reassembled the body's parts, placed them a little further apart, and announced his plans: "We'll make a car a little wider than this Buick. We'll have it a little longer; more leg room. Put your regular hood and radiator on it. It will look like an Olds and it will run. Paint it; upholster it—and there's your Oldsmobile for the coming year."[8] Durant's new model sold at $1250—against $1000 for the Buick—and Oldsmobile was quickly overwhelmed with demand.

One deal followed another. Next—in 1909—came the Oakland Motor Car Company. Oakland was later renamed after one of its top-performing vehicles (renowned for its hill climbing): the Pontiac. Then came the $4.5 million purchase of Cadillac.

The boom couldn't last. As the Model T swept the world, sales of other vehicles collapsed. In 1910, eighteen car makers disappeared. GM had to sell off some of its companies at a loss, and Durant was forced out.

He didn't go quietly. Far from it. Indomitable, Durant promptly founded another company, with backing from businesspeople anxious to leave the expiring wagon and buggy industry. A former Buick racing driver, Swiss-born Louis Chevrolet, was his designer, and Chevrolet's name went on the company.

By 1916, Durant was able to trade Chevrolet for a majority share of GM stock, putting himself back in the driver's seat at the company he had founded. This time, his era was short-lived. Between 1917 and 1919, the du Ponts paid $49 million for 29 percent of GM. (They later added a further $84 million of GM stock to this investment. It proved an outstandingly astute investment. When they began divesting GM shares in 1962, they had received $2 billion in dividends and the shares were worth over $3 billion.)[9]

The intervention of the du Ponts came at the right time for General Motors. Durant's seat-of-the-pants management style fit the fledgling days of the car industry but was increasingly ill suited when the going became corporate. In one classic story, Durant was involved in discussions about where to locate a company office building. An out-of-town location was suggested by one of his executives, who argued that city center property prices were too high and a car company didn't need to be in the middle of Detroit. Durant agreed and they visited a site outside Detroit. Durant saw it and instructed his junior to buy it and made a mark on the ground—randomly it seemed—up to which they should buy. The result was, eventually, a $20 million building.

Before Durant's final departure in 1920, GM acquired dozens of automobile and supplier companies—including the Fisher Body Company, Dayton Metal Products, the Dayton-Wright Airplane Company, and the T.W. Warner Company (a gear manufacturer). Thanks largely to Durant, GM had grown to eight times its 1916 size in just four years.

But the postwar depression put paid to Durant's colorful career. GM shares plummeted—from $400 to $12—and he departed. Durant went on to start Durant Motors, which produced the low-cost "Star." Like so many others, Durant Motors eventually failed. Durant was bankrupted and finished up running a chain of bowling alleys back in Flint.[10]

The Modern Executive

Watching, working, and waiting in the wings as Durant flared like a brilliant entrepreneurial comet was Alfred Pritchard Sloan Jr. (1875–1966). Immediately prior to Durant's departure, Sloan had been on the verge of resigning from the company. He and his wife went to Europe for a vacation. Sloan ordered a Rolls Royce and contemplated touring around Europe. The tour was postponed. On returning Sloan changed his mind—"I was a manufacturer, and this could be made the grandest manufacturing enterprise the world had ever seen. I did not want to leave," Sloan later recalled.[11]

Sloan was precociously brilliant. He initially failed to get into the Massachusetts Institute of Technology because he was thought to be too young. When he was allowed in, to study electrical engineering, he was the youngest member of his class.

Sloan then began his working career as a draftsman in a small machine shop, the Hyatt Roller Bearing Company of Newark, New Jersey. Hyatt made Sloan. His influence, in spite of his age, was immediate. He pointed the company toward making antifriction bearings for cars, and in 1899—still only twenty-four—Sloan became the company's president. Hyatt was a beneficiary of the huge expansion in the car industry. Its bearings became the industry standard and it grew rapidly.

In 1916 Hyatt merged with the United Motors Corporation. A variety of other car industry suppliers also joined the company and Sloan became president. In 1918, United Motors was acquired by General Motors, and Sloan became vice president in charge of accessories and a member of GM's Executive Committee.

Sloan, methodical and intellectually rigorous, worked closely with the dedicatedly entrepreneurial Durant. "Everybody said Durant was amazingly resourceful. Some said he was reckless to the point of danger. Perhaps both viewpoints were to an extent right, but neither really reflects the great contribution Durant made," Sloan later reflected. "Our methods of approaching operating problems were entirely different. But I liked him even when I disagreed with him. Durant's integrity? Unblemished. Work? He was a prodigious worker. Devotion to General Motors? Why, it was his baby!"[12]

But at the same time that Sloan recognized Durant's virtues, he was also sure that Durant's management style was a thing of the past. It had helped get GM to where it was, but was ill suited to enable it to cope with the challenges Sloan envisaged it encountering in the future. "In bringing General Motors into existence, Mr. Durant had operated as a dictator," said Sloan. "But such an institution could not grow into a successful organization under a dictatorship. Dictatorship is the most effective way of administration, provided the dictator knows the complete answers to all questions. But he never does and he never will. That is why dictatorships eventually fail. If General Motors were to capitalize its wonderful opportunity, it would have to be guided by an organization of intellects. A great industrial organization requires the best of many minds."[13]

Central to Sloan's concern about Durant's approach was the issue of organization. Durant had helped create a corporate colossus, but one that was largely unmanageable. Toward the end of Durant's period with the company, Sloan suggested that it would be beneficial to examine the way the organization worked. Durant promptly rejected the proposed "organization study." But when Pierre du Pont (1870–1954) took over the reins in 1920, he approved Sloan's plan to examine how and why the company was organized.

Indeed, du Pont provided a powerful role model for Sloan. In 1902 he and his cousins, Coleman and Alfred, had taken control of the family explosives company, DuPont. As the company treasurer, Pierre du Pont introduced a series of innovative financial measures and systems. In 1903, du Pont introduced return on investment as a measure of organizational performance and went on to devise a formula to compare the performance of various departments. Du Pont, aided by his deputy John Raskob, basically instilled professional vigor into corporate accounting and financial systems. (Prior to this, in the nineteenth century, cost accounting had been developed by J. Edgar Thomson at the Pennsylvania Railroad.)

Sloan's examination of the company's organization was to prove the foundation for the achievements of the rest of his career. In 1923, Sloan became the company's president. Sloan's predecessor, du Pont, said at the time: "The greater part of the successful development of the Corporation's operations and the building of a strong manufacturing and sales organization is due to Mr. Sloan. His election to the presidency is a natural and well merited recognition of his untiring and able efforts and successful achievement."

Sloan replaced Durant's erratic, one-man leadership with clearly formulated policies and talented executives. Over five decades, he reshaped General Motors and reinvented how it was managed.[14] His major achievements were twofold. First, Sloan created a new cadre of highly professional, dispassionate, intelligent managers who made decisions on the basis of the information available rather than always following their intuition. Decision making was the heart of management—as Chester Barnard argued. Sloan was the first great professional manager. "As exemplified by Sloan, the executive is a professional first and foremost: objective, dispassionate, open-minded. His insistence on facts, on ample documentation, on considering all sides of a question, prevent his being opinionated, let alone bigoted," wrote Peter Drucker.[15] More damningly, *Fortune* later observed: "Alfred P. Sloan Jr. was himself a man of limited interests who immersed himself totally in the construction of the company."[16]

"Alfred Sloan did for the upper layers of management what Henry Ford did for the shopfloor: he turned it into a reliable, efficient, machine-like process," the *Economist* recently observed.[17] Sloan, trained as an engineer, was driven by a love of systematic reasoning, of weighing up the pros and cons and then making a decision. He turned managerial decision making from a tumultuous, spontaneous art into an informed, commercially driven process. He took the amateurism (and some of the fun) out of business and replaced it with sober, respectable professionalism.

Organizing the Colossus

Sloan's second achievement was no less important. He created a new organizational form, a means of managing Durant's meandering colossus. The fruit of Sloan's organization study was an organizational model that combined decentralized operations with coordinated, centralized policy control.

As a result of his organization study, in the early 1920s Sloan organized the company into eight divisions—five car divisions and three component divisions. In the jargon (invented fifty years later) they were strategic business units.

Ford had been able to achieve standardization and mass production by producing as narrow a product range as possible. Sloan wanted to produce a far greater range from the industrial ragbag accumulated by Durant. He set about creating a coherent organization from his motley collection of companies.

Previously GM cars had competed for the same markets; to prevent that, Sloan gave each car division its own price and style categories. He also introduced annual model changes, creating a market for used cars. Each car division became an independent brand.

While Ford remained fixated on the Model T, GM moved progressively forward. The company's model changes were backed by extensive and carefully planned research, development, and testing. GM's expertise grew. The 1920s saw the introduction of Buick's four-wheel brakes (1923), Cadillac's shatter-resistant safety glass (1926), chromium plating, automatic engine temperature control, hydraulic shock absorbers, automatic choking, adjustable front seats, and numerous advances in performance, dependability, and manufacturing technology. (For this Sloan was thankful to Charles Kettering (1876–1958) who had sold his company Delco—Dayton Engineering Laboratories Co.—to GM in 1916. Kettering and his team developed improved fuels, shock absorbers, and the refrigerant Freon.)

After years of the simple Model T, the car-buying public embraced GM's innovations with enthusiasm. The one millionth Buick was built in 1923; the five millionth GM car was a 1926 Pontiac. In 1927, GM vehicles outsold Fords for the first time. By 1931, Oldsmobile's new eighty-five-acre complex in Lansing, Michigan, could send a new car off the line every forty-one seconds, shipping eight hundred cars a day. And the beauty of it all was that costs fell as volume increased.

As GM thrived, its organization took firmer shape. Each of the company's units was made responsible for all its commercial operations. Each had its own engineering, production, and sales departments, but was supervised by a central staff responsible for overall policy and finance. The operating units were semiautonomous, charged with maintaining market share and sustaining profitability in their particular area. In a particularly innovative move, the components divisions sold products not only to other GM companies but also to external companies.

Meanwhile the company's headquarters was kept to a manageable size. Its business was number crunching. Using the systems devised by du Pont the center could carefully measure and keep up-to-date with the return-on-assets performance of each and every division. GM's chief financial officer, Donaldson Brown, was another key figure in the emergence of the company from Ford's shadow.

Sloan's organizational model gave business units far more responsibility than ever before. The clarification of who was responsible for what was central to his approach. In a similar, parallel organizational development Procter & Gamble (P&G) developed the concept of brand management. This reached fruition in 1931 and basically involved creating an entire business function charged with brand management. With brands like Ivory and Camay bath soaps, P&G believed that the best way to organize itself would be to give responsibility to a single individual: a brand manager. The brand management system began to take shape in the 1920s. But it was in 1931 that Neil McElroy, the company's promotion department manager, created a marketing organization based on competing brands managed by dedicated groups of people.

Prior to the development of brand management, brands were left unattended at the corporate fringes. By introducing a systematic brand management approach, P&G proved that providing some sort of framework can be very powerful and that inclusion is better than bemused or ad hoc exclusion. The system did not transform the world overnight, but gradually brand management became an accepted functional activity. By 1967, 84 percent of large consumer packaged goods manufacturers in the United States had brand managers.

Similarly, once responsibilities were decided on at General Motors, Sloan believed that it was inappropriate as well as unnecessary for top managers at the corporate level to know much about the details of division operations. Poor performance led to changes in management at divisional level. Simple as that. For this reason Sloan invested a great deal of time in personnel selection. If GM got it right in the first place, the divisional chiefs should be up to standard. Good performers were promoted and, eventually, found themselves based at GM HQ.

Sloan's multi-divisional form meant that executives had more time to concentrate on strategic issues and that operational decisions were made by people in the front line rather than at a distant headquarters. It required a continuous balancing act. But it worked.

In effect, Sloan took advantage of the company's size without making it cumbersome. Companies like Buick, Pontiac, and Cadillac retained their powerful feeling of independence and their individual brand identity. At the same time, GM as a whole offered a coherent superstructure. "The multi-divisional organization was perhaps the single most important administrative innovation that helped companies grow in size and diversity far beyond the limits of the functional organization it replaced," say contemporary thinkers Sumantra Ghoshal and Christopher Bartlett.[18]

The multi-divisional form created a trend among large organizations for decentralization. In 1950 around 20 percent of Fortune 500 corporations were decentralized; this had increased to 80 percent by 1970. Among those taking the plunge was IBM—in 1956, IBM chief Thomas Watson Jr. announced his plans to decentralize the company into six autonomous divisions, each focusing on a product line. Later—in the 1980s—AT&T joined in when it attempted to make the shift from being a production-based bureaucracy to a marketing organization.

One of the key supporters of this trend was Alfred Chandler. His classic book, *Strategy and Structure,* lauded Alfred Sloan's work at General Motors. Chandler argued that the chief advantage of the multi-divisional organization was that "it clearly removed the executives responsible for the destiny of the entire enterprise from the more routine operational responsibilities and so gave them the time, information and even psychological commitment for long-term planning and appraisal."

Another who celebrated GM was Peter Drucker. Drucker's connection with GM had begun in the fall of 1943, when he took a call from the company's public relations director, Paul Garrett. Out of the blue, Garrett invited Drucker to study the company. (This was actually the idea of GM's vice chairman, Donaldson Brown.) This effectively launched the career of the century's foremost management thinker. The resulting book, *Concept of the Corporation* (1946), was a groundbreaking examination of the intricate internal working of the company and revealed the auto giant to be a labyrinthine social system rather than an economic machine. In the United Kingdom the book was retitled *Big Business* as, Drucker later explained, "both Concept and Corporation [were] then considered vulgar Americanisms."

After being celebrated as a managerial exemplar by both Chandler and Drucker, the deficiencies of Sloan's model gradually became apparent. The decentralized structure built up by Sloan revolved around a reporting and committee infrastructure that eventually became unwieldy. As time went by, more and more committees were set up. Stringent targets and narrow measures of success stultified initiative. By the end of the 1960s the delicate balance that Sloan had brilliantly maintained between centralization and decentralization was lost—finance emerged as the dominant function and GM found itself paralyzed by what had once made it great.

The multi-divisional form, say Christopher Bartlett and Sumantra Ghoshal, was handicapped by having "no process through which institutionalized wisdoms can be challenged, existing knowledge bases can be overturned, and the sources of the data can be reconfigured. In the absence of this challenge, these companies gradually become immobilized by conventional wisdoms that have ossified as sacred cows, and become constrained by outmoded knowledge and expertise that are out of touch with their rapidly changing realities."

Sloan's organizational model was right for its time. It brought much-needed clarity to organizational life. During the 1920s, 1930s, and 1940s, it worked brilliantly. That GM failed to move forward from it

State of Play: Corporate Stars in 1930[19]

AT&T: The first $5 billion company. In 1930 AT&T recorded profits of $202 million. Sources of income were the 15.7 million Bell System phones—from a total of 20.2 million phones in the United States. A near monopoly perhaps, but *Fortune* noted: "There can be no question of the sincerity of the company. It is committed to a policy of distributing excess profits not to stockholders in cash but to its public in service."

DRUG INCORPORATED: At the time, owner of the largest chain of drug stores in the world. Drug Inc. was the holding company for Life Savers, the Bayer Company, the Vick Chemical Company, and Bristol-Myers. Its origins lay in United Drug, founded in Boston by Louis Liggett. By 1930 one of Drug Inc.'s bases was New York's Liggett Building. "Our price policy is simple: the lowest possible price to the consumer consistent with good business," said the company's Charles McCallum in 1930.

A.O. SMITH CORPORATION: Milwaukee-based manufacturer of frames for the booming car market. In 1930, A.O. Smith had sales of $60 million. Its products—frames for Pontiacs, Chevrolets, Chryslers, Buicks—departed on 30,000 freight cars every year. At the time it was investing in the future with a new $1.5 million research center that, it was planned, would be home to 1,000 engineers. Little wonder, A.O. Smith was expanding at the speed of a latter day Amazon.com—its net income rose from $2.83 million in 1928 to $5.5 million in 1930.

THE GREAT ATLANTIC & PACIFIC TEA COMPANY OF AMERICA: Atlantic & Pacific (A&P) then sold over $1 billion worth of food every year. (Tea remained a minority interest, despite the company's name—it was its worst seller.) "To get all this food and drink to the right place at the right time so that each of the 5,000,000 families will daily make its sixty-five-cent purchase is, needless to say, a triumph of organization, for which, in a war, all the orders of all the crowned heads would be pinned on somebody's breast," concluded *Fortune*.

State of Play: Corporate Stars in 1930 (continued)

R.J. REYNOLDS TOBACCO COMPANY: From Winston-Salem, R.J. Reynolds was then recording sales estimated at $300 million. Housed in a state-of-the-art twenty-three-floor skyscraper, Reynolds had brought the world the Camel brand—"Camels lead the world" was the slogan—as well as Prince Albert pipe tobacco and Brown's Mule chewing tobacco, among others. In 1930, Reynolds had twelve thousand employees producing eight hundred cigarettes a minute. It was, however, looking over its shoulder somewhat anxiously at the growing competitive threat from American Tobacco's Lucky Strikes.

INTERNATIONAL TELEPHONE & TELEGRAPH CORPORATION: In 1921 the Behn brothers came to New York to expand their fledgling communications business, which had proved highly successful in Cuba and Puerto Rico. They succeeded. The company's gross earnings rose from $5.85 million in 1924 to $104.47 million in 1930: ITT had arrived. The master plan of the Behns, according to *Fortune,* was to create "an American communications system."

---

was a fault of its more recent executives rather than the organizational model. Instead of a company building from Sloan's legacy, GM has increasingly resembled a company with little idea what to do with the legacy. As recently as 1998, an article in *Fortune* noted: "As one executive explained: 'The die was cast 70 years ago when everything was bought, rather than built from within.' If you're keeping score at home, 70 years ago was during the Coolidge Administration—and GM still hasn't fully integrated those companies! Not until later this year will Buick and Oldsmobile move out of their old headquarters in Flint and Lansing to Detroit. GM still awards a corporate vice presidency to the head of each division, another relic of their former independence."[20] GM has manifestly failed to live with its past, as surely as Ford failed to live with the inheritance of its founder.

The Top American Companies of 1929

Rank	Company	Assets ($ million)
1.	U.S. Steel	2,286
2.	Standard Oil of New Jersey	1,767
3.	General Motors	1,131
4.	Standard Oil of Indiana	850
5.	Bethlehem Steel	802
6.	Ford Motor	761
7.	Mobil Oil	708
8.	Anaconda	681
9.	Texaco	610
10.	Standard Oil of California	605
11.	General Electric	516
12.	DuPont	497
13.	Shell Oil	486
14.	Armour	452
15.	Gulf Oil	431
16.	Sinclair Oil	401
17.	International Harvester	384
18.	General Theaters Equipment	360
19.	Swift	351
20.	Kennecott Copper	338

Source: A.D.H. Kaplan, *Big Enterprise in a Competitive System.* Westport, Conn.: Greenwood, 1964

The Dow Jones Industrial Average Companies as of October 1, 1928

Allied Chemical	Nash Motors
American Can	North American
American Smelting	Paramount Publix
American Sugar	Postum Inc.
American Tobacco B	Radio Corp.
Atlantic Refining	Sears, Roebuck
Bethlehem Steel	Standard Oil of New Jersey
Chrysler	Texas Corporation
General Electric	Texas Gulf Sulphur
General Motors	Union Carbide
General Railway Signal	U.S. Steel
Goodrich	Victor Talking Machine
International Harvester	Westinghouse Electric
International Nickel	Woolworth
Mack Truck	Wright Aeronautical

The Management Century Timeline

1921

U.S. unemployment goes over 20 percent. Congress limits immigration and establishes the national origin quota system.

Sony founder Akio Morita born in Nagoya, Japan.

1922

Ray Kroc, later of McDonald's fame, begins work as a salesman for Lily Tulip Cup Co. and moonlights as a piano player.

The first management congress—in Prague—is organized by Herbert Hoover, then U.S. Secretary of Commerce, and Thomas Masaryk, the historian and founding president of the new Czechoslovak Republic.[21]

Wallace Donham, dean of Harvard Business School, oversees the launch of the *Harvard Business Review.* "The Effect of Hedging upon Flour Mill Control" hardly set the pulse racing, but was the beginning of a publishing success story and a prestigious addition to the Harvard brand. For more than seventy-five years the *Harvard Business Review* has been influential in shaping management thinking around the globe.

1923

Walt Disney opens a cartoon studio in Hollywood.

Gillette produces a gold-plated razor—a real steal at a dollar.

The American Management Association is founded.

Pan American Airways and Hertz Drive-Ur-Self car rentals created.

Time magazine appears.

1924

The case study method is established as the primary method of teaching at Harvard Business School.

Computing-Tabulating-Recording Company becomes International Business Machines.

Ford produces its ten millionth car.

1925

After failing to convince Montgomery Ward to move into retailing, Robert E. Wood (1879–1969) is hired by Sears, Roebuck in 1924. Julius Rosenwald liked the idea of moving into retail stores; Sears opens its first retail store in 1925 and becomes the world's largest general merchandiser. By 1928 Sears had 192 retail stores. A heady pace of expansion was maintained—during a single year in the 1920s a new Sears store opened every other business day.

Scripps-Howard newspaper empire formed.

1926

Congress passes the Railway Labor Act, requiring employers to bargain with unions.

Greyhound Corporation, Prestone antifreeze, National Broadcasting Company created.

Coca-Cola sets up a foreign sales department.

1927

Hostess Cakes, Wonder Bread, Gerber Baby Food, Volvo cars introduced.

1928

First TV program is broadcast in the United States.

On Sunday November 18, Mickey Mouse features in one of the only cinematic epics of seven minutes in length: *Steamboat Willie.* This is the first cartoon to synchronize sound and action.

Columbia Broadcasting System introduced; Transamerica Corporation founded.

1929

Stock market crashes. The Dow didn't recover the ground lost in the Crash of 1929 until 1954. The Great Depression begins.

Kodak color movies are invented.

Chapter 4
1931–1940: Discovering People

Many people tell me what I ought to do and just how I ought to do it, but few have made me want to do something.
—MARY PARKER FOLLETT[1]

Turning on the Lights

In 1926, the Laura Spelman Rockefeller Foundation awarded a grant of $100,000 a year for five years to the Committee on Industrial Physiology of Harvard University. This was hardly headline news. But the research undertaken proved truly groundbreaking.

Among the members of the committee was an Australian called Elton Mayo (1880–1949). Mayo had a colorfully peripatetic background. He trained in medicine in London and Edinburgh, spent time in Africa, worked in an Adelaide printing company, and taught at Queensland University. He also worked on psychoanalyzing sufferers of shell shock after the First World War.[2] Mayo arrived in the United States in 1923 and worked at the University of Pennsylvania before joining Harvard in 1926 to work on the business school's new research program.

The grant from the foundation was used to explore the reality of working life. How did people really work in factories? What concerned and motivated the people actually doing the work? What factors affected their morale and productivity? At the time businesses were still mystified as to why scientific management had failed to revolutionize productivity and behavior. On paper its logic seemed powerful and irrefutable. In practice, however, morale was often lowered by the introduction of mass production and scientific management techniques. The humanistic strand of management thinking was ignited not by concern for fellow human beings but by desperation. Companies wanted to maximize productivity.

In asking such questions the researchers were taking a radically different route from their predecessors. Their aim was later described as to achieve an "intimate, habitual, intuitive familiarity with the phenomena."[3] This eventually produced over twenty thousand interviews that were diligently recorded and transcribed for posterity.

The resulting experiments, run by Mayo but involving a coterie of other researchers (among those who later wrote about the findings were Harvard's Fritz Roethlisberger and William Dickson), were carried out at Western Electric's Hawthorne plant in Cicero, Illinois, between 1927 and 1932.[4]

The Hawthorne studies began with experiments in which the lighting in the factory was altered. The theory was that brighter light would raise morale and, as a result, increase productivity. The trouble was that lighting was expensive. Mayo and his researchers set out to establish the lighting level that maximized productivity without being prohibitively expensive. This seemed straightforward, simply a question of finding the balance between cost and effect.

Hawthorne workers were separated into two groups. In one group the lighting levels were increased: productivity increased. In the other group the lighting remained at its normal level: productivity increased. Lighting levels were further increased, but still the productivity levels in the two groups remained much the same.

This seemed surprisingly inconclusive. How could productivity rise when the lighting remained exactly the same? The researchers, therefore, started decreasing lighting levels. They reduced the lighting in one group drastically: productivity increased. Eventually, the light was reduced to extreme dinginess. It was expected that the workers would be depressed and irritable working in moonlight. In fact, their productivity remained at a similar level, and sometimes increased. To prove the point, two workers were isolated in a very small room indeed with minimal lighting. Their productivity continued at a healthy level.

The researchers shook their heads and contemplated what all this meant. They were confused—but, being researchers, returned with a more complicated experiment. In the factory's relay assembly test room, a group of six women who assembled telephone relay switches were selected and isolated. There they were diligently observed. Conditions were changed and tinkered with. But nothing seemed to reduce productivity.

The conclusion from the research team was that they had missed something. This something was the relationships, attitudes, feelings, and perceptions of the people involved. The research program had revolved around selecting small groups of workers to be studied. This, not surprisingly, made them feel special. For the first time they actually felt that management was interested in them. The second effect was that the people felt like they belonged to a select team. They identified with their group. "The desire to stand well with one's fellows, the so-called human instinct of association, easily outweighs the merely individual interest and the logic of reasoning upon which so many spurious principles of management are based," commented Mayo.

The Harvard research team then determined to look more closely at how groups operated. Was social structure behind the formation and behavior of such groups? The researchers chose the bank wiring room at the factory for this next stage in their experiments. This contained nine wiremen, three soldermen, two inspectors, and the observer.

The job of the soldermen was to service the wiremen. Each was designated three wiremen. The wiremen attached wires to panels, while the soldermen soldered the connections. The inspectors then tested the connections electrically. Of the nine wiremen, three worked solely on selectors while the remaining six concentrated on connectors.

The group appeared small and relatively simple to understand. But the more the researchers looked at the group's behavior, the more they uncovered. First, there were a variety of social structures at work in the group. Being a wireman granted workers greater prestige—though not as much as being an inspector. This was revealed in the usual ways human beings find to express their superiority—soldermen were dispatched to get lunch for the group; wiremen exercised control over whether the windows were open or closed. The good news for the soldermen was that there were people lower than them in status. These were the truckers who brought supplies and took away finished products. Truckers were put in their place by a variety of tricks and treats—including spitting on the completed terminals. All truckers were treated the same. New recruits were automatically treated in the same way as all other truckers. This was not written down in some corporate manual. It simply happened. Truckers were nobodies, end of story.

The second feature of the group's behavior was the constant series of games the workers engaged in. They played card games, shot craps, and made obscure bets on numbers in their paychecks. They argued and horsed around. In this they were basically split into two groups—those at the front and those at the back of the room.

A third element was the complex array of individual dynamics at work. Some workers were more popular than others. There were outcasts and more popular members of the group whom people would offer to help. There were cliques. Membership in the cliques was determined by not working too much (rate-busting), not working too little (chiseling), not running to tell all to the supervisors, and not trying to act like an inspector.

The cliques served the purpose of protecting workers against management. Clique members covered for each other, inventing and embellishing stories to help each other out. Solidarity, based on contempt, ensured that the group could stand firm against any changes—especially to their piece rates.

The group created a complex world of their own. They exerted control over it. Sometimes their reasoning and perceptions were completely at odds with the truth. The researchers found that the workers did not, for example, understand the company's payment system. Misconceptions were handed down from one worker to the next and quickly became accepted as truth.

From an organizational perspective, the experiment in the bank wiring room provided a salutary lesson. It seemed that apparently well-organized and rigorously managed groups were nothing of the kind. Instead of being tightly controlled, easily regulated, and understandable, they were an intricate web of relationships and dynamic forces. If people worked together for any length of time, they formed their own status system, culture, and structures, which often served as protection against management. "Man's desire to be continuously associated in work with his fellows is a strong, if not the strongest, human characteristic," wrote Mayo. "Any disregard of it by management or any ill-advised attempt to defeat this human impulse leads instantly to some form of defeat for management itself."[5] The conclusion was inescapable: Understanding the structures and relationships in such informal groups is essential to successful management of any organization. "So long as commerce specializes in business methods which take no account of human nature and social motives, so long may we expect strikes and sabotage to be the ordinary accompaniment of industry," Mayo concluded.

The New Human Deal

The significance of the Hawthorne experiments is only fully understood when you consider the dearth of humanity in the theories and practice of Frederick Taylor, Henry Ford, or Alfred P. Sloan. To Taylor, people were Schmidt and the like, human fodder for industry. To Ford, people were instruments of production and purchasing. There seemed little human warmth in between. And Sloan's *My Years with General Motors* is one of the most clinically empty books of all time. Sloan's many decades at General Motors were, it seems, devoid of any human confrontation or any personality.

Taylor discovered work. Ford discovered work on a massive scale. Sloan organized work. And no one discovered the people doing the work.

There were notable exceptions, oases where people were treated with fairness and decency. These, however, were few and far between. For the most part, managers were concerned with coming to terms with production and organization rather than the human arts of management.[6]

Motivation, for example, was generally ignored. Inevitably, this did not stop Henry Ford having an opinion on the subject. "Thinking men know that work is the salvation of the race, morally, physically, socially," said Ford. "Men work for two reasons. One is for wages, and one is for fear of losing their jobs." People worked through financial necessity and through a built-in belief in the goodness of work. Martin Luther's Protestant work ethic—whose lingering effects are still felt—insisted that work and prayer were closely linked. Working was good for the soul. Work was inextricably tied up with religion. Work was unquestioned, almost above question. To work was good. "All men possess a calling in the world and the fulfilment of its obligation is a divinely imposed duty," said Martin Luther. John Calvin wrote, "Disciplined work raises a person above the calling into which he was born and is the only sign of his election by God to salvation." Given the assumptions about the positive nature of work it is perhaps little wonder that the nature of work had gone unquestioned for so long and that Taylor, Ford, and others had a highly pliable workforce to mold to their methods. If your work is your salvation, you are more likely to do as you are told.

The industrialists of the early part of the twentieth century were not an isolated instance. Sensitive management of people is usually notable by its absence as you scan the history books. Look and you are left grasping at straws—the Emperor Hadrian's human resource management—Hadrian's army was forged on his willingness to share the same conditions as his troops. One anecdote describes his refusal to wear his cloak or cap no matter what the weather. Similarly, Hadrian was reputed to join his troops on lengthy marches in full armor. Or you can point to Napoleon's belief in meritocracy—Napoleon said that talent was no respecter of birth. Careers should, he said, be "open to talents without distinction of birth or fortune." Napoleon recruited and promoted on the grounds of ability rather than nobility. As a child of the middle classes, he wasn't about to elevate noble lords above their ability.

These are exceptions. The rest is brute force masquerading as leadership.

A handful of nineteenth-century philanthropists stand out from the crowd. But their example was usually relegated to the industrial fringes. Given the paucity of good practice—or even considered practice—it is perhaps not all that surprising that it took so long for theorists to consider the human side of management.

This is even more clear when you consider that the dominant metaphor of working life was that of a machine. Corporations were machines, gigantic engines of capitalism. Imagine the surprise of readers when they came across Elton Mayo's book, *The Human Problems of an Industrial Civilization* (1933). Mayo proposed new images. As a biologist, he regarded corporations as organic systems, complex and perpetually altering beings. "Living organism is best conceived as a number of variables in equilibrium with each other in such a fashion that a change in any one will introduce changes throughout the whole organization," wrote Mayo.[7]

Mayo recognized that human organizations were as prone to dysfunctional behavior as human beings themselves. "Although Mayo was for the opportunity for growth for everybody, everywhere, he recognized the possibility of lopsided growth," wrote his colleague Fritz Roethlisberger. "He saw that many things, both desirable ones and undesirable ones, can be both functional and dysfunctional. Restriction of output among workers, for instance, although functional for the solidarity of the group and the emotional security of its members, is dysfunctional for the group's identity with the economic objectives of the enterprise."[8]

Dynamic People

In 1926 Lyndal Urwick was a senior manager with the English chocolate manufacturer Rowntree. At the behest of his boss he canceled a weekend with his wife to attend a lecture by an American woman he had never heard of. Her name was Mary Parker Follett.

"There was rather a dull paper on the Friday evening. Mary Follett spoke in the subsequent discussion. But I was feeling tired and rather fed up. I wasn't particularly struck by her contribution," Urwick later recalled. "After the meeting was over, [Seebohm] Rowntree grabbed me and introduced us. As I looked at her I remember thinking, 'What on earth is my dear Seebohm up to? He's always most considerate of those working with him. And here he's practically forced me to cancel a weekend to which I had greatly looked forward in order to meet this gaunt Boston spinster. From what she said in the discussion she's a pure academic. What in the world can we have in common?' Then Mary started to talk with me. And in two minutes I was at her feet, where I remained for the rest of her life."

The gaunt Boston spinster, Mary Parker Follett (1868–1933), was born in Quincy, Massachusetts. She attended Thayer Academy and the Society for the Collegiate Instruction of Women in Cambridge, Massachusetts (now part of Harvard University). She also studied at Newnham College, Cambridge (in the United Kingdom), and in Paris. Her first published work was *The Speaker of the House of Representatives* (1896), which she wrote while still a student.

Follett's career was largely spent in social work though her books appeared regularly—*The New State* (1918), an influential description of Follett's brand of dynamic democracy, and *Creative Experience* (1924), Follett's first business-oriented book. In her later years she was in great demand as a lecturer. After the death of long-time partner Isobel Briggs in 1926, she moved to London.

Generally ignored, Follett was decades ahead of her time. She was discussing issues such as teamworking and responsibility (now reborn as empowerment) in the first decades of the twentieth century. Follett was a female, liberal humanist in an era dominated by reactionary males intent on mechanizing the world of business.[9]

The breadth and humanity of her work was a refreshing counter to the dehumanized visions of Taylor and others. "We should remember that we can never wholly separate the human from the mechanical sides," warned Follett in *Dynamic Administration*.[10] "The study of human relations in business and the study of the technology of operating are bound up together."

The simple thrust of Follett's thinking was that people were central to any business activity—or, indeed, to any other activity. "I think we should undepartmentalize our thinking in regard to every problem that comes to us," said Follett. "I do not think that we have psychological and ethical and economic problems. We have human problems, with psychological, ethical and economical aspects, and as many others as you like."

In particular, Follett explored conflict. She argued that as conflict is a fact of life "we should, I think, use it to work for us." Follett pointed out three ways of dealing with confrontation: domination, compromise, or integration. The latter, she concluded, is the only positive way forward. This can be achieved by first "uncovering" the real conflict and then taking "the demands of both sides and breaking them up into their constituent parts." "Our outlook is narrowed, our activity is restricted, our chances of business success largely diminished when our thinking is constrained within the limits of what has been called an either-or situation. We should never allow ourselves to be bullied by an 'either-or.' There is often the possibility of something better than either of two given alternatives," Follett wrote.

Follett advocated giving greater responsibility to people—at a time when the mechanical might of mass production was at its height. "At present nearly all our needs are satisfied by external agencies, government or institutional. Health societies offer health to us, recreation associations teach us how to play, civic art leagues give us more beautiful surroundings, associated charities give us poor relief. A kind lady leads my girl to the dentist, a kind young man finds employment for my boy, a stern officer of the city sees that my children are in their places at school. I am constantly being acted upon, no one is encouraging me to act. Thus am I robbed of my most precious possession—my responsibilities—for only the active process of participation can shape me for the social purpose."[11] No participation without responsibility, was Follett's persuasive message. Few read her lips.

Follett's views were a large step beyond those of Mayo and the Hawthorne investigators. While Mayo offered a humanistic view of the workplace, it was still one that assumed that the behavior of workers was dictated by the "logic of sentiment" while that of the bosses was by the "logic of cost and efficiency." A Japanese manager, quoted in Richard Pascale's *Managing on the Edge,* made an important observation: "There is nothing wrong with the findings. But the Hawthorne experiments look at human behavior from the wrong perspective. Your thinking needs to build from the idea of empowering workers, placing responsibility closest to where the knowledge resides, using consistently honored values to draw the separate individuals together. The Hawthorne experiments imply smug superiority, parent-to-child assumptions. This is not a true understanding."[12] Nor was it Mary Parker Follett's understanding.

There was also a modern ring to Follett's advice on leadership: "The most successful leader of all is one who sees another picture not yet actualized." Follett saw the leader's tasks as coordination, defining the purpose of the business, and anticipation—"We look to the leader to open up new paths, new opportunities." Follett suggested that a leader was someone who saw the whole rather than the particular, organized the experiences of the group, offered a vision of the future, and trained followers to become leaders. The leader was a conduit to greater knowledge: "If leadership does not mean coercion in any form, if it does not mean controlling, protecting or exploiting, what does it mean? It means, I think, freeing. The greatest service the teacher can render the student is to increase his freedom—his free range of activity and thought and his power of control."[13]

Follett was concerned that the actual term *leadership* was unhelpful—it smacked of dictatorship, being told what to do. Her vision of leadership was of "reciprocal leadership," "a partnership in following, of following the invisible leader—the common purpose."[14] Indeed, Follett's work is among the first to highlight the role of followers—followership was later rediscovered fifty years later. "If the followers must partake in leadership, it is also true that we must have followership on the part of leaders. There must be a partnership of following," wrote Follett.[15]

In addition, Follett was an early advocate of management training and the concept that leadership could be taught. "The theory has been of personal domination, but study the political leaders, the party bosses, and notice how often they have gained their positions by their ability to bring into harmonious relation men of antagonistic temperaments, their ability to reconcile conflicting interests, their ability to make a working unit out of many diverse elements."

Follett's work was largely neglected in the West. Peter Drucker, now an admirer, recalls that when he was seeking out management literature in the 1940s, no one even mentioned Follett's name. Once again, however, a Western thinker was honored in Japan—which even boasts a Follett Society.

The Human Reality

Mary Parker Follett may have been ignored, but the human side of business was the abiding issue of the depression-struck 1930s. People were the future.

Roosevelt's New Deal played a central role in making this happen. It brought the phrase "industrial democracy" to the forefront of the business agenda—though not necessarily into best practice. In 1933, working conditions and laws were improved with startling rapidity. In July the cotton textile code was signed—this gave American workers a forty-hour week and $12 minimum weekly wages, and abolished child labor. Later in the same month, Roosevelt sent five million "re-employment agreements" to as many employers, of whom three million signed. In August the National Labor Board was created to settle the wave of strikes created by the resurgence of organized labor. "A truce on selfishness, a test of patriotism," cried General Johnson.[16]

"Whatever the phrase 'industrial democracy' may mean, it is the heart of the President's recovery program. As embodied in the NRA, 'industrial democracy' no longer terrifies U.S. businessmen," observed *Time* magazine, declaring Roosevelt to be Man of the Year.

Change was in the air. William S. Knudsen, executive vice president of General Motors, declared his support for the New Deal "without reservations." *Time* announced, "The days of cut-throat competition and laissez faire are over. Few industrialists want them back. Many of them would agree with NRA's Divisional Administrator Arthur Dare Whiteside, Dun & Bradstreet executive, one of the most experienced practical businessmen in the Administration, who said last week: 'It is obvious in retrospect that four years ago this month the old industrial order which existed for generations broke down forever. Today we have set up a new order which has been built on a foundation which I firmly believe will prove indestructible, although I am definitely convinced that it will be necessary to make alterations.'"[17]

And the new humanity was reflected in the business practice of those setting up in business during the 1930s. Their numbers included Bill Hewlett and David Packard. They began their company, Hewlett-Packard, in 1937—with a mere $538 in a rented garage in Palo Alto, California. The two had met while students at nearby Stanford. Their ambitions were typical of many young people starting a business. "We thought we would have a job for ourselves. That's all we thought about in the beginning," said Packard. "We hadn't the slightest idea of building a big company." That garage was the birthplace of Silicon Valley and of a more responsible and humane form of management.

The Dow Jones Industrial Average Companies as of January 1, 1939

Allied Chemical	Procter & Gamble
American Can	Johns-Manville
American Smelting	Loew's
DuPont	General Foods
Eastman Kodak	National Kelvinator
Goodyear	Sears, Roebuck
Bethlehem Steel	Standard Oil of New Jersey
Chrysler	Texas Corporation
General Electric	National Distillers
General Motors	Union Carbide
American Tobacco B	U.S. Steel
Standard Oil of California	International Business Machines
International Harvester	Westinghouse Electric
International Nickel	Woolworth
Corn Products Refining	National Steel

The Management Century Timeline

1930

National Unemployed Council is formed.

The State Department orders the hiring of foreign laborers to stop.

Hostess Twinkies introduced.

1931

An article in *Fortune* observes: "With the Census of Occupations as a base, I found that of 42,000,000 Americans gainfully employed, not more than 10,000,000 spent their working hours in close contact with machinery. Further analysis discloses that only about 5,000,000 can properly be called robots at all in that they surrender their personalities to the machine. The other 5,000,000 either are handicraft men and other helpers about factories who have little to do with machinery, or—and this is important—they themselves dominate the mechanism and thus let some of its energy into their own veins."[18]

U.S. Congress passes Davis-Bacon Act providing for payment of prevailing wages to workers.

The biggest one-day percentage gain for the Dow: 14.9 percent on October 6. Nonetheless, 1931 is the Dow's worst year—it ends at 77.90, down 52.67 percent.

1932

The Dow hits its lowest point ever: 41.22.

IBM is added to the Dow though it is dropped in 1939 and only returns to the index forty years later. Meanwhile it had gained 22,000 percent during those four decades.

1933

A severe banking crisis looms in Michigan. GM intervenes and puts up half the cash ($12,500,000) to form a new and liquid bank, the National Bank of Detroit. This saves the state and the fledgling motor industry from chaos.

U.S. cotton textile code sets 40-hour week and minimum weekly wage for men.

Edwin Armstrong invents FM radio.

Federal Deposit Insurance Corporation (FDIC) established.

Gold standard abandoned in United States.

1934

Federal Communications Commission and Securities and Exchange Commission established.

1935

Roosevelt signs the Social Security Act into law.

1936

Concerned about the development of automatic looms, Kiichiro Toyoda decides that the future of his family's business lies in carmaking. He changes the company's name to Toyota in 1936. (The name Toyota emerged from a competition—Toyota in Japanese characters conveys speed and uses eight strokes, a number suggesting prosperity. From the Western perspective it is pronounceable and attractively meaningless.)

Walter Reuther leads first ever sit-down strike.

Henry Ford establishes the Ford Foundation.

1937

Walt Disney premiers *Snow White,* the first full-length animated film.

United States establishes minimum wage for women.

Dale Carnegie's *How to Win Friends and Influence People* published.

1938

Congress passes the Fair Labor Standards Act (FLSA) establishing the forty-hour workweek and the minimum wage, and banning child labor.

Chester Carlson produces the first xerographic image in his laboratory in Queens in New York City. Later, in 1947, the Haloid Company acquires the license to basic xerographic patents taken out by Carlson from Battelle Development Corporation of Columbus, Ohio. A year later, the two companies announce the development of xerography, and the words "Xerox" and "xerography" are patented.

DuPont introduces nylon.

Chester Barnard's *Functions of the Executive* published.

1939

Pan Am starts regular transatlantic and transpacific service.

1940

The two McDonald brothers—Dick and Maurice (known by all as Mac)— open up a restaurant in San Bernardino, California. It is nothing unusual— a barbecue and car-hop place. As they become more experienced, the McDonalds realize that their customers want food in a hurry. They don't necessarily want to be waited on. They just want their food quickly. So, in December 1948, Dick and Mac move into fast food. Their new restaurant is topped by a large neon sign proclaiming that Speedee the Chef works there.

Chapter 5
1941–1950: Lessons in War

The vanguard of the fightingest nation in the world.
—WARTIME ADVERTISEMENT FROM
THE INDIAN MOTORCYCLE COMPANY

Fighting the Good Fight

Wars have always concentrated managerial minds wonderfully. They have made and broken companies. When war broke out in 1914, 150,000 Americans found themselves trapped in Europe. Who could they turn to for help? The line at the American Express office at 11, Rue Scribe, in Paris was soon a hundred meters long and six people deep as Americans tried to escape Europe. American Express rose to the occasion and posted money to points all across Europe. In some countries, the locals preferred to trade in American Express travelers checks rather than trust the local currency. What price would you put on such branding?

In addition, wars tend to push the frontiers of invention. Companies create and innovate at a hectic pace and can create the basis of their future success. In 1917 (during the First World War), for example, Kodak developed aerial cameras and trained aerial photographers for the U.S. Signal Corps.

And then there are the lucrative military orders, which can make a company—and introduce millions to its products. In 1917 the U.S. government placed an order for 3.5 million razors and 36 million blades with Gillette. The entire army needed a shave.

The Second World War (1939–1945) was one of the most important events in the evolution of management practice and theory. It coalesced the fledgling human relations school of thinking with the mass production techniques that had been mastered over the preceding forty years.

Production was on a massive scale. Donald Nelson of Sears, chairman of the War Production Board from 1942 to 1944, later tried to put things in perspective: "The American war-production job was probably the greatest collective achievement of all time. It makes the seven wonders of the ancient world look like the doodlings of a small boy on a rainy Saturday afternoon."

This may have overstated things slightly—and it is difficult to compare the creation of the Hanging Gardens of Babylon with the mass production of bombers. But the raw statistics are impressive. The United States produced twice as much as Japan and Germany combined. Productivity went through the roof. The depressed economy was kick-started in spectacular fashion. American GDP shot from $91.3 billion in 1941 to $166.6 billion in 1945. Thanks to wartime production, manufacturing output almost doubled and agricultural output rose 22 percent. The investment in winning was enormous. The American government doubled its total expenditure, spent a total of $400 billion (double what it had actually spent in its entire history prior to 1940), and, by the end of the war, was saddled with around $260 billion of debt.[1]

In total America produced 86,000 tanks, 296,000 aircraft, 15 million rifles, 41 billion rounds of ammunition, 5,400 merchant ships, and 6,500 warships. This was achieved through virtually all industrial output being turned over to the war effort.

Department of the Army Dollar Expenditures (by fiscal year)[2]

1940	907,160,000
1941	3,938,943,000
1942	14,325,508,000
1943	42,525,562,000

America's entry into the Second World War saw the entire Harley-Davidson production dispatched to the military. A 1942 Harley-Davidson brochure read: "Off the assembly lines they roll, sleek, streamlined Harley Davidsons for Uncle Sam's forces and the armies of our allies."

IBM placed its facilities at the government's disposal and expanded its product line to include items such as Browning automatic rifles. IBM chief Thomas Watson set a nominal profit of 1 percent, the proceeds of which went toward a fund for the widows and orphans of IBM war casualties. IBM kept all employees enlisting in the armed services on the payroll.

Central to the American war effort was General Motors president William S. Knudsen, who was responsible for industrial production at the National Defense Advisory Council and then in charge of production for the War Department. General Motors became America's largest defense contractor. More than 90 percent of GM's total production between 1942 and 1945 was of war material.[3] By 1943, American automobile industry output was double its prewar capacity and as the war reached its finale in fall 1945, the car factories accounted for around 20 percent of the total amount of weapons and war material produced in the United States. Plants that had been idle before the war, thanks to the effects of the Great Depression, burst into life. By spring 1941 U.S. airplane production was hitting record levels—in March of that year 1,216 were produced.

Two-thirds of the war items produced by GM and other carmakers were entirely new to them. Cadillac and Chrysler made tanks; Oldsmobile made heavy caliber shells. Other companies found themselves shifting businesses—AC Spark Plug made machine guns, Fisher Body made B-25 airframes, and Packard made engines for PT boats.[4] (Of course, this wasn't the preserve of American companies. Elsewhere companies were venturing into unfamiliar territory. In Japan Konosuke Matsushita made ships and planes as part of the Japanese war effort—even though he had no experience in either area.)

But it wasn't simply a war dominated by manufacturing industry. Wartime also cemented the role of management consultants and business schools. At Harvard Business School all regular civilian instruction was suspended for the duration of the war and 5,921 military students were involved in war training programs. Harvard's Advanced Management Program began life in 1943 as a wartime management training program.

Leading management researchers also had a part to play. The government funded a training program run by a colleague of Elton Mayo's to teach foremen how to work with people and treat people as individuals. And Rensis Likert (1903–1981) was involved in national surveys and the Strategic Bombing Survey's morale division.[5] Its unenviable task was to calculate the effect on morale of bombing. It looked at Germany and then Japan. The findings included the suggestion that "light" bombing decreased morale while blanket bombing had little extra impact. This has influenced government policy in the United States and beyond ever since—witness the NATO strategy in Kosovo in the 1999 conflict.

Consultants were also in demand as the government sought to come to terms with the massive management exercise involved. In 1940, consulting firm Booz·Allen responded to a request from Secretary of the Navy Frank Knox to help prepare the U.S. Navy for war. Throughout the war, "Management Engineers" cut through the red tape of military bureaucracy to get fast results.

At the same time, there was growing appreciation that cooperation between workers and management was fruitful—not to mention necessary if the war was to be won. In many ways, the war was a better place to work. Unemployment dropped dramatically as men went to war and women worked in their place. Discord was, for a while at least, put to one side. The American Federation of Labor (AFL) and Congress of Industrial Organizations (CIO) gave no-strike pledges for the duration of the war in 1941. With a highly motivated workforce, clear goals, and manufacturing might, the Allied juggernaut was unstoppable.

Brands for the Boys

To this formidable war effort was added an extra ingredient: marketing. The war marked the advent of mass marketing. It did so in an unusual way. The troops sitting in their trenches in northern France were granted a preview of the consumerist future. The troops were a captive audience.[6] The big brands came running. The war effort became a time to cement names and products in the public's imagination. The war was a breeding ground for the world to come.

The best-known example of this phenomenon was Coca-Cola. The company boldly and ambitiously promised that any U.S. soldier would be able to buy a Coke for a nickel. The Coke became the symbol of American taste and consumption. To fulfill its promise Coke built sixty mobile bottling plants and sent them along with the army. Each could be run by two men and produce 1,370 bottles an hour. (The more cynical and worldly slant on this story is that Coke convinced the government that its drink was vital to the well-being and happiness of U.S. troops to get around the potential threat of sugar rationing.)

The war cemented Coke's place at the heart of American society. *Time* magazine celebrated Coke's "peaceful near-conquest of the world." (Coke's competitors complained of favoritism and hyperbole.) The postwar years saw Coke expand its corporate empire in the quest for what it engagingly called "share of throat."

Other brands were bolstered by wartime. The war boosted consumption of Wrigley's chewing gum as the Allied armed forces purchased large quantities. Chewing gum was believed to ease tension, promote alertness, and improve morale generally. In 1944, Wrigley's entire production was turned over to the U.S. Armed Forces overseas and at sea (as was the production of Hershey chocolate). It may have lost some of its appeal today, but the slogan "Got any gum, chum?" was a big hit with military personnel at the time.

Similarly, when Allied troops landed in Normandy in 1944 they carried self-heating cans of Heinz soup. Heinz's wartime slogans included the memorable "Beans to bombers" and "Pickles to pursuit planes." The war also saw demand for Nescafé instant coffee (at the time, a comparatively recent invention) go through the roof—Nestlé's total sales increased from $100 million to $225 million and the entire output of Nestlé's U.S. plant—in excess of one million cases—was reserved for military use.

There were other curious tales of brand triumphs. Contrary to popular myth, Spam, the manufactured ham substitute made by the Hormel

Company in Minnesota, was not an integral part of GI rations. (Despite Eisenhower's claim, "I ate Spam along with millions of soldiers.") Nor was it dropped on bombing runs. In fact, fifteen million cans a week of Spam were dispatched to feed the British and the Russians. The postwar Soviet leader Nikita Khrushchev later observed: "Without Spam, we wouldn't have been able to feed our army." On such endorsements great brands were made.

Seeds of the Future

In 1924, a physicist called Walter Shewhart (1891–1967) came up with the idea of a production control chart. A year later, he joined Western Electric as an engineer and discovered that the desire for exactitude found in theory was inevitably disappointed by practice. Shewhart's response was to develop a statistical approach to quality that emphasized the stability of production and supply and applied the standards of the end user to the producer. Basically, Shewhart argued that minimal variation in production and maximum human cooperation were the most productive routes forward.

During the war, the U.S. War Department, anxious to enhance productivity as much as possible, brought in Western Electric's Bell Telephone Laboratories to promote its quality control methods. The armaments industry was given a crash course in Shewhart-style quality. Its impact was generally seen as positive. Indeed, Lord Cherwell, wartime scientific adviser to Winston Churchill, said that the Shewhart quality philosophy was the single most significant U.S. contribution to the whole Allied war effort.

Such steps forward seemed to suggest that the Allied victors had the industrial world at their feet. Wartime had been a proving ground for modern management and manufacturing. They had emerged triumphant, able to produce reliable goods quickly in huge quantities.

In the immediate postwar years, however, the pursuit of *more* once again became the driving economic force. Shewhart was largely forgotten in the rush to get on with business life. Quality initiatives like those at Western Electric disappeared . . . from the United States at least.

Meanwhile, the scale and speed of the revival of the countries defeated and devastated by the war was startling. The destruction was enormous, beyond parallel at an individual, national, and corporate level. In Germany, the huge Siemens corporation was all but destroyed. By 1945, only about four hundred of the twenty-four thousand machine tools originally installed were still operative in the company's Berlin plants. After only fourteen days of occupation, the Allied powers allowed work to resume; by the end of 1945, around fourteen thousand workers were employed at Siemens's Berlin plants, cleaning up the damage and making a bizarre collection of products including bicycle tires, coal shovels, cooking pots, and coal-fired stoves.

On September 2, 1945, the Japanese surrendered on board the U.S.S. *Missouri.* However, the Japanese had begun planning their future before their final defeat. (As had German industrialists. "Group directorates" were already established in southern and western Germany by Siemens in the final months of the war. These directorates were later able to start the reconstruction work independently of the head office in Berlin.) In the summer of 1945 Japanese ministers met secretly to discuss the future revival of their country. The aim, according to the country's foreign minister, Shigeru Yoshida, was to ensure that "we could indeed rebuild Imperial Japan out of this way of defeat. . . . Science will be advanced, business will become strong with the introduction of American capital, and in the end our Imperial country will be able to fulfil its true potential. If that is so, it is not so bad to be defeated in this war." This combination of pragmatism, optimism, planning, and blind faith was characteristic of the rebuilding of the country.

The Japanese were greatly helped by General MacArthur's commitment to rebuilding the country. He wanted to rebuild not through reestablishing the old elite but through elevating the middle ranks to take charge. One of the immediate postwar objectives was to set up a Japanese radio receiver industry so that the occupying powers could communicate directly to the people. The team of engineers charged with helping Japan's radio industry included a number who had worked at Western Electric and were, as a result, aware of the concept of quality control.

Indeed, the approach of the American team of engineers in postwar Japan was greatly influenced by Shewhart's work. The team included

Homer Sarasohn, W.S. Magil, Frank Polkinghorn, and Charles Protzman. Magil used Shewhart's quality control theories at the Nippon Electric Company in 1946 and lectured on the subject while in Japan.

Then Sarasohn and Protzman were supported by MacArthur in their idea of establishing a management training program to ensure that their approaches reached as many people in industry as possible. During 1949 and 1950, Sarasohn and Protzman organized a series of eight-week courses on industrial management to which only top executives in the Japanese communications industry were invited. The students included Matsushita Electric's Masaharu Matsushita, Mitsubishi Electric's Takeo Kato, Fujitsu's Hanzou Omi, Sumitomo Electric's Bunzaemon Inoue, and Akio Morita and Masaru Ibuka, the founders of Sony.

Another postwar initiative was the creation (in August 1946) of Japan's Federation of Economic Organizations (FEO). This sounds like a glorified talking shop. It wasn't. FEO became one of the mainsprings of Japanese economic renewal, with over 750 large corporations and 100 major national trade associations. FEO was the power behind the revival of Japan Inc. and announced its main purpose as "to maintain close contact with all sectors of the business community for the purpose of adjusting and harmonizing conflicting views and interests of the various businesses and industries represented in its huge membership. It is the front office of the business community and is in effect a partner of the government." FEO's first president was Ichiro Ishikawa, a successful industrialist, who was also president of the Japan Union of Scientists and Engineers (J.U.S.E.), Japan's most important quality control organization, founded in 1946.

Quality control was, therefore, well under way to becoming established in Japan very soon after the end of the war. Its impetus was to become irreversible.

The next move forward came when Ishikawa invited a Census Bureau statistician called W. Edwards Deming (1900–1993) to give a lecture to Tokyo's Industry Club in July 1950. Deming had first visited Japan in 1947 to aid in the development of what was to become the 1951 census. His message was different from the usual quality control theory in that he emphasized the deficiencies of management. If quality was to happen it had to be led by management. The new generation had to seize the day.

As Ishikawa had sent out the invitations, the lecture was well attended, with twenty-one company presidents (some have suggested there were up to forty-five) in attendance. "I did not just talk about quality. I explained to management their responsibilities," Deming recalled. "Management of Japan went into action, knowing something about their responsibilities and learning more about their responsibilities."[7]

Deming eventually delivered a series of lectures. He asked for no fee but J.U.S.E. sold reprints. The money raised through reprint sales was used to create the Deming Application Prize. This award for outstanding total quality programs was first awarded in 1951 to Koji Kobayashi.

Leading the Rebirth

The dramatic revitalization of Japan was not simply a matter of the application of quality control. At its root was robust entrepreneurial vigor and enterprise combined with management with a social and human conscience.

Determined pragmatism ruled. In the postwar years the Yamaha president, Genichi Kawakami, decided to make use of the company's old production machinery by setting up a motor bike production line. It took a few years to sort the line out and develop the first model— understandable as the company usually made pianos and organs.

The epitome of the Japanese revival was the rise of Sony. Akio Morita (born 1921) was an officer in the Japanese Navy during the Second World War. Trained as a physicist and scientist, Morita could have followed family tradition and gone into sake production. (He refers to himself as "the first son and fifteenth generation heir to one of Japan's finest and oldest sake-brewing families.") Instead, he founded a company with Masaru Ibuka (1908–1997) immediately after the end of the war. The duo invested the equivalent of $530 and set themselves up in business in a bombed-out Tokyo department store. Ibuka was the technical expert, Morita the salesman. The company was christened Tokyo

Tsushin Kogyo KK (Tokyo Telecommunications Engineering Corporation). Not a good name to put on a product, Morita later ruminated. Initially, the company made radio parts and a rice cooker, among other things. Its rice cooker was unreliable. Today, Ibuka and Morita's organization is a $45 billion company with over 100,000 employees. According to one Harris poll, the company is America's most respected brand.

In 1957 the company produced a pocket-sized radio and a year later renamed itself Sony (*sonus* is Latin for sound). The Sony name remains prominent on all of its products. In 1960 Sony produced the first transistor TV in the world.

And increasingly the world was Sony's market. Its combination of smaller and smaller products at the leading edge of technology proved irresistible.

In 1961 Sony Corporation of America was the first Japanese company to be listed on Wall Street. In 1989, Sony bought Columbia Pictures—and by 1991 it had more foreigners on its 135,000 payroll than Japanese.[8]

Morita and Sony's story parallels the rebirth of Japan as an industrial power. "We in the free world can do great things. We proved it in Japan by changing the image of Made in Japan from something shoddy to something fine," said Morita. When Sony was first attempting to make inroads into Western markets it cannot be forgotten that Japanese products were sneered at as being of the lowest quality. Surmounting that obstacle was a substantial business achievement.

Morita became famous as the acceptable face of Japanese industry. Sophisticated and entrepreneurial, he did not fit the Western stereotype of the uncreative, devoted Japanese corporate servant. (He also advocated a more assertive Japanese approach in *The Japan That Can Say No*, which he wrote with a Japanese politician, Ishihara Shintaro.)

Morita and Sony's gift was to invent new markets. Describing what he called Sony's "pioneer spirit," Morita said: "Sony is a pioneer and never intends to follow others. Through progress, Sony wants to serve the whole world. It shall be always a seeker of the unknown. . . . Sony has a principle of respecting and encouraging one's ability . . . and always tries to bring out the best in a person. This is the vital force of Sony."

Apart from his marketing and entrepreneurial prowess, Morita has emphasized the cultural differences in Japanese attitudes toward work. "Never break another man's rice bowl," he advises, observing, "Japanese people tend to be much better adjusted to the notion of work, any kind of work, as honorable." Management is regarded by Morita as where the buck stops and starts: "If we face a recession, we should not lay off employees; the company should sacrifice a profit. It's management's risk and management's responsibility. Employees are not guilty; why should they suffer?"

Sony was not alone. Konosuke Matsushita (1894–1989) created a similarly enormous and entrepreneurial empire. Brought up in poverty in a small village near Wakayama, Matsushita left school in 1904 and was apprenticed to a maker of charcoal grills. Matsushita later worked his way up to become an inspector in the Osaka Electric Light Company and, in 1917, founded his own company, Matsushita Electric.

Matsushita's first product was a plug adapter. He had suggested the idea to his previous employer but it had shown no interest—this was hardly surprising as Matsushita had little idea of how to actually make the product. It took Matsushita and four others four months to figure out how to make the adapter. No one bought the product.

Matsushita's major break was an order to made insulator plates. He delivered the goods on time and with high quality. Matsushita began to make money. He then developed an innovative bicycle light. By 1932 Matsushita had over a thousand employees, ten factories, and 280 patents. In the postwar years expansion continued. The eventual result was a $42 billion revenue business, one of the world's most successful brands (Panasonic), and a personal fortune of $3 billion.

Matsushita understood customer service before anyone in the West had even thought about it. "Don't sell customers goods that they are attracted to. Sell them goods that will benefit them," he said. "After-sales service is more important than assistance before sales. It is through such service that one gets permanent customers."

The other pillars of his management were entrepreneurialism and paternalism. Matsushita took risks and backed his beliefs at every stage. The classic example of this is the development of the video cassette. Matsushita developed VHS video and licensed the technology. Sony developed Betamax, which was immeasurably better, and failed to license the technology. The world standard is VHS and Betamax is consigned to history.

At the same time, Matsushita advocated business with a conscience. There was nothing new in this—at least in Japan. In the early nineteenth century, the leading Japanese bankers, Yamagata Banto (1748–1821) and Kusama Naokata (1753–1831) defined capital as a "social property" to be kept in circulation for the benefit of the public rather than amassed for private gain. In the early part of the twentieth century, Japanese worker groups and engineers had power delegated to them to a far greater degree than ever contemplated in Western enterprises.[9]

Matsushita's commitment was manifested in his paternalistic employment practices. During a recession early in its life the company did not make any people redundant. This cemented loyalty. "It's not enough to work conscientiously. No matter what kind of job, you should think of yourself as being completely in charge of and responsible for your own work," said Matsushita. "The mission of a manufacturer should be to overcome poverty, to relieve society as a whole from misery, and bring it wealth." While the Allied powers luxuriated in victory, such sentiments and insights were the preserve of the Japanese.

The Management Century: Tale of the Tape

	Unemployment (percentage)	
	1900	*1998*
Germany	2.0	11.5
Britain	2.5	4.9
United States	5.0	4.6
France	6.8	12.1

Source: Time, April 13, 1998.

The Dow Jones Industrial Average Companies as of January 1, 1949

Allied Chemical	Procter & Gamble
American Can	Johns-Manville
American Smelting	Loew's
DuPont	General Foods
Eastman Kodak	United Aircraft
Goodyear	Sears, Roebuck
Bethlehem Steel	Standard Oil of New Jersey
Chrysler	Texas Corporation
General Electric	National Distillers
General Motors	Union Carbide
American Tobacco	U.S. Steel
Standard Oil of California	American Telephone & Telegraph
International Harvester	Westinghouse Electric
International Nickel	Woolworth
Corn Products Refining	National Steel

The Management Century Timeline

1940

General Motors produces its 25 millionth car—a silver Chevrolet.

U.S. Office of Production Management set up to regulate defense production and facilitate shipment of war materials.

Goodrich introduces first synthetic tire for commercial use.

Debut of network television in the United States.

1941

U.S. carmakers agree to reduce output by one million units annually.

Henry Ford reluctantly agrees to union presence at Ford. United Auto Workers sign with Ford Motor Company.

Mary Parker Follett's *Dynamic Administration* published.

1942

The United States enters the war and, a few weeks later, the government halts civilian car production. The last cars produced before production stopped included chromeless "blackout" models.

Car makers transform all their operations into a vast international network of military plants, suppliers, and subcontractors.

1943

President Roosevelt proclaims a forty-eight-hour minimum workweek for war plants.

1944

IBM produces the first large-scale calculating computer—Mark 1. No laptop—more than fifty feet long and eight feet high, it weighs in at nearly five tons.

Bretton Woods conference establishes the World Bank.

1945

Wal-Mart first comes to life in Newport, Arkansas. Aged twenty-seven, Sam Walton acquires a franchise licence for a five-and-dime store. His first year is good. Sales total $80,000. By the third year, the store is generating sales of $225,000. Then, in 1950, the lease came to an end. Walton moved to Bentonville, Arkansas, and opened "Walton's." Soon after he added another store and, in 1962, opened his first large-scale rural discount store.

The Advanced Management Program becomes a regularly scheduled part of Harvard Business School's activities.

Just two days after resumed production is authorized, Ford drives its first 1946 model off the line at its Rouge Assembly Plant. The vehicle astounded WPB forecasters, who had predicted no vehicles would be seen until sixty days after "go day."

1946

The first electronic digital computer, known as ENIAC, is introduced.

Masaru Ibuka and Akio Morita invest $530 to start their company.

A postwar strike wave sweeps the United States.

American crime syndicate expands into "legitimate" business with the Flamingo Hotel in Las Vegas.

1947

Congress passes the Taft-Hartley Act (Labor Management Relations Act) restricting union practices.

The Marshall Plan for reconstruction of Europe is proposed.

Max Weber's *Theory of Social and Economic Organization* published.

Henry Ford dies at his estate, Fair Lane.

1949

Sony develops magnetic recording tape and, in 1950, sells the first tape recorder in Japan.

Nationwide steel strike shuts down U.S. steel industry for six weeks.

AT&T antitrust suit begins.

1950

Peter Drucker becomes professor of management at New York University— "The first person anywhere in the world to have such a title and to teach such a subject," he later said.

Chapter 6
1951–1960: Living the Dream

Our voices swell in admiration
Of T.J. Watson proudly sing
He'll ever be our inspiration
To him our voices loudly ring.
— IBM SONG LYRIC

The Western Project and Corporate Man

The Western dream: a house with a white fence, a car in the driveway, an attractive wife, beautiful children. Ball games, perhaps a relaxing beer; the reassurance of a steady job. The safe accumulation of material possessions.

In the 1950s the Western dream became the thing of reality. After the tumult of the 1940s, comfort and material wealth came home. (In the 1950s, the median family income in the United States was $4,418 while an average house cost $9,650. Between 1948 and 1962 the number of cars in the United States increased 146 percent and telephones by 131 percent.[1]) The man forced to war was transformed into the man with the pipe and carpet slippers. The 1950s was the decade of plenty. The Dow Jones Industrial Average gained 239.5 percent during the decade (its best performance over any decade except for the 1990s).

Life had an air of predictability at home and at work. The 1950s saw the rise of corporate man. Corporate man was loyal. Corporate man saw his career and life mapped out predictably and reassuringly in front of him. (Corporate woman was not yet contemplated, let alone invented.)

The life of corporate man was brilliantly and poignantly described by William Whyte in his 1956 book *Organization Man*. (Whyte went on to forge a career as an urbanologist, studying human behavior in urban situations. Among his revealing findings was that a large percentage of companies that moved from New York City ended up in locations less than eight miles from the homes of their chief executives. Whyte also found that the corner outside Bloomingdale's at 59th Street and Lexington Avenue had the most daytime pedestrian traffic.)

Reviewing the book in the *New York Times,* C. Wright Mills wrote that Whyte "understands that the work-and-thrift ethic of success has grievously declined—except in the rhetoric of top executives; that the entrepreneurial scramble to success has been largely replaced by the organizational crawl."[2]

"It was *Fortune*'s William H. Whyte Jr. who made the 'Organization Man' a household word—and the organization wife too. His was a fine achievement in sociological reporting. In it he related the phenomenon of the business organization to questions of human personality and values. The kind of people who are eager to hear the worst about American society assumed that Mr. Whyte was predicting the destruction of individualism by the organization," *Fortune*-founder Henry Luce later commented. "Whyte was not a doomsayer. True he was uneasy about corporate life, which seemed to stifle creativity and individualism. He was uneasy about the subtle pressures in the office and at home that called for smooth performance rather than daring creativity. But he did not urge the organization man to leave his secure environment. Rather he urged them to fight the organization when necessary and he was optimistic that the battle could be successful."[3] In the 1950s there were few volunteers.

Implicit in the career of corporate man was the understanding that loyalty and solid performance brought job security. This was mutually beneficial. The executive gained a respectable income and a high degree of security. The company gained loyal, hardworking executives. Win-win.

This unspoken pact became known as the *psychological contract*. The originator of the phrase was the MIT-based social psychologist Edgar Schein (born 1928). Schein's interest in the employee-employer relationship developed during the late 1950s, as he looked at the approaches taken by the various management training institutes companies were beginning to develop.

GE established its Management Development Institute at Crotonville in 1956. It was CEO Ralph Cordiner's most important legacy and has helped imbue the GE culture into generations of managers. Its tradition is carried on by today's CEO Jack Welch. "I want a revolution, and I want it to start at Crotonville," Welch pronounced in the early 1990s.[4] Welch is a regular visitor and teacher at the center—it is estimated that in 250 sessions he has personally talked to some fifteen thousand of the company's executives. Crotonville's professed mission is "to leverage GE's global competitiveness as an instrument of cultural change, by improving business acumen, leadership abilities and organization effectiveness of GE professionals." Echoing Welch, Noel Tichy (now of the University of Michigan and an ex-Crotonville director) has called Crotonville "a staging ground for a corporate revolution."[5]

Ed Schein expressed reservations about the revolutionary zeal of places like Crotonville. His first paper spoke of management development as a "process of influence" that applied the brainwashing model from prison camps to the corporate world. "There were enormous similarities between the brainwashing of the POWs [in Korea] and the executives I encountered at MIT," says Schein. "I didn't see brainwashing as bad. What was bad were the values of the Communists. If we don't like the values, we don't approve of brainwashing."[6] The dynamics of groups and Schein's knowledge of brainwashing later led him to develop an interest in corporate culture, a term which Schein is widely credited with inventing.

As Schein's link with brainwashing suggests, there was more to the psychological contract than a cozy mutually beneficial deal. It raised a number of issues.

First, the psychological contract was built around loyalty. Executives were expected to be blindly loyal. "The most important single contribution required of an executive, certainly the most universal qualification, is loyalty [allowing] domination by the organization personality," noted Chester Barnard in *The Functions of the Executive* (1938). The word "domination" suggests which way Barnard saw the balance of power falling. While loyalty is a positive quality, it can easily become blind. What if the corporate strategy is wrong or the company is engaged in unlawful or immoral acts? Also there is the question, Loyal to what? In the 1950s, corporate values were assumed rather than explored or questioned.

The second issue raised by the psychological contract was that of perspective. With careers neatly organized, executives were hardly encouraged to look over the corporate parapets to seek out broader viewpoints. The corporation became a self-contained and self-perpetuating world supported by a complex array of checks, systems, and hierarchies. The company was right. Customers, who existed in the ethereal world outside the organization, were often regarded as peripheral. In the fifties, sixties, and seventies, no executive ever lost a job by delivering poor quality or indifferent service. Indeed, in some organizations, executives only lost their jobs by defrauding their employer or insulting their boss. Jobs for life was the refrain and, to a large extent for executives, the reality.

Clearly, such an environment was hardly conducive to the fostering of dynamic risk-takers. The psychological contract rewarded the steady foot soldier, the safe pair of hands. It was not surprising, therefore, that when Harvard Business School's Rosabeth Moss Kanter came to examine corporate life for the first time in her 1977 book, *Men and Women of the Corporation,* she found that the central characteristic expected of a manager was "dependability."

The reality was that the psychological contract placed a premium on loyalty rather than ability and allowed a great many poor performers to seek out corporate havens. It was also significant that the psychological contract was regarded as the preserve of management. Lower down the hierarchy, people were hired and fired with abandon no matter how great their loyalty.

The corporate archetype of the 1950s was International Business Machines. IBM—"Big Blue"—became the apotheosis of the modern corporation. IBM executives were the living embodiment of corporate men. With their regulation somber suits, white shirts, plain ties, zeal for selling, and company song, IBMers played hard; they were loyal and had their loyalty reciprocated. (Loyalty is always reciprocated when things are going well.)

IBM's origins lay in the awkwardly named Computing Tabulating & Recording Company, which began life in 1911 after a merger between the Computing Scale Company of America, the Tabulating Machine Company, and the International Time Recording Company. Based in New York City, C-T-R initially employed 1,300 people.

In 1914 Thomas Watson Sr. (1874–1956) joined C-T-R as general manager, having been fired as general sales manager of the National Cash Register Company.

Under Watson the company's revenues doubled from $4.2 million to $8.3 million by 1917. Initially making everything from butcher's scales to meat slicers, its activities gradually concentrated on tabulating machines, which processed information mechanically on punched cards. In 1924 Watson boldly renamed the company International Business Machines.[7] This was, at the time, overstating the company's credentials—though IBM Japan was established before the Second World War.

IBM began producing calculating machines and entered the typewriter business. The only black mark against it was the U.S. government's antitrust suit against the company (launched in 1932 and followed by a second suit in 1952). The government took with one hand and gave with the other.

IBM's development was helped by the 1937 Wages-Hours Act, which required U.S. companies to record hours worked and wages paid. Existing machines couldn't cope, and Watson instigated work on a solution. The result was what the company called the contract for "the biggest accounting operation of all time"—to help the U.S. government set up and maintain the employment records for 26 million Americans after Congress passed the Social Security Act 1935.

In 1944 the Mark 1 was launched, followed by the Selective Sequence Electronic Calculator in 1947. By then IBM's revenues were $119 million and it was set to make the great leap forward to become the world's largest computer company and one of the world's most valuable brands.

While Thomas Watson Sr. created IBM's service-centered brand and strong corporate culture, his son, Thomas Watson Jr. (1914–1994), moved it from being an outstanding performer to world dominance. Watson Jr. brought a vision of the future to the company that his father had lacked. In 1987 Watson was hailed by *Fortune* as "the most successful capitalist in history." (This overstated his credentials and was a prelude to the company's dramatic collapse at the beginning of the 1990s.)

Watson Jr. became chief executive in 1956 and retired in 1970. (He was then U.S. ambassador in Moscow until 1980.) Watson Jr. codified and clarified what IBM stood for—most notably in his book, *A Business and Its Beliefs* (1963). Under Watson Jr., the corporate culture, the company's values, and the company brand became all-important. They were the glue that kept a sprawling international operation under control. The three basic beliefs on which IBM was built were give full consideration to the individual employee, spend a lot of time making customers happy, and go the last mile to do things right. Beliefs, said Watson, never change. Change everything else, but never the basic truths on which the company is based—"If an organization is to meet the challenges of a changing world, it must be prepared to change everything about itself except beliefs as it moves through corporate life. . . . The only sacred cow in an organization should be its basic philosophy of doing business."[8]

The growth of strong corporate cultures by powerful corporations was a significant development. It attached a level of meaning and importance never previously applied to companies. It was recognition that companies shaped lives and were more than mere legal shells. Companies could create powerful worlds of their own.

And it is here that a crucial difference from the Japanese model was obvious. The Japanese linked corporate success with the broader context of society, individual betterment, and the Japanese economy as a whole. In the West, however, success was ring fenced. The corporation was all.

The Joy of Marketing

These companies existed in an era of brimming opportunities. The world was out there waiting to be sold something. Companies began to systematize and consider the process of connecting to their markets with far greater rigor than ever before. Modern marketing was born.

As with so many ideas, it was kick-started by Peter Drucker, the undoubted doyen of management thinking in the twentieth century. Drucker's first attempt at creating the managerial bible was his 1954 book, *The Practice of Management* ("a fairly short book of fundamentals," according to him). He largely succeeded. The book is a masterly exposition on the first principles of management. Drucker put the customer at center stage in a way never before contemplated. In one of the most quoted and memorable paragraphs in management literature, Drucker gets to the heart of the meaning of business life: "There is only one valid definition of business purpose: to create a customer. Markets are not created by God, nature or economic forces, but by businessmen. The want they satisfy may have been felt by the customer before he was offered the means of satisfying it. It may indeed, like the want of food in a famine, have dominated the customer's life and filled all his waking moments. But it was a theoretical want before; only when the action of businessmen makes it an effective demand is there a customer, a market."[9]

The actual nitty-gritty of clarifying the exact nature and extent of marketing was taken on by others. In 1960 E. Jerome McCarthy took the marketing mix (defined by marketing's éminence grise, Philip Kotler, as "the set of marketing tools that the firm uses to pursue its marketing objectives in the target market") and identified its critical ingredients as product, price, place, and promotion. This became known as the Four P's of marketing. It is a mantra that has stood the test of time. It is still recited by students and known by virtually everyone in business. (The renown of marketing's Four P's is such that purchasing sought to follow its example with its own Four O's.)

Despite its popularity and longevity, it would be wrong to view the idea of the Four P's as anything other than a catchy and fairly accurate aide-mémoire. Knowing what the Four P's are is unrelated to your ability or willingness to do anything with them. In the same way as the Seven S framework of the 1980s is not going to transform a company's performance, the Four P's are unlikely to turn a company into a marketing superstar.

Even so, at the time of their inception, the Four P's encapsulated the essence of traditional marketing. A company that successfully focused its attention on all of the Four P's *could* develop a soundly based marketing strategy. A company that failed to do so—or allowed its focus to shift—was unlikely to excel at marketing.

Examining the four categories, first there is the product (or the service) being offered. This appears straightforward enough—though Philip Kotler, author of the definitive textbook *Marketing Management,* noted: "The idea of a product seems intuitive; yet there is a real problem in knowing exactly what it embraces." Kotler eventually settled for a definition of a product as "a bundle of physical, services, and symbolic particulars expected to yield satisfaction or benefits to the buyer." (This has since been distilled down to "A product is something that is viewed as capable of satisfying a want.")

Next comes the self-explanatory issue of pricing. In recent years this has become ever more complex, with an array of pricing strategies covering everything from premium pricing to seasonal or even daily pricing.

The other two elements, place and promotion, are more wide ranging. Place embraces how and where the company makes the product accessible to potential customers. This includes, therefore, distribution and logistics.

Finally, you come to promotion. This hides a multitude of activities, all of which have enjoyed an explosion of growth over the last twenty or so years. These include communication, personal selling, advertising, direct marketing, sales promotion, and public relations.

The attraction of the Four P's is that they give four easily remembered categories under which marketing activities can be considered. At a basic level this may be useful, but it is less useful in a complex modern organization—especially one in a service industry. The Four P's suggest that the categories can be viewed in isolation. In reality, there are myriad relationships between the various components of any marketing mix. To religiously follow the Four P's structure runs the risk of overlooking such relationships.

Over the years since the Four P's were first introduced, a series of thinkers have regularly offered alternative classifications. Indeed, there are an endless array of potential combinations. Albert Frey, in *Advertising,* advocates separation between the offering (made up of product, packaging, brand, price, and service) and methods and tools (distribution channels, personal selling, advertising, sales promotion, and publicity). In their book *Managerial Marketing,* William Lazer and Eugene Kelly suggest three mixes—the goods and service mix, the distribution mix, and the communications mix.

Others, including Philip Kotler, have correctly pointed out that the Four P's present essentially a seller's mix rather than a buyer's mix. The 1950s was, after all, a seller's decade. They suggest that more attention be paid to a buyer's marketing mix—the Four C's of customer needs and wants, cost to the customer, convenience, and communication. Similarly, it has been suggested that the provision of customer service should be added to the list. (Philip Kotler counters this, arguing that customer service is an aspect of product strategy.) Yet another author suggests that people, physical evidence, and processes should supplement the original Four P's.[10]

Emulation is largely futile. The Four P's were a useful summary of the dominant parts of the marketing mix in the 1950s when mass industrial marketing was the order of the day. However, the nature of business has changed. No longer is the emphasis on volumes, it is on customer delight. No longer does a company blindly start with the product and then attempt to find a market; it takes the customer as the starting point.

The nature of marketing has also fundamentally changed. The divisions between the Four P's are increasingly blurred, sometimes nonexistent. For example, the Four P's are of limited value if you are marketing and selling your products over the Internet. Despite great technological leaps forward, product, price, place, and promotion are still important. The trouble is that defining their exact meaning, role, and potential is more and more difficult.

From Joy to Myopia

From a theoretical point of view, the next crucial step forward in the development of marketing came in the July-August 1960 issue of the *Harvard Business Review.* It included an article by a Harvard Business School academic, Ted Levitt (born 1925), titled "Marketing Myopia." The article has since sold over 500,000 reprints and has entered the select group of articles that have genuinely changed perceptions.

The article propelled the German-born Levitt to prominence. It was, he admits, a lucky break. In 1975 he reflected: "'Marketing myopia' was not intended as analysis or even prescription; it was intended as manifesto. Nor was it a new idea—Peter F. Drucker, J.B. McKitterick, Wroe Alderson, John Howard, and Neil Borden had each done more original and balanced work on *the marketing concept.* My scheme, however, tied marketing more closely to the inner orbit of business policy."[11]

In "Marketing Myopia" Levitt argued that the central preoccupation of corporations should be with satisfying customers rather than simply producing goods. Companies should be marketing-led rather than production-led and the lead must come from the chief executive and senior management—"Management must think of itself not as producing products but as providing customer-creating value satisfactions."

At the time of Levitt's article, the fact that companies were production-led was not open to question. Henry Ford's success in mass production had fueled the belief that low-cost production was the key to business success. Ford persisted in his belief that he knew what customers wanted, long after they had decided otherwise. (Even so, Levitt saluted Ford's marketing prowess, arguing that the mass production techniques he used were a means to a marketing end rather than an end in themselves.)

Levitt observed that production-led thinking inevitably led to narrow perspectives. He argued that companies must broaden their view of the nature of their business. Otherwise their customers will soon be forgotten. "The railroads are in trouble today not because the need was filled by others . . . but because it was not filled by the railroads themselves," wrote Levitt. "They let others take customers away from them because they assumed themselves to be in the railroad business rather than in the transportation business. The reason they defined their industry wrong was because they were railroad-oriented instead of transportation-oriented; they were product-oriented instead of customer-oriented." The railroad business was constrained, in Levitt's view, by a lack of willingness to expand its horizons. Levitt went on to level similar criticisms at other industries. The film industry, for example, failed to respond to the growth of television because it regarded itself as being in the business of making movies rather than providing entertainment.

Growth, wrote Levitt, can never be taken for granted—"In truth, there is no such thing as a growth industry." Growth is not a matter of being in a particular industry, but in being perceptive enough to spot where future growth may lie. History, said Levitt, is filled with companies that fall into "undetected decay"—usually for a number of reasons. First, they assume that the growth in their particular market will continue so long as the population grows in size and wealth. Second, they fall into the belief that a product cannot be surpassed. Third, they place their faith in the ability of improved production techniques to deliver lower costs and therefore higher profits.

In "Marketing Myopia" Levitt also made a telling distinction between the tasks of selling and marketing. "Selling concerns itself with the tricks and techniques of getting people to exchange their cash for your product. It is not concerned with the values that the exchange is all about. And it does not, as marketing invariably does, view the entire business process as consisting of a tightly integrated effort to discover, create, arouse, and satisfy customer needs," he wrote. This was picked up again in the 1980s when marketing underwent a resurgence and companies began to heed Levitt's view that they were overly oriented toward production.

Levitt's article—and his subsequent work—pushed marketing to center stage. Indeed, in some cases it led to what Levitt labeled "marketing mania" with companies "obsessively responsive to every fleeting whim of the customer." Even so, the main thrust of the article has stood the test of time. ("I'd do it again and in the same way," commented Levitt in 1975.)

Land of Plenty

Away from the academic discussions, the 1950s created a world led by consumption. Getting and spending were the twin pillars of capitalist joy.

And meeting these new needs was an entirely new generation of brands. Instead of being decorative adornments, brands became business drivers. The most powerful brand reincarnation of the time was that of Marlboro.

At the beginning of the 1950s, the tobacco company R.J. Reynolds had reason to feel complacent. Its market share was approaching 35 percent. It was the dominant force in the American cigarette industry. Among those trailing, breathlessly behind—in sixth place—was the Philip Morris Company, whose market share was less than 10 percent. Executives at R.J. Reynolds no doubt lay back in their executive-style chairs and inhaled deeply on one of their successful products.

Meanwhile plans were being hatched at Philip Morris. They smacked of desperation. One of its brands, Marlboro, was targeted at the female smoker. It had first been launched in the 1920s with the suitably feminine slogan: "Mild as May." During wartime, Marlboro production halted as Camel, Lucky Strike, and Chesterfield dominated the market. In the heavy-smoking fifties, those three brands continued to exert a stranglehold on the market.

Marlboro was brought back on the market in the early 1950s but remained a women's cigarette. There were fears of lung cancer and Marlboro was filtered—men regarded Marlboro's filters as effeminate.

Philip Morris brought in the Leo Burnett ad agency to consider how it could make Marlboro appealing to men as well as women. The result was a 1955 ad campaign based around a tattooed man. The Marlboro smoker was reincarnated "as a lean, relaxed outdoorsman—a cattle rancher, a Navy officer, a flyer—whose tattooed wrist suggested a romantic past, a man who had once worked with his hands, who knew the score, who merited respect." Marlboro sales exploded. In New York sales increased 5,000 percent in eight months.

The original Marlboro man was highly talkative—he had quite a lot of explaining to do. In the early ads, he cheerfully gave his life story—"I'm a rancher. Grew up in this part of the country . . ."—before lapsing into silence in later years. The brand's development was helped by a strongly designed box with recognizable colors. The box was the membership card. You, too, became a cowboy—even if you lived in the middle of the city and wouldn't know one end of a cow from the other.

By 1989, Marlboro accounted for a quarter of all American cigarette sales; Philip Morris had 43 percent of the U.S. market. All was well in Marlboro country, though only for a while—the drama of Marlboro

Friday, when the company dramatically reduced the brand's prices, awaited.

The new world of brands then discovered that service industries were ripe for branding. Indeed, services offered huge vistas of opportunity. A single bright idea could change the world. And some did.

In the summer of 1951, the Wilson family of Memphis set off on a motoring vacation. There was nothing special about it. Just a couple and their five children heading to Washington, D.C. Mr. Wilson, Kemmons Wilson (born 1913) was a Memphis builder and realtor. He and his family became exasperated as their vacation progressed. It was not a great deal of fun staying in expensive and poor-quality motels.

"A motel room only cost about $8 a night, but the proprietors inevitably charged $2 extra for each child. So the $8 charge soon ballooned into an $18 charge for my family," Wilson later recounted. "If we could get a room with two beds, our two daughters slept in one, and Dorothy and I slept in the other. Our three boys slept on the floor in sleeping bags. Sometimes there was a dollar deposit for the key and another dollar for the use of a television."

So, Wilson decided to build his own—"I was seized by an idea: I could build a chain of affordable hotels, stretching from coast to coast. Families could travel cross-country and stay at one of my hotels every night." Wilson envisaged four hundred such motels. It sounded outrageously ambitious, but Wilson didn't hang around. He began work while still on vacation. He measured rooms and looked at facilities. His conclusion was that features such as televisions, telephones, ice machines, and restaurants should be universal. In his imagined hotel chain, children would stay free.

When the family returned home, Wilson got straight to work. He asked a draftsman to draw up some plans. The draftsman had seen a Bing Crosby film the previous evening and labeled the plan *Holiday Inn* from the Crosby movie. Wilson liked it. The name stuck.

The first Holiday Inn was opened at 4985 Summer Avenue, Memphis, in 1952. (This fared better than Wilson's first house, which he mistakenly built on the wrong lot.) After coming up with the idea and having launched the first Holiday Inn, Kemmons Wilson attempted to franchise the idea. Opening four Holiday Inns in just over a year in

Memphis had stretched his finances to their limits. Twelve franchises were sold to house builders for $500 each. Only three were eventually built. Wilson thought again and sold 120,000 shares at $9.75.

The rest is motel history.

This provided the impetus necessary to create a nationwide chain. The fiftieth Holiday Inn was opened in 1958, the hundredth in 1959, the five hundredth in 1964. Clean and cheap, Holiday Inns sprouted up throughout the United States and then the world. "He changed the way America travels," Senator John Glenn concluded of Wilson. "Kemmons Wilson has transformed the motel from the old wayside fleabag into the most popular home away from home," noted *Time.* By the time Wilson retired in 1979, Holiday Inn was the world's largest lodging chain. Today there are 1,643 Holiday Inn hotels with 327,059 rooms.[12]

The 1950s also saw the emergence of McDonald's and many other now famous brands. In 1954 Kroc bought the American franchise to McDonald's for $2.7 million; in 1961 he bought the world rights. In 1958 the classic green American Express card was launched in the United States, the perfect complement to the first golden era of consumer brands. Brand after brand first saw the light of day in the 1950s.

Not all hit the high points from the very start. In 1959 the Japanese motorcycle company, Honda, created the American Honda Motor Co. It was the company's first foray in the U.S. market dominated by Harley-Davidson, the British companies BSA, Triumph, and Norton, and the Italian manufacturer Motto-Guzzi.

At this time, Japanese products were still regarded with suspicion. Generally they were seen as inferior, cheap imitations of the real thing. So the hopes for Honda in the United States appeared fairly forlorn.

Honda decided to launch its bikes into Los Angeles, as part of a grand strategy to sell into the United States. Its HQ was at 4077 Pico Boulevard. Honda sent two of its executives to California, expecting to promote its larger bikes. Honda believed that its 250 cc and 350 cc models were the most suitable for the American market. The trouble was that these machines proved unreliable, with oil leaks and clutch problems.

In order to get around town, the Honda sales people used some of the newly developed small 50 cc bikes. These attracted a lot of attention wherever they went. Eventually the sales team received inquiries, not from motorcycle dealers, but from sports shops and other retailers. It seemed that fewer people were interested in the large machines, and against Mr. Honda's and the American team's expectations the 50 cc bikes were to become the biggest seller.

Honda changed tack, overturned Mr. Honda's wisdom and started promoting the smaller machines—with the slogan "You meet the nicest people on a Honda." This effectively opened up the U.S. market to Honda. New motorcycle owners flocked to Honda—in the 1960s 65 percent of its buyers were buying a motorcycle for the first time. Within four years Honda was marketing almost 50 percent of all motorcycles sold in the United States. By 1974, Honda had sold over ten million Honda 50s.

Honda's change of direction had an element of luck. But note that even in 1960 Honda employed seven hundred people in its research team while its competitors averaged around one hundred; Honda's production per man-year was 159 units in 1962, a figure Harley-Davidson only reached in 1974. Honda invested in the future; Western companies barely looked further than tomorrow.

And increasingly, Japanese companies were looking West. Honda wasn't the only Japanese company making cautious inroads into Western markets. In 1953 Yamaha president Genichi Kawakami made his first overseas inspection trip. A flurry of inventiveness followed. In 1954 the company developed a hi-fi player, launched the Yamaha Music School system, and also, somewhat bizarrely, began producing its 125 motor bikes. In 1955 it established the Yamaha Motor Company. Its next moves were into archery equipment, a new type of electronic organ, and the development and marketing of FRP skis. (This was capped brilliantly in 1964 when the company began producing bathtubs. Trumpets, guitars, and drums inevitably followed.) As the West was buying, the Japanese were learning.

The Motivation to Work

The great irony of these times was that amid this sea of consumer-led contentment, leading academics began to examine and question motivation.

The interest in motivation was not born through a sudden move toward humanitarian management. Businesses simply recognized that with virtually full employment, improving the efficiency of workers was central to improving industrial performance.

At a superficial level, what motivated people appeared clear. In the first decades of the century, fear and need motivated. Then consumer-led desire. The transition, as a series of brilliant minds found, was not so straightforward. Among the luminaries contemplating motivation were Douglas McGregor (1906–1964), Abraham Maslow (1908–1970), Chris Argyris (born 1923), and Frederick Herzberg (born 1923).

Though their influences, ideas, and careers differed, this group is widely labeled the human relations school. This is accurate in the sense that they all studied human behavior in relation to business situations. Their insights, perspectives, and conclusions, however, were significantly different.

Abraham Maslow took an approach popular among business writers past and present, from Machiavelli to Stephen Covey: look at successful, fulfilled people and attempt to identify common characteristics. Among those studied by Maslow were Albert Einstein and Eleanor Roosevelt. "The study of crippled, stunted, immature, and unhealthy specimens can yield only a cripple psychology and a cripple philosophy," wrote Maslow in *Motivation and Personality*—taking a none-too-subtle swipe at Freudian psychology. He was also not enamored with the other popular psychological approach of the time, that championed by B.F. Skinner. Skinner had studied how to motivate animals through rewards and repetition. Maslow saw this as dry, joyless, and statistically driven. He preferred an approach that was more positive—motivating through play rather than rewards—and one that recognized the individuality and idiosyncrasies of people.

Maslow was fundamentally optimistic and positive about human nature. He concluded that there were general needs—deficiency needs: physiological, safety, love, and esteem—that have to be satisfied before a person can act unselfishly. Trying to satisfy these needs is healthy.

Once these deficiency needs are met, we move on to seek out other needs. This process continues as we satisfy one need after another. The result is Maslow's hierarchy of needs. The hierarchy of needs (first published in 1943) parallels the human life cycle. First are the fundamental physiological needs of warmth, shelter, and food. "It is quite true that man lives by bread alone—when there is no bread. But what happens to man's desires when there is plenty of bread and when his belly is chronically filled?" Maslow asked.

Once basic physiological needs are met, others emerge to dominate. "If the physiological needs are relatively well gratified, there then emerges a new set of needs, which we may categorize roughly as the safety needs," wrote Maslow in *Motivation and Personality.* "A man, in this state, if it is extreme enough and chronic enough, may be characterized as living almost for safety alone."[13]

Next on the hierarchy are social or love needs, and ego or self-esteem needs. Ultimately, as man moves up the scale, with each need's satisfaction comes what Maslow labeled *self-actualization.* The need for self-actualization is "the desire to become more and more what one is, to become everything that one is capable of becoming." Self-actualization is when individuals achieve their own personal potential. "A musician must make music, an artist must paint, a poet must write, if he is to be ultimately at peace with himself. What a man be, he must be," said Maslow.

While the hierarchy of needs provides a rational framework for motivation, its flaw lies in the nature of humanity. Man always wants more. When asked what salary they would be comfortable with, people routinely—no matter what their income—name a figure around twice their current income.

To test out his theories, in the summer of 1962 Maslow worked at a Southern California company, Non-Linear Systems, to observe the work environment and organizational practices. The result was a book titled *Eupsychian Management.* This, said Maslow, was "enlightened management."

To Maslow, several factors defined enlightened management:

- *Values:* "It is really fantastic to me that one book after another will make a pious statement about this new development and about organizational theory and management theory and then proceed to say nothing whatsoever about values and purpose except in some vague way that any high school senior could match."[14]

- *Goals and Vision:* "It seems clear to me that in an enterprise, if everybody concerned is absolutely clear about the goals and directives and far purposes of the organization, practically all other questions then become simple technical questions of fitting means to the ends. But it is also true that to the extent that these far goals are confused or conflicting or ambivalent or only partially understood, then all the discussions of techniques and methods and means in the world will be of little use."[15]
- *Teamworking:* "Generosity can increase wealth rather than decrease it. The more influence and power you give to someone else in the team situation, the more you have yourself."[16]

The second major figure in the human relations school was Frederick Herzberg. Herzberg received a grant to investigate the entire field of attitudes to work when he was research director at Psychological Services in Pittsburgh. A review of the literature left Herzberg bemused.

"We could make no sense out of it," Herzberg later recalled. "It seemed that the human being was forever debarred from rational understanding as to why he worked. We looked again at some of the data describing what people wanted from their jobs and noticed that there was a hint that the things people said positively about their job experiences were not the opposite of what they said negatively about their job experiences; the reverse of the factors that seemed to make people happy in jobs did not make them unhappy. So what happens in science, when your research leads to ambiguity? You begin to suspect your premises. In my Public Health School days I had conceived the concept that mental health was not the opposite of mental illness; that mentally healthy people were not just the obverse of mentally sick people. So I took a stab on the basis of mental health not being the opposite of mental illness and came up with a new concept."[17]

The new concept was job satisfaction. Herzberg argued that job satisfaction and job dissatisfaction are separate entities with their own characteristics and produced by different stimuli. Herzberg's next research project, therefore, focused on two questions. He asked people, What makes you happy on the job? and What makes you unhappy on the job?

Herzberg and his fellow researchers took their questions to over two hundred people drawn from nine companies in the Pittsburgh area. (Three steel manufacturers, two machinery manufacturers, one instrument manufacturer, one consumer goods manufacturer, one shipbuilder, and one utility company.) Herzberg focused the research on engineers and accountants as previous research suggested they were better than other types of workers at describing events.

Looking at the results, Herzberg was able to separate the motivational elements of work into two categories—those serving people's animal needs (hygiene factors) and those meeting uniquely human needs (motivation factors). "Hygiene operates to remove health hazards from the environment of man. It is not a curative; it is, rather, a preventative. . . . Similarly, when there are deleterious factors in the context of the job, they serve to bring about poor job attitudes. Improvements in these factors of hygiene will serve to remove the impediments to positive job attitudes," wrote Herzberg and his coauthors in the resulting 1959 book, *The Motivation to Work.*

Hygiene factors—also labeled maintenance factors—were determined to include supervision, interpersonal relations, physical working conditions, salary, company policies and administrative practices, benefits, and job security. "When these factors deteriorate to a level below that which the employee considers acceptable, then job dissatisfaction ensues," observed Herzberg. Hygiene alone is insufficient to provide the "motivation to work." Indeed, Herzberg argued that the factors that provide satisfaction are quite different from those leading to dissatisfaction.

True motivation, said Herzberg, comes from achievement, personal development, job satisfaction, and recognition. The aim should be to motivate people through the job itself rather than through rewards or pressure.

Herzberg went on to broaden his research base. This further confirmed his conclusion that hygiene factors are the principal creator of unhappiness in work and motivational factors the route to satisfaction.

After the success of *The Motivation to Work,* there was a hiatus until Herzberg returned to the fray with the publication of an influential article in the *Harvard Business Review* in 1968. The article—"One More

Time: How Do You Motivate Employees?"—has sold over one million copies in reprints, making it the *Review*'s most popular article ever. Herzberg asked, "What is the simplest, surest, and most direct way of getting someone to do something? Ask? But if the person responds that he or she does not want to do it, then that calls for psychological consultation to determine the reasons for such obstinacy. Tell the person? The response shows that he or she does not understand you, and now an expert in communication methods has to be brought in to show you how to get through. Give the person a monetary incentive? I do not need to remind the reader of the complexity and difficulty involved in setting up and administering an incentive system. Show the person? This means a costly training program. We need a simple way." The article introduced the helpful motivational acronym KITA (kick in the ass) and argued: "If you have someone on a job, use him. If you can't use him get rid of him." Herzberg said that KITA came in three categories: negative physical, negative psychological, and positive. The latter was the preferred method for genuine motivation.

Herzberg also coined the now popular phrase, "job enrichment." He believes that business organizations could be an enormous force for good, provided they liberate both themselves and their people from the thrall of numbers and get on with creative expansion of individuals' roles within them.

The final key figure in the motivational triumvirate was Douglas McGregor, who remains one of the most influential and most quoted thinkers in human relations. His work influenced and inspired the work of thinkers as diverse as Rosabeth Moss Kanter, Warren Bennis, and Robert Waterman. Most notably, McGregor is renowned for his motivational models, Theories X and Y.

Detroit-born McGregor was the son of a clergyman. He graduated from the City College of Detroit (now Wayne University) in 1932. He then went on to Harvard to study for a Ph.D. Following his Ph.D. McGregor worked at Harvard as an instructor and tutor in social psychology. He then moved to MIT as an assistant professor of psychology. In 1948 he became president of Antioch College in Yellow Springs, Ohio. Antioch was renowned as a progressive liberal college. In 1954

McGregor returned to MIT as a professor of management. He became Sloan Fellows Professor of Industrial Management in 1962. At MIT McGregor attracted some of the emerging generation of thinkers to work with him, including Bennis and Schein.

Theories X and Y were the centerpiece of McGregor's 1960 classic, *The Human Side of Enterprise.* Theory X was traditional carrot-and-stick thinking built on "the assumption of the mediocrity of the masses." This assumed that workers were inherently lazy, needed to be supervised and motivated, and regarded work as a necessary evil to provide money. The premises of Theory X, wrote McGregor, were "(1) that the average human has an inherent dislike of work and will avoid it if he can, (2) that people, therefore, need to be coerced, controlled, directed, and threatened with punishment to get them to put forward adequate effort toward the organization's ends and (3) that the typical human prefers to be directed, wants to avoid responsibility, has relatively little ambition, and wants security above all."

McGregor lamented that Theory X "materially influences managerial strategy in a wide sector of American industry," and observed, "if there is a single assumption that pervades conventional organizational theory it is that authority is the central, indispensable means of managerial control."

"The human side of enterprise today is fashioned from propositions and beliefs such as these," wrote McGregor, before going on to conclude that "this behavior is not a consequence of man's inherent nature. It is a consequence rather of the nature of industrial organizations, of management philosophy, policy, and practice." It is not people who have made organizations, but organizations that have transformed the perspectives, aspirations, and behavior of people.

The other extreme was described by McGregor as Theory Y, based on the principle that people want and need to work. If this were the case, then an organization would need to develop each individual's commitment to its objectives, and then to liberate the individual's abilities on behalf of those objectives. McGregor described the assumptions behind Theory Y: "(1) That the expenditure of physical and mental effort in work is as natural as in play or rest—the typical human doesn't inherently dislike work; (2) external control and threat of punishment are not the only means for bringing about effort toward a company's ends; (3) commitment to objectives is a function of the rewards associated with their achievement—the most important of such rewards is the satisfaction of ego and can be the direct product of effort directed toward an organization's purposes; (4) the average human being learns, under the right conditions, not only to accept but to seek responsibility; and (5) the capacity to exercise a relatively high degree of imagination, ingenuity, and creativity in the solution of organizational problems is widely, not narrowly, distributed in the population."

"It is well to treat working people as if they were high type Theory Y human beings, not only because of the Declaration of Independence and not only because of the Golden Rule and not only because of the Bible or some religious precepts or anything like that, but also because this is the path to success of any kind whatsoever, including financial success," commented Abraham Maslow.[18]

Theories X and Y were not simplistic stereotypes. McGregor was realistic: "It is no more possible to create an organization today which will be a full, effective application of this theory than it was to build an atomic power plant in 1945. There are many formidable obstacles to overcome."

Theories X and Y have tended to be simply interpreted as a people-oriented manifesto with McGregor arguing that more efficient managers tend to value and trust people while less effective managers are cynical and mistrust people. In fact, McGregor did not view the world so simplistically. He acknowledged that it was possible for Theory X managers to be corporate dictators while still trusting people. Nor did he regard Theory Y managers as paragons—they could trust people and treat them fairly and still make a mess of running a business. McGregor was observing the facts of motivational life rather than prescribing the way forward. "The motivation, the potential for development, the capacity for assuming responsibility . . . are all present in people. Management does not put them there," he said.

Even so, it is worth noting that Theory Y was more than mere theorizing. In the early 1950s, McGregor helped design a Procter & Gamble plant in Georgia. Built on the Theory Y model with self-managing teams, its performance soon surpassed other P&G plants.

The common complaint against McGregor's Theories X and Y is that they are mutually exclusive, two incompatible ends of an endless spectrum. To counter this, before he died in 1964, McGregor was developing Theory Z, a theory that synthesized the organizational and personal imperatives. The concept of Theory Z was later seized upon by William Ouchi. In his book of the same name, he analyzed Japanese working methods. Here, he found fertile ground for many of the ideas McGregor was proposing for Theory Z—lifetime employment, concern for employees including their social life, informal control, decisions made by consensus, slow promotion, excellent transmittal of information from top to bottom and bottom to top with the help of middle management, commitment to the firm, and high concern for quality.

The Dow Jones Industrial Average Companies as of January 1, 1959

Allied Chemical	Procter & Gamble
American Can	Johns-Manville
American Smelting	International Paper
DuPont	General Foods
Eastman Kodak	United Aircraft
Goodyear	Sears, Roebuck
Bethlehem Steel	Standard Oil of New Jersey
Chrysler	Texas Corporation
General Electric	National Distillers
General Motors	Union Carbide
American Tobacco B	U.S. Steel
Standard Oil of California	American Telephone & Telegraph
International Harvester	Westinghouse Electric
International Nickel	Woolworth
Corn Products Refining	National Steel

The Harvard 100

Top Five HBR *Articles Published in the 1950s*	Ranking in Top 100
"How to Choose a Leadership Pattern," Robert Tannenbaum and Warren H. Schmidt—March-April 1958	3
"Barriers and Gateways to Communication," Carl R. Rogers and F.J. Roethlisberger—July-August 1952	7
"Skills of an Effective Administrator," Robert L. Katz—January-February 1955	11
"An Uneasy Look at Performance Appraisal," Douglas McGregor—May-June 1957	14
"Listening to People," Ralph G. Nichols and Leonard A. Stevens—September-October 1957	74

Source: "The 100 Best-Selling Articles."

The Management Century Timeline

1950

Diner's Club introduces first credit card.

1951

Employment of women reaches its highest point in history, even higher than during World War Two.

Launch of the Deming Prize.

The first commercial color TV broadcast airs.

AT&T is first company with more than a million stockholders.

1953

New York Curb Exchange renamed American Stock Exchange.

TV Guide and *Playboy* launched.

1954

Peter Drucker's biblically proportioned *The Practice of Management* published.

The Tonight Show debuts on NBC.

Abraham Maslow's *Motivation and Personality* is published.

Anglo-Iranian Oil Company renamed British Petroleum.

Volvo enters the U.S. market with the PV444. Observers suggest comparisons with selling refrigerators to Eskimos.

1955

The New York Stock Exchange prices are the highest quoted since 1929.

Ray Kroc forms a new franchising company called McDonald's System Inc., which becomes the McDonald's Corporation in 1960.

IBM introduces first business computer.

AFL-CIO merger.

Disneyland opens in Anaheim, Calif.

1956

Ford Motor Company goes public.

1957

Factory wages average $82.99 per week.

Hewlett-Packard crafts the first set of corporate objectives, which lead to the H-P Way. "The achievements of an organization are the result of the combined efforts of each individual in the organization working toward common objectives. These objectives should be realistic, should be clearly understood by everyone in the organization, and should reflect the organization's basic character and personality."

1958

A serious recession results in 7.7 percent joblessness in the United States.

C.N. Parkinson's hilarious *Parkinson's Law* raises chuckles at management's expense.

1959

Two reports on business education from the Carnegie Foundation and the Ford Foundation are highly critical of business schools.

Xerox Corporation introduces the first xerographic copier for commercial use.

Barbie first sees the light of day at the annual Toy Fair in New York. She is now a $1.9 billion industry.

The 100th McDonald's opens.

Frederick Herzberg's *The Motivation to Work* published.

1960

Sony introduces all-transistor portable television.

Unimation sells first industrial robots.

Douglas McGregor's *The Human Side of Enterprise* published.

Chapter 7
1961–1970 : Understanding Strategy

To be practical, any plan must take account of the enemy's power
to frustrate it; the best chance of overcoming such obstruction is to
have a plan that can be easily varied to fit the circumstances met;
to keep such adaptability, while still keeping the initiative, the best
way is to operate along a line which offers alternative objectives.
—B.H. Liddell Hart[1]

Planning the Future

Peter Ferdinand Drucker was born in Austria in 1909. His father,
Adolph, was the chief economist in the Austrian civil service. (Freud
had lectured in psychiatry to his mother.) In Austria during the 1920s
and 1930s Drucker witnessed the steady descent of Europe into chaos.
This he attributed to inept management.

He left Austria for London, where he worked as a journalist before
moving to America in 1937. Drucker has been writing prolifically and
bluntly challenging managers with his innovative and rigorous thinking
ever since. The ideas he has contributed to management thinking are
many and varied. Among the most significant emerged from Drucker's
phenomenal 1954 book, *The Practice of Management*.

In *The Practice of Management* and the equally enormous *Management: Tasks, Responsibilities and Practices* (1973) Drucker established five basics of the managerial role: to set objectives, to organize, to motivate and communicate, to measure, and to develop people. "The function which distinguishes the manager above all others is his educational one," he wrote. "The one contribution he is uniquely expected to make is to give others vision and ability to perform. It is vision and moral responsibility that, in the last analysis, define the manager." This morality is reflected in the five areas identified by Drucker "in which practices are required to ensure the right spirit throughout management organization":

1. There must be high performance requirements; no condoning of poor or mediocre performance; and rewards must be based on performance.
2. Each management job must be a rewarding job in itself rather than just a step on the promotion ladder.
3. There must be a rational and just promotion system.
4. Management needs a "charter" spelling out clearly who has the power to make "life-and-death" decisions affecting a manager; and there should be some way for a manager to appeal to a higher court.
5. In its appointments, management must demonstrate that it realizes that integrity is the one absolute requirement of a manager, the one quality that he has to bring with him and cannot be expected to acquire later on.

At the time, the idea from *The Practice of Management* that was seized upon was what became known as management by objectives (MBO). "A manager's job should be based on a task to be performed in order to attain the company's objectives . . . the manager should be directed and controlled by the objectives of performance rather than by his boss," Drucker wrote. Hijacked as yet another bright idea, MBO became a simplistic means of setting a corporate goal and heading toward it and bore little relation to Drucker's broader interpretation. (The entire MBO concept was developed most fruitfully by a number of others including George Odiorne and the United Kingdom's John Humble.)

Drucker identified managing by objectives as the first of "seven new tasks" for the manager of the future. Given that these were laid down over forty years ago, their prescience is astounding.

1. Manage by objectives.
2. Take more risks and for a longer period ahead.
3. Make strategic decisions.
4. Build an integrated team, each member of which is capable of managing and of measuring personal performance and results in relation to the common objectives.
5. Communicate information fast and clearly.
6. See the business as a whole and integrate the manager's own function with it. The traditional limited knowledge of one or more functions will no longer be enough.
7. See the business in relation to business in general. The traditional specialization in a few products or one industry will also no longer be enough.

The concept of managing by objectives was a creature of its times. The affluence and security of the 1950s eased gently into the 1960s. Corporations rolled powerfully on. The world seemed predictable. The future could be planned. It seemed sensible, therefore, for executives to identify their objectives. They could then focus on managing in such a way that these objectives were achieved. They could then set some more objectives.

This was the capitalist equivalent of the Soviet Union's five-year plans. MBO provided a framework to express managerial certainty. Not for nothing did one of the leading management theorists of the 1960s suggest that the best-managed organizations in the world were the Standard Oil Company of New Jersey, the Roman Catholic Church, and the Communist Party. The belief was that if the future was mapped out, it would happen. In an era of steady growth, technological maturity, and opening markets, management by objectives was an expression of confidence.

Military Models

The antecedents of management by objectives lay in military strategy. Military strategy shared a similar approach: identify where you want to be and mobilize every resource to get there. You took one hill, then moved onto the next. Given time, you could conquer the world, hilltop to hilltop.

Indeed, military analogies with business thinking and practice are especially strong and long lasting. Best military practice has often been pillaged by modern management thinkers. How about Wellington's managerial style, as outlined by John Keegan in his book, *The Mask of Command:* "[Wellington's methods] required a particularly intense 'managerial' style—'taking trouble' with the battle, as Wellington himself would later put it. The general must make himself the eyes of his own army . . . must constantly change position to deal with crises as they occur along the front of his sheltered line, must remain at the point of crisis until it is resolved and must still keep alert to anticipate the development of crises elsewhere."[2] Dress it up and this passage would fit comfortably in most modern management texts.

Books as diverse as Carl von Clausewitz's *On War* (1831), B.H. Liddell Hart's *Strategy* (1967), and Miyamoto Mushashi's *Book of Five Rings* (1974) have explored the military-management link. Military role models—Wellington, Napoleon, Montgomery, MacArthur, Colin Powell, Norman Schwarzkopf—are keenly seized upon by executives. The military, with its elements of logistics management, human resource management, strategy, and leadership, is alluring. The link between the military and business worlds has existed since time immemorial. Its starting point, as far as it is possible to discern, is Sun-Tzu's *Art of War,* written 2,500 years ago.[3]

The attraction of military analogies is that it is clear who your enemy is. When your enemy is clear, the world appears clearer whether you are a general or a CEO. Sun-Tzu is an aggressive counterpoint to the confusion of mere theory. After all, among his advice was the following: "Deploy forces to defend the strategic points; exercise vigilance in preparation, do not be indolent. Deeply investigate the true situation, secretly await their laxity. Wait until they leave their strongholds, then seize what they love."

To many, Sun-Tzu is the apogee of strategy. Managers appear to lap up such brazen brutality—the book returned to the best-seller lists in the 1980s. Yet *The Art of War* is more sophisticated than that. Why destroy when you can win by stealth and cunning? "If you are near the enemy, make him believe you are far from him. If you are far from the enemy, make him believe you are near," wrote the master. Michael Porter never made it that simple. "A sovereign should not start a war out of anger, nor should a general give battle out of rage. For while anger can revert to happiness and rage to delight, a nation that has been destroyed cannot be restored, nor can the dead be brought back to life," wrote Sun Tzu. "To subdue the enemy's forces without fighting is the summit of skill. The best approach is to attack the other side's strategy; next best is to attack his alliances; next best is to attack his soldiers; the worst is to attack cities."

Sun-Tzu's take on strategy tends to become lost in neat but ultimately unhelpful aphorisms. "For the shape of an army is like that of water," said Sun-Tzu. "The shape of water is to avoid heights and flow towards low places; the shape of the army is to avoid strength and to strike at weakness. Water flows in accordance with the ground; an army achieves victory in accordance with the enemy." Quite what the manager in Hickory, North Carolina, makes of such Confucian wisdom it is difficult to determine.

More coherent and more contemporary are the insights into strategy of the Prussian general Carl von Clausewitz (1780–1831), author of (the unfinished and posthumously published) *On War* (1831).

As a kind of historical stepping stone to von Clausewitz are the strategic insights of Nicolo Machiavelli (1469–1527). The Florentine diplomat portrayed a world of cunning, intrigue, and brutal opportunism. "I believe also that he will be successful who directs his actions according to the spirit of the time, and that he whose actions do not accord with the time will not be successful," he wrote. "Because men are seen, in affairs that lead to the end which every man has before him, namely, glory and riches, to get there by various methods; one with caution, another with haste; one by force, another by skill; one by patience, another by its opposite; and each one succeeds in reaching the goal by a different method." If it works, do it. Opportunism *uber alles*. Machiavelli was a combination of Sun-Tzu and Dale Carnegie, sugary persuasion mixed with clinical brutality.

Von Clausewitz was influenced by Machiavelli in that he saw strategy as a political game. "Rather than comparing it [war] to art we could more accurately compare it to commerce, which is also a conflict of interests and activities; and it is still closer to politics, which in turn may be considered as a kind of commerce on a larger scale," wrote the Prussian.[4] Most famously, he observed that war "is merely the continuation of policy by other means."

Von Clausewitz was, in a colorful military career, at one time director of the Prussian war college. He coined the phrase "grand strategy"—the overall objective of the military campaign. This was a precursor of management by objectives in that it simply stated that everything needs to be subsumed beneath the overall military objective. Nowhere are the similarities between von Clausewitz's view of strategy and MBO more clear than in his comment, "By looking on each engagement as part of a series, at least insofar as events are predictable, the commander is always on the high road to his goal."[5] Just remember that the low road is the route to unemployment.

The Summer of Strategy

In the business world, Peter Drucker's 1964 book *Managing for Results* was, he says, the "first book ever on what we now call strategy." Perhaps. But Alfred Chandler (born 1918) could argue equally powerfully that his *Strategy and Structure* (1962) was the first installment in modern understanding of the strategic beast.

A business historian, Chandler defined strategy as "the determination of the long-term goals and objectives of an enterprise, and the adoption of courses of action and the allocation of resources necessary for carrying out these goals." He argued that strategy came before structure. Having developed the best possible strategy, companies could then determine the most appropriate organizational structure to achieve it.

In the early sixties, this was speedily accepted as a fact of life—no one had previously considered strategy in such terms.

More recently, Chandler's premise has been persistently questioned. "I think he got it exactly wrong," Tom Peters has commented with typical forthrightness. "For it is the structure of the organization that determines, over time, the choices that it makes about the markets it attacks."[6] Others suggest that the entire process is far messier than Chandler asserted. In a perfect world, companies would hatch perfect strategies and then create neat structures and organizational maps. Reality, however, is a mess in which strategy and structure mix madly.

Contemporary strategist Gary Hamel provides a more positive perspective on Chandler's insights. "Those who dispute Chandler's thesis that structure follows strategy miss the point," Hamel argues. "Of course, strategy and structure are inextricably intertwined. Chandler's point was that new challenges give rise to new structures. The challenges of size and complexity, coupled with advances in communications and techniques of management control, produced divisionalization and decentralization. These same forces, several generations on, are now driving us towards new structural solutions—the *federated organization,* the multicompany coalition, and the virtual company. Few historians are prescient. Chandler was."[7] Further plaudits come from *Business Week,* which has noted, "In the history of business, BC stands for Before Chandler."

While Drucker and Chandler could argue between themselves about who got there first, third prize undoubtedly goes to Igor Ansoff (born 1918). Ansoff trained as an engineer and mathematician. After leaving Brown University, he worked for the RAND Corporation,[8] initially in the mathematics department, and then the Lockheed Corporation where he was a vice president.

In 1963 he left industry for academia, joining Carnegie-Mellon's Graduate School of Business Administration. He then taught at Vanderbilt University, the European Institute for Advanced Studies in Management in Belgium, and the San Diego–based U.S. International University.

Ansoff's experiences at Lockheed provided the impetus for his first book, *Corporate Strategy* (1965), in which he sought to make sense of the broader implications of what he had learned at the company. Ansoff believed that there was "a practical method for strategic decision making within a business firm" that could be made accessible to all.

This, he believed, was especially important in a world he perceived to be struggling to cope with relentless change. Ansoff expressed concern at the "deluge of technology, the dynamism of the world-wide changes in market structure, and the saturation of demand in many major United States industries." He worried that in industries such as electronics, pharmaceuticals, plastics, and aerospace, change was so fast that companies needed to "continually survey the product-market environment" for new opportunities. Ansoff concluded that no business "can consider itself immune to threats of product obsolescence and saturation of demand." In retrospect, these seem tame observations. At the time they flew in the face of contemporary, and rather complacent, wisdom.

Ansoff identified four different but standard types of decision: decisions regarding strategy, policy, programs, and standard operating procedures. Policy, programs, and procedures solved commonplace and regularly occurring issues and problems. The management input was minimal. On the other hand, strategic decisions were different. Situations differ and they demand management attention and energy.

Ansoff divided decisions into those that were "strategic" (concerned with products and markets), "administrative" (concerned with structure and resource allocation), and "operating" (concerned with budgeting, supervising, and controlling). Ansoff moved beyond Chandler's linking of strategy and structure to add systems.

The result was a rational model by which strategic and planning decisions could be made. A creature of its times, the model concentrated on corporate expansion and diversification rather than strategic planning as a whole. (When interviewed by the Lockheed CEO, Ansoff had asked what was meant by diversification. The CEO did not know—even though this was the strategy the company was then pursuing.) From this emerged the Ansoff Model of Strategic Planning, an intricate and somewhat daunting sequence of decisions.

Central to this was the reassuringly simple concept of gap analysis: see where you are, identify where you wish to be, and identify tasks that will take you there. Ansoff can also lay claim to introducing the word *synergy* into the management vocabulary. He explained it with persuasive brevity as "2 + 2 = 5."

Unfortunately, in their enthusiasm to overturn the basic rules of math, executives usually found that 2 + 2 = 3.5. Synergy became the de rigueur explanation for every unlikely corporate marriage. And in the 1960s there were many startling examples of how not to synergize. Among the best—or worst—examples is that of RCA. In 1965 RCA chief Bobby Sarnoff took over a company that was performing well in broadcasting, manufacturing, and recording. It was also moving into the fledgling computer market. The future looked promising. Then Sarnoff, son of the legendary David Sarnoff, took the fashionable route for the 1960s and tried to turn RCA into ITT through a series of gloriously ill-advised acquisitions. In 1967, RCA bought Arnold Palmer Enterprises. "Perhaps someone at the network thought it would be a good idea to have Palmer on board in some capacity," recalled an executive. "Or it might have been they wanted to play golf with him. Also, Arnold Palmer was a hell of a better symbol than Nipper the Dog for the 1960s." As it turned out, RCA would have been better off sticking with Nipper. RCA also bought Hertz, a frozen foods packaging company, a real-estate company, and then a carpet maker. "He would take great intuitive leaps from an unwarranted assumption to foregone conclusion," lamented one of Sarnoff's colleagues.

Igor Ansoff would not have approved. His approach was more analytical and prescriptive. Ansoff regarded strategic management as "the part of management which develops a firm's future profit potential by assuring that it does business in markets which have the potential of satisfying its objectives; that it offers products/services which these markets want; and that it offers them in a way which assures it a competitive advantage." He distinguished this from what he called *operating management*—"the part of management which, using the profit potential, optimizes a firm's profitability through efficient production, distribution and marketing its products/services generated by strategic management."

Analysis was the bedrock of strategic management. Early converts to strategic planning as outlined by Ansoff found that "paralysis by analysis" was a very real threat. "In retrospect, the incidence of strategic planning failure should not have been surprising. After all, it was a practical invention designed by staffs in business firms as a solution to a problem which was poorly understood, and in the absence of a theory which could have guided the design," Ansoff has reflected.

A measure of the argumentative power, if not the practical achievements, of strategic management can be seen by the fact that it took over twenty-five years for a comprehensive development of the debate, a rewriting of the fundamentals and a rebuttal of Ansoff's approach, to emerge. This came from Henry Mintzberg (born 1939) in *The Rise and Fall of Strategic Planning* (1994). Mintzberg defined planning as "a formalized system for codifying, elaborating and operationalizing the strategies which companies already have." In contrast, strategy is either an "emergent" pattern or a deliberate "perspective." Mintzberg argued that strategy cannot be planned. While planning is concerned with analysis, strategy making is concerned with synthesis. Today's planners are not redundant but are only valuable as strategy finders, analysts, and catalysts. They are supporters of line managers, forever questioning rather than providing automatic answers. Their most effective role is in unearthing "fledgling strategies in unexpected pockets of the organization so that consideration can be given to (expanding) them."

Mintzberg identified three central pitfalls to today's strategy-planning practices.

First, the assumption that discontinuities can be predicted. Forecasting techniques are limited by the fact that they tend to assume that the future will resemble the past. This gives artificial reassurance and creates strategies that are liable to disintegrate as they are overtaken by events. He points out that our passion for planning mostly flourishes during stable times such as the 1960s. Confronted by a new world order, planners are left seeking to re-create a long-forgotten past.

Second, the way that planners are detached from the reality of the organization. Mintzberg is critical of the "assumption of detachment." "If the system does the thinking," he writes, "the thought must be detached from the action, strategy from operations, [and] ostensible thinkers from doers. . . . It is this disassociation of thinking from acting that lies close to the root of [strategic planning's] problem."

Planners have traditionally been obsessed with gathering hard data on their industry, markets, competitors. Soft data—networks of contacts, talking with customers, suppliers, and employees, using intuition and using the grapevine—have all but been ignored.

Mintzberg points out that much of what is considered "hard" data is often anything but. There is a "soft underbelly of hard data" typified by the fallacy of "measuring what's measurable." The results are limiting—for example, a pronounced tendency "to favor cost-leadership strategies (emphasizing operating efficiencies, which are generally measurable) over product leadership strategies (emphasizing innovative design or high quality, which tends to be less measurable)."

To gain real and useful understanding of an organization's competitive situation soft data needs to be dynamically integrated into the planning process. "Strategy-making is an immensely complex process involving the most sophisticated, subtle and at times subconscious of human cognitive and social processes," wrote Mintzberg. "While hard data may inform the intellect, it is largely soft data that generate wisdom. They may be difficult to 'analyze,' but they are indispensable for synthesis—the key to strategy making."

The third and final flaw identified by Mintzberg is the assumption that strategy making can be formalized. The left side of the brain has dominated strategy formulation with its emphasis on logic and analysis. Overly structured, this creates a narrow range of options. Alternatives that do not fit into the predetermined structure are ignored. The right side of the brain needs to become part of the process, with its emphasis on intuition and creativity. "Planning by its very nature," concluded Mintzberg, "defines and preserves categories. Creativity, by its very nature, creates categories or rearranges established ones. This is why strategic planning can neither provide creativity, nor deal with it when it emerges by other means." Mold-breaking strategies "grow initially like weeds, they are not cultivated like tomatoes in a hothouse. . . . [They] can take root in all kinds of places."

Strategy making, as presented by Mintzberg, displays the following characteristics:

- It is derived from synthesis.
- It is informal and visionary, rather than programmed and formalized.
- It relies on divergent thinking, intuition, and using the subconscious. This leads to outbursts of creativity as new discoveries are made.
- It is irregular, unexpected, ad hoc, instinctive. It upsets stable patterns.
- It regards managers as adaptive information manipulators—opportunists rather than aloof conductors.
- It is done in times of instability characterized by discontinuous change.
- It results from an approach that takes in broad perspectives; it is therefore visionary, and involves a variety of actors capable of experimenting and then integrating.

The Rise and Fall of Strategic Planning attracted a great deal of attention and some vituperative debate—not least an entertaining spat between Ansoff and Mintzberg—but it was a debate that had been held over while analysis traveled the world and changed the nature of managerial work.

Analysis in Practice

Igor Ansoff's carefully constructed world of strategic management was a wonder to behold. But who would make all this happen? Who could carry out the analysis and reach the best business decision? The answer: professional managers. The 1950s and 1960s saw the emergence of management as a profession.

"Professionalism is here to stay awhile," concluded a 1966 *Fortune* article. "The scientist, engineer, and lawyer are indispensable to management and so are professional communicators and others whose skill lies in the coordination and leadership of specialists. The professional man in management has a powerful base of independence—perhaps a firmer base than the small businessman ever had in his property rights. The highly trained young man entering management today can look for corporate aid in enhancing his competence and hence his base of independence. He need not aspire to become the top officer of the firm who holds the only human job in an organization conceived on the old line of a machine with all its decision-making initiative concentrated in the operator at the top. Today's management recruit can—and, in fact, does—have more rational and less frustrating ambition of a life of ever widening responsibility and choices. The prospect for a managerial career today is more adventurous than it ever was, because by the year 2000 there will be hundreds of thousands, perhaps millions, of Americans whose influence on the quality of life in their more fluid society will be greater than that of any past captain of industry."[9]

Alfred Chandler attributed the evolution of management to increases in scale in industry. Bigger companies producing bigger quantities required a new breed of professionals. The "visible hand" of management was required to coordinate the flow of product to customers more efficiently than Adam Smith's "invisible hand."

The chief providers of this new generation of professionals were the growing ranks of business schools. In the 1960s they began to cover the world. Invented in the United States, the business school as we know it can be traced to the Wharton School at the University of Pennsylvania, which was founded in 1881. The Wharton approach to business was numerical. Its bedrock was finance, and it was the management of money that was drummed into students from the earliest days. Other schools soon followed. These institutions grew out of a desire to train and educate future generations in management techniques and practices, an aspiration often supported by generous donations from industrialists.

Toward the end of the nineteenth century this desire had led to the creation of a number of specialized departments and schools attached to leading U.S. universities. For the first time commercial practices, and the philosophies that underpinned them, were elevated to the same sort of level as other academic disciplines. They have been unlikely and often uncomfortable bedfellows ever since.

The origins of the MBA, the best known business school qualification, date back to this period. Founded in 1900, the Tuck School at

Dartmouth claims to have had the first graduate program in management. Although not technically an MBA, the first graduate degree was offered by Tuck in 1900. Originally it was a "three, two" program, with three years study at undergraduate level at Dartmouth followed by two years at Tuck.

Postgraduate entry courses followed. Harvard Business School claims to have been the first business school to require a university degree for entry to its management program. Founded in 1908, the school awarded its first master's degree in the discipline in 1910.

The idea of business education quickly took off. In some cases it was integrated into other professional disciplines. As early as 1914, for example, the Massachusetts Institute of Technology offered business training for engineers, and its masters degree in management dates back to 1925. Elsewhere it was given a helping hand by a section of the local business community. The Edwin L. Cox School of Business, at the Southern Methodist University in Dallas, for example, was founded in 1921 with the help of Dallas businessmen and women. The need to establish some sort of quality control resulted in the creation of the American Association of Collegiate Schools of Business (AACSB) in 1916.

Throughout the 1940s interest in business schools grew rapidly in the United States. After World War Two a number of private business schools were started, including the American Graduate School of International Management, known as Thunderbird. But by the end of the 1950s business schools were under attack. In 1959 two reports on the state of American management education were published, one—by Robert A. Gordon and James E. Howell—was sponsored by the Ford Foundation and the other—by Frank C. Pierson—had the financial backing of the Carnegie Corporation. Both complained that business schools were little more than vocational colleges, with mediocre students and second-rate teachers. Business schools were criticized for failing to produce original research and being out of touch with business.

Business schools took the criticism to heart. Academic credibility was a raw nerve. In the coming years, it was to become an issue that dictated their priorities. The business schools hit back by raising admission and teaching standards. They also initiated the research programs for which the U.S. schools are now well known.

It was also at this time that the classic two-year American MBA model was born, with the first year devoted to the core disciplines and the second year offering more specialization through electives. The business schools were determined to be taken seriously. They would put management on the academic map. If large sums of cash were generated from these programs to pay for more research, then so much the better.

The MBA bandwagon was under way. Over the next forty years it would call at countless new business schools, providing job mobility for the several million business school graduates it picked up along the way.

While American institutions boarded the bandwagon with enthusiasm, in Europe there was a tepid response. In Europe, structured study of management is a much more recent phenomenon. With a few exceptions, Europeans took little interest in business schools in the first half of the twentieth century. (One of the notable exceptions was the Paris Chamber of Commerce and Industry, which introduced a management course in 1931. In many ways it was a precursor of the executive MBA—a part-time program aimed at managers between thirty and forty, though it did not involve a degree.)

After the Second World War, the impact of the Marshall Plan and other U.S.-led initiatives to rebuild Europe's industrial base brought American ideas to Europe. These included recognition that the business leaders of the future required special training.

By the late 1940s and 1950s business schools were springing up on the European mainland. The origins of the Institute for Management Development (IMD), at Lausanne, Switzerland, for example, can be traced back to 1946. In 1958, the European Institute of Business Administration, better known as INSEAD, was established in Paris. INSEAD offered an MBA for the first time in 1959. (The dearth of European business education opportunities was such that in 1970 only one member of INSEAD's faculty had a business doctorate—all now do.)

In the United Kingdom, too, seeds were being sown for the business schools that followed. In 1965, Manchester and London Business Schools were opened. They joined others including Henley Management College and Cranfield, which were already running courses in management education. But the two new British schools had the backing of the

British government and were deliberately created to be centers of excellence that would rival their American counterparts. This represented an important development. The British government of the time believed that the creation of such centers was a necessary precondition to maintain the competitiveness of the national economy.

The American model was the one to follow. Elsewhere in Europe many of the newer schools were heavily influenced by U.S. business schools. Harvard professor Georges Doriot was the driving force behind the creation of the French school, INSEAD. A Ford Foundation grant provided impetus at the school's genesis and Harvard helpfully provided books to begin INSEAD's library. IESE at the University of Navarra in Barcelona was also inspired by Harvard, and still makes extensive use of the Harvard case study method. Harvard supported the founding of Paris's Centre de Perfectionnement aux Affaires in 1931. In the Netherlands, Erasmus University's close links with the University of Michigan helped it create Rotterdam School of Management in the early 1970s.

Harvard's influence stretched around the world. The Indian Institute of Management, for example, was established with Harvard's support and remains a devout follower to this day. In Asia the Manila-based Asian Institute of Management was launched in 1968 and initially used material from Harvard for all of its programs. Harvard even offers a one-year program in applied economics with the Ho Chi Minh City Economics University in Vietnam—thus achieving by stealth what the United States failed to achieve through warfare.

Today, business schools operate from within the walls of some of the most respected universities in the world—though those august academic institutions, Cambridge and Oxford, have only embraced management in the last decade. Business schools have influenced and changed the business world and created a cadre of professional managers.

The Analysts Take Charge

Thanks to a combination of ideas and education, the manager was effectively reinvented as an information analyst. The apotheosis of the analyst-manager was Harold Geneen (1910–1997). Geneen, the "legendary conglomerateur" according to *BusinessWeek,* was a remorselessly driven workaholic who believed that analytical rigor could—and surely would—conquer all.

Geneen allowed for no frivolity and, even in his late eighties, worked a ten-hour day at his office in New York's Waldorf-Astoria Hotel running Gunther International, a company he bought into in 1992. "If I had enough arms and legs and time, I'd do it all myself," said Geneen.[10] He combined hard work with an apparently slavish devotion to figures "Putting deals together beats spending every day playing golf," he once said.

Behind the mythology, Harold Geneen qualified as an accountant after studying at night school. He then began climbing the executive career ladder working at American Can, Bell & Howell, Jones & Laughlin, and finally Raytheon, which was taken over by ITT. ITT had started life in 1920 as a Caribbean telephone company. Geneen joined the board of ITT in 1959 and set about turning the company into the world's greatest conglomerate.

His basic organizational strategy was that diversification was a source of strength. There was nothing halfhearted in Geneen's pursuit of diversity. Under Geneen, ITT bought companies as addictively as Imelda Marcos once bought shoes. ITT's spending spree amounted to 350 companies and included Avis Rent-A-Car, Sheraton Hotels, Continental Baking, and Levitt & Sons—among many others. By 1970 ITT was composed of 400 separate companies operating in seventy countries.

The ragbag collection was a managerial nightmare. Keeping the growing array of companies on track was a complex series of financial checks and targets. Geneen managed them with intense vigor. Few other executives could have done so, but he brought a unique single-mindedness to the task. As part of his formula, every month over fifty executives flew to Brussels to spend four days poring over the figures. Geneen didn't believe in traveling light. *Fortune* reported on his working arrangements: "When Geneen is in New York, he operates from a thirty-three foot office complete with eight telephones and a clock that shows what parts of the world are in sunlight, what parts in darkness. Ten suitcase-sized leather dispatch cases are spread around the window ledges. When Geneen travels, a half dozen of these cases are likely to travel with him. They contain a couple of hundred pounds of paper—bulky copies of the reports and other communications relevant to the operation of ITT divisions and subsidiaries everywhere in the world."[11]

Geneen was armed against the unexpected. Analysis could iron out the wrinkles of reality. "I want no surprises," announced Geneen. He hoped to make people "as predictable and controllable as the capital resources they must manage." While others would have watched as the deck of cards fell to the ground, Geneen kept adding more cards—and managing to know the pressures and stresses each was under.

Facts were the lifeblood of the expanding ITT—and executives sweated blood in their pursuit. "The highest art of professional management requires the literal ability to *smell* a *real fact* from all others—and, moreover, to have the temerity, intellectual curiosity, guts and/or plain impoliteness, if necessary, to be sure that what you do have is indeed what we will call an *unshakeable fact*," said Geneen.

By sheer force of personality, Geneen made his approach work. (More cynically, you could say that ITT was a success in the parameters created by Geneen.) Between 1959 and 1977 ITT's sales went from $765 million to nearly $28 billion. Earnings went from $29 million to $562 million and earnings per share rose from $1 to $4.20. Geneen stepped down as chief executive in 1977 and as chairman in 1979.

A company built around the drive and energy of one man will not last longer than that man's career. ITT rapidly disintegrated following Geneen's departure. Indeed, the writing was on the wall before that—the company's profits fell in 1974 and 1975. "Running a conglomerate requires working harder than most people want to work and taking more risks than most people want to take," said Geneen. His followers were unable to sustain his uniquely driven working style. The underside of ITT was exposed—it had worked with the CIA in Chile and been involved in offering bribes. The deck of cards tumbled. In the month of Harold Geneen's death, ITT was taken over.

Geneen epitomized the new professional manager—corporate man with added analytics. "The best people to run companies are not the geniuses. They're too difficult to get along with. The best people are

well-rounded men with ambition," said Geneen, before going on to categorize himself as a "difficult person."[12] But it was a managerial model
that was not to everyone's taste. It seemed, to some, to stifle the entrepreneurial spirit, to dampen creativity. Among those voicing such skeptical heresies was Robert Townsend (1920–1998), president of Avis
Rent-a-Car from 1962 until it was absorbed into the ITT empire in
1965. In 1970 Townsend's *Up the Organization* provided a clarion call
to those not taken in by the relentless quest for data. The book's subtitle
was "How to Stop the Corporation from Stifling People and Strangling
Profits." If Harold Geneen was Bill Haley, Townsend was management's
Jimi Hendrix.

"In the average company the boys in the mailroom, the president,
the vice-presidents, and the girls in the steno pool have three things in
common: they are docile, they are bored, and they are dull," wrote
Townsend. "Trapped in the pigeonholes of organization charts, they've
been made slaves to the rules of private and public hierarchies that run
mindlessly on and on because nobody can change them."

There was a serious side to Townsend, underlying the humor. His
argument was that management wasn't some sort of superspecies—"top
management (the board of directors) is supposed to be a tree full of
owls—hooting when management heads into the wrong part of the forest. I'm still unpersuaded they even know where the forest is"—and that
business was fundamentally about people rather than numbers. "There's
nothing fundamentally wrong with our country except that the leaders
of all our major organizations are operating on the wrong assumptions,"
he wrote. "We're in this mess because for the last two hundred years
we've been using the Catholic Church and Caesar's legions as our patterns for creating organizations. And until the last forty or fifty years it
made sense. The average churchgoer, soldier, and factory worker was
uneducated and dependent on orders from above. And authority carried considerable weight because disobedience brought the death penalty
or its equivalent."

The message from Townsend was timely and accurate: managers
could be professional without regarding themselves as some sort of superspecies who were always right. There was more to management than
numbers.

Chiefs Past

CEOs of Major Companies in 1968:

Company	CEO
First National City Bank	George S. Moore/Walter Wriston
General Motors	James M. Roache
Ford Motor	Henry Ford II
IBM	Thomas Watson Jr.
General Electric	Fred Borch
Travelers Insurance	Sterling T. Tooker
U.S. Steel	Roger M. Blough
Mobil Oil	Albert L. Nickerson
American Telephone & Telegraph	Haakon I. Romnes
Prudential Insurance	Orville E. Beal
Bank of America	Rudolf A. Peterson
Standard Oil of New Jersey	Michael J. Haider
Bankers Trust	William H. Moore
Texaco	J. Howard Rambin Jr.
Gulf Oil	Ernest D. Brockett
Sears, Roebuck	Gordon M. Metcalf
General Telephone & Electronics	Leslie H. Warner
Irving Trust	George A. Murphy
Wells Fargo Bank	Richard P. Cooley
Chase Manhattan Bank	George Champion/David Rockefeller

Source: "The Top of the Top," *Fortune,* June 15, 1968.

Comings and Goings

While the world enjoyed the Summer of Love, the business world found 1967 hard going. Net income among the Fortune 500 declined—down for the first time in six years. GM, Ford, and U.S. Steel all reported declines in sales. These are the Fortune top 20—the largest industrial corporations for 1967:

1. General Motors
2. Standard Oil of New Jersey
3. Ford Motor
4. General Electric
5. Chrysler
6. Mobil Oil
7. International Business Machines
8. Texaco
9. Gulf Oil
10. U.S. Steel
11. Western Electric
12. Standard Oil of California
13. DuPont (EI) de Nemours
14. Shell Oil
15. Radio Corporation of America
16. McDonnell Douglas
17. Standard Oil of Indiana
18. Westinghouse Electric
19. Boeing
20. Swift

The Dow Jones Industrial Average Companies as of January 1, 1969

Allied Chemical	Procter & Gamble
American Can	Johns-Manville
Anaconda	International Paper
DuPont	General Foods
Eastman Kodak	United Aircraft
Goodyear	Sears, Roebuck
Bethlehem Steel	Standard Oil of New Jersey
Chrysler	Texas Corporation
General Electric	Owens-Illinois Glass
General Motors	Union Carbide
American Tobacco B	U.S. Steel
Standard Oil of California	American Telephone & Telegraph
International Harvester	Westinghouse Electric
International Nickel	Woolworth
Swift & Co.	Aluminum Co.

The Harvard 100

Top Five HBR *Articles Published in the 1960s*	*Ranking in Top 100*
"One More Time: How Do You Motivate Employees?" Frederick Herzberg—January-February—1968	1
"Pygmalion in Management," J. Sterling Livingstone—July-August 1969	4
"The Management Process in 3-D," Alec MacKenzie—November-December 1969	5
"Marketing Myopia," Theodore Levitt—July-August 1960	6
"Who Are Your Motivated Workers?" M. Scott Myers—January-February 1964	9

Source: "The 100 Best-Selling Articles."

The Management Century Timeline

1961

A bill setting the U.S. minimum wage at $1.25 an hour is signed by President Kennedy.

Twenty-nine electric-equipment manufacturers are convicted of price fixing.

IBM's Selectric typewriter hits the market.

1962

AT&T launches first communications satellite.

IBM chief Thomas Watson Jr. decides to develop the System/360 family of computers. This decision cost the company $5 billion—more than the development of the atomic bomb. The result was the first mainframe computer even though IBM's market research suggested it would only sell two units worldwide. System/360 formed the basis of IBM's success in the 1970s and 1980s.

Ted Levitt's *Innovation in Marketing* is published.

Alfred Chandler reawakens the corporate world to strategy with *Strategy and Structure.*

1963

Thomas Watson Jr.'s *A Company and Its Beliefs* is published.

The Morita family moves to the United States so that Akio Morita can study the American market. Morita is the cofounder of Sony.

Alfred P. Sloan recounts a corporate life in *My Years with General Motors.*

Kodak introduces the Instamatic camera.

Philips Corporation introduces music-quality cassette tapes.

1964

Walt Disney conceives EPCOT, which opens in Orlando, Florida, in 1971.

Phil Knight launches Nike with Bill Bowerman, his former track coach at the University of Oregon.

Civil Rights Act of 1964 outlaws workplace discrimination and establishes Equal Employment Opportunity Commission.

IBM launches System/360 (*Fortune* calls it "Tom Watson Jr.'s $5 billion gamble"). Some gamble. The revolutionary System/360 helps IBM's base of installed computers jump from eleven thousand in early 1964 to thirty-five thousand in 1970, and its revenues more than double, to $7.5 billion. At the same time, IBM's market value soars from about $14 billion to more than $36 billion.

Mitsubishi reaches a point where it is made up of over fifty companies employing a quarter of a million Japanese and generating sales in excess of $3 billion. Few notice in the West.[13]

1965

Igor Ansoff's *Corporate Strategy* is published.

General Motors becomes ever bigger. Its 1965 operating revenues exceed the 1964 gross national product of all but nine nations in the free world. Its 1965 sales are $20,734 million and it employs more than 735,000 people—a total greater than the population of Boston.[14]

1966

Walt Disney dies in Los Angeles.

The Dow Jones breaks 1,000 points.

1967

The General Agreement on Tariffs and Trade is signed in Geneva by the United States and forty-five other country representatives.

First McDonald's outside the United States opens.

Commissioner Pete Rozelle asks Booz·Allen to help structure the newly formed National Football League.

GM builds its 100 millionth automobile.

Philip Kotler's *Marketing Management* is published.

1968

Gordon Moore and Robert Noyce leave Fairchild Semiconductor to establish their own company, Intel. The rest is a whirlwind of technological history and huge commercial success. They are joined in their adventure by employee #4, Andy Grove.

1969

Peter Drucker's *Age of Discontinuity* predicts the corporate future with inspired accuracy and introduces the concept of knowledge work.

The U.S. government files a third antitrust suit against IBM; IBM "unbundles" its products.

Astronaut Neil Armstrong walks on the moon. Meanwhile, not so far out in space, Boeing launches the 747.

1970

Sony is the first Japanese firm on the New York Stock Exchange.

Robert Townsend's *Up the Organization* provides a humorous counter to corporate seriousness.

Amtrak is created.

Chapter 8

1971–1980: Organized Paralysis

Now that they are needed by the millions, white-collar workers are also expendable. The lifetime sinecure is rapidly disappearing as management experts figure out yet another way to streamline the job, get in another machine, and cut down overhead.
—*FORTUNE,* 1970[1]

Under the Parapet

In the early 1970s, Western capitalism seemed in a healthy state. Management had made large leaps forward in being accepted as a profession. Managers had erected the full panoply of professionalism around themselves—educational bodies, institutions, associations. The evidence of the growing power of professional managers was there for all to see as they cast their eyes around the great corporations, the industrial juggernauts pressing relentlessly forward. The modern corporation was a colossus comfortable with its size. Bloated by the concept of synergy, corporations had erected labyrinthian hierarchies. Dusty recesses where little could—or needed to—be done were commonplace.

Complacency was in the air. Pricking the bubble were a very few thinkers, rare voices of doubt in a world of cast-iron belief and faith. At the radical end of the doubt-mongers was the futurist Alvin Toffler (born 1928). Toffler first came to prominence with his 1970 book, *Future Shock*. Its messages were not easily contemplated by managers reared on a diet of certainty. *"Future Shock* suggested that businesses were going to restructure themselves repeatedly," Toffler later observed. "That they would have to reduce hierarchy and [adopt] what we termed ad-hocracy. This sounded sensational to many readers."[2] It also sounded highly implausible. After decades of assembling carefully constructed hierarchies and ornate bureaucracies, companies saw no reason to dismantle them.

The book's origins lay in Toffler's time in Washington where he came to the conclusion that the political systems were hopelessly outdated. (Virtually every other Washington correspondent comes to the same conclusion. Most do not go on to consider how things should be changed.) Some of the ideas were flagposted in a 1965 article, "The Future as a Way of Life," which suggested that accelerating change and uncertainty were going to be characteristics of the future. Toffler regarded the term *future shock* as "an analogy to the concept of culture shock. With future shock you stay in one place but your own culture changes so rapidly that it has the same disorienting effect as going to another culture."[3]

As a counterpoint to Toffler's views, it is worth quoting those of *Fortune* founder Henry Luce. As Toffler contemplated a world beset with change and uncertainty, Luce felt able to pronounce: "The American economy has now reached an extraordinary point, one rarely, if ever, reached by any large human construct. The American economy has arrived at the point where it meets all, or very nearly all, the demands put upon it. It meets the demands both of 'capitalism' and of 'socialism.' It meets the demands of businessman that it should provide ample opportunity for production for profit—and it also meets the demands of the welfare of all the people."[4]

Little wonder then that Toffler's theorizing came as a rude awakening to many readers. At the beginning of the 1970s corporate America was at the height of its powers. Toffler was not taken in by the burgeoning overconfidence of the time. His starting point was that things needed to change dramatically. The second crucial area of difference was that Toffler had a keen awareness of the technological potential. The future he envisaged was driven by technology and knowledge. "The image of the office of the future is too neat, too smooth, too disembodied to be real. Reality is always messy. But it is clear that we are rapidly on our way, and even a partial shift towards the electronic office will be enough to trigger an eruption of social, psychological, and economic consequences. The coming word-quake means more than just new machines. It promises to restructure all the human relationships and roles in the office as well," he later wrote in *The Third Wave*.

Toffler was right. Reality was—and is—messy. The trouble is that the entire edifice of professional management had been erected around neatness and order. Strategy was interpreted as an analytically led means of reaching a decision rather than a subject requiring a degree of creativity. Even management education was orderly. The chief educational building block of MBA programs throughout the world was the case study.

The case study method—established as the primary method of teaching at Harvard Business School as long ago as 1924—presented students with a corporate example. From the narrative, they were expected to reach conclusions about what was the right or wrong thing to do, identify best and worst practice, and learn something about managerial behavior. The case study was introduced to bring a level of reality to a student in a remote environment so that theoretical concepts could be brought to life. The trouble was that it also stimulated an unwillingness to do anything or decide on anything unless there was a supportive case.

The second figure pricking the bubble of managerial complacency was the familiar one of the Canadian Henry Mintzberg (born 1939). Mintzberg has forged a career out of challenging conventional orthodoxies. He usually wins—the argument at least.

Mintzberg graduated in mechanical engineering from McGill University in 1961 and completed a general arts degree in the evenings. Between 1961 and 1963, he worked in the operational research branch of Canadian Railways before going on to MIT's Sloan School, where his Ph.D. dissertation was titled "The Manager at Work: Determining His Activities, Roles and Programs by Structured Observation." It formed the basis of his first book, *The Nature of Managerial Work* (1973). This involved Mintzberg's—in true engineering fashion—examining how managers worked. Not surprisingly, managers did not do what they liked to think they did.

Instead of spending time contemplating the long term, Mintzberg found that managers were slaves to the moment, moving from task to task with every move dogged by another diversion, another call. The median time spent on any one issue was a mere nine minutes. Mintzberg identified the characteristics of the manager at work:

- Performs a great quantity of work at an unrelenting pace
- Undertakes activities marked by variety, brevity, and fragmentation
- Has a preference for issues that are current, specific, and nonroutine
- Prefers verbal rather than written means of communication
- Acts within a web of internal and external contacts
- Is subject to heavy constraints but can exert some control over the work

From these observations, Mintzberg identified the manager's "work roles" as follows:

Interpersonal Roles

Figurehead: representing the organization or unit to outsiders
Leader: motivating subordinates, unifying effort
Liaiser: maintaining lateral contacts

Informational Roles

Monitor: keeping track of information flows
Disseminator: distributing information to subordinates
Spokesman: transmitting information to outsiders

Decisional Roles

Entrepreneur: initiating and designing change
Disturbance handler: handling nonroutine events
Resource allocator: deciding who gets what and who will do what
Negotiator: promoting the organization's advantage in discussions
　　with others outside or within its ranks

Mintzberg's research prodded at the flabby, hidden belly of management. It was not a pretty sight. On the surface, managers were concerned with the big strategic issues. Professional decision making was their métier. In reality, they were driven by circumstances from one task to another. In the 1970s the management nirvana created by corporate men of the fifties and the great corporations of the 1960s imploded. Happiness was a myth. The nice white house with the picket fence was home to domestic discord. "There is a terrible, striking contrast between the fun-filled mobile existence of the young opulents of America as shown on television, and the narrow, constricting, un-fun existence that is the lot of most white-collar workers at the lower job levels," observed *Fortune.* "You can't buy much of what television is selling on the salaries these young workers earn. . . . The result is frustration, sometimes bitterness, even anger."[5]

A 1974 study revealed that 75 percent of workers didn't like their jobs. Between 1972 and 1981, the average number of days lost per year per thousand workers was telling evidence of an underlying problem: Britain, 531; United States, 382; France, 187; Germany, 31; and Japan, 96.[6] Consumed and miserable—though highly qualified—the manager began to ask the unaskable: was there a better way?

The Other Way

Managers did not know where to turn—or to whom. With the seismic effects of the oil crisis and endemic industrial unrest, the old certainties disappeared. The future, so carefully mapped out, would be different and require different insights and new skills. But where could the skills be learned and who already had them?

For the first time, the American management model had to look elsewhere for inspiration. Best practice was elusive. One of those charged with seeking it out was a young McKinsey & Company consultant called Thomas J. Peters (born 1942). In 1976 McKinsey launched three "practices" to consider the nature of the relationship between strategy, structure, and management effectiveness.

Peters was told to seek out best organizational practice wherever it was to be found in the world. He had eight weeks to gather information. During the spring of 1977 he left his San Francisco base and traveled the world, visiting twelve business schools and a number of companies in the United States and Europe. His first port of call was Scandinavia. "Tom called me and asked who should he see in Scandinavia," recalls Lennart Arvedson, a long-time Swedish friend of Peters who was then based in Stockholm working with the Business and Social Research Institute. "He arrived in Sweden after seeing Herb Simon at Carnegie-Mellon and I set up a few meetings in Norway and Sweden."[7]

Among the meetings organized by Lennart Arvedson was one with Einar Thorsrud, a former wartime resistance leader and friend of Eric Trist, the British champion of industrial democracy. Thorsrud was founder of the Arbeidspsykologisk Institut in Oslo, which had become the focal point for Scandinavian experiments in industrial democracy. At the time of Peters's visit, Thorsrud was applying the ideas of self-government to work teams on Norwegian oil tankers. This was about as far removed as you could get from the American corporate giants Peters was used to dealing with. In Scandinavia, Peters also visited Volvo's factory floor, where technicians were taking over the flow of work, and the Scania factory outside Stockholm, which was following a new sociotechnical design. It was big industry, but not as Americans knew it.

"Tom was fascinated with what was going on in work-organization in Scandinavia—it was a concerted movement to find new ways of organizing work which tapped into human talent and made organizations more human and more effective. It really interested him," says Peters's Scandinavian guide, Lennart Arvedson.[8]

For the first time, American management looked to Europe for inspiration. As Peters's experiences suggest, it found it in some unusual places. (Usually when found it was examined and then disregarded with a quizzical or disappointed look.) The strands of European management practice that resurfaced in the 1970s had their roots in a number of postwar experiments and thinkers who had generally received scant attention outside Europe.

One of the most important was a long-term experiment in industrial democracy at the United Kingdom's Glacier Metal Company between 1948 and 1965. The experiment was driven forward by the vision and political ideas of the company's chairman and managing director, Wilfred Brown. Brown served in the Labour government of Harold Wilson and later became Lord Brown.

Glacier introduced a number of highly progressive changes in working practices. A works council was introduced. This was far removed from the usually toothless attempts at worker representation. Indeed, no change of company policy was allowed unless all members of the works council agreed. Any single person on the council had a veto. Contrary to what experts and observers anticipated, the company did not grind to an immediate halt. Other innovations at Glacier included the abolition of "clocking on," the traditional means of recording whether someone had turned up for work.

The emphasis was on granting people responsibility and of understanding the dynamics of group working. "I'm completely convinced of the necessity of encouraging everybody to accept the maximum amount of personal responsibility, and allowing them to have a say in every problem in which they can help," said Elliott Jaques, one of the most influential researchers involved. Jaques was brought into the project as a facilitator, though his role was more expansive than that. "We spent the first month just having widespread discussions through the company and gradually we worked through things," is how Jaques remembers his introduction.[9]

The Glacier research led to Jaques's 1951 book, *The Changing Culture of a Factory.* "The project itself produced none of the successors we had anticipated. It was a decade ahead of any form of organizational development," said Eric Trist. What the experiment did successfully highlight was the redundancy of conventional organization charts, the potential power of corporate culture (a concept then barely understood), and the potential benefits of running organizations in a fair and mutually beneficial way.

Later, in *The General Theory of Bureaucracy* (1976), Jaques presented his theory of the value of work. This was ornate, but aimed to clarify something Jaques had observed during his research: "The manifest picture of bureaucratic organization is a confusing one. There appears to be no rhyme or reason for the structures that are developed, in number of levels, in titling, or even in the meaning to be attached to the manager-subordinate linkage." His solution was labeled the *time span of discretion*, which contended that levels of management should be based on how long it was before their decisions could be checked, and that people should be paid in accordance with that time. This meant that managers were measured by the long-term impact of their decisions. The effects of the Glacier project are difficult to gauge. It was generally greeted with apathy. But it did register somewhere in the overall managerial consciousness. It was a part of the jigsaw, but no one really knew what the finished picture would look like.

Something similar can be said of one of the more idiosyncratic strands of management theorizing at this time, the work of the singular British thinker called Reg Revans (born 1907). In the 1920s, Revans (a former Olympic athlete) worked at Cambridge's Cavendish Laboratories alongside five Nobel Prize winners. In the quest to split the atom, the eminent scientists tended to champion their own particular field. To break the logjam, physicist Lord Rutherford decided that the team should hold a meeting every week to discuss their difficulties and ask fresh questions. "Even though they had won Nobel Prizes, they were willing to acknowledge that things could be going on elsewhere. They asked questions," Revans remembers.[10]

If leading thinkers could introduce humility and the sharing of knowledge into their working practices, why couldn't others? After the war, Revans moved on to become the first director of education and training at the U.K. National Coal Board and set about applying his ideas. He concluded that colliery managers and miners themselves needed to acknowledge the problems they faced and then attempt to solve them. "When doctors listen to nurses, patients recover more quickly; if mining engineers pay more attention to their men than to their machinery, the pits are more efficient. As in athletics and nuclear research, it is neither books nor seminars from which managers learn much, but from here-and-now exchanges about the operational job in hand."

With characteristic frankness, Revans announced that he saw no need to employ a team of specialist tutors: "The ultimate power of a successful general staff lies not in the brilliance of its individual members, but in the cross-fertilization of its collective abilities." Revans spent two years underground to examine the real problems facing miners. This reinforced his idea that learning comes when problems are aired and shared in small groups of "comrades in adversity." The pits that tried Revans's methods recorded a 30 percent increase in productivity.

At the Coal Board Revans worked with E.F. Schumacher, author of *Small Is Beautiful*— "Small is dutiful," is Revans's retort. "You must seek to understand each other's problems and develop a sense of responsibility for each other through working in small groups." Revans's approach was not well received by management and he eventually resigned. He then dedicated his career to the promotion of his theory of *action learning.*

Revans's greatest success came in the 1970s. As other countries wrestled with the various crises, Revans was leading an experiment in Belgium launched by the Foundation Industrie-Université with the support of the country's leading businesspeople and five universities. "Brussels had been selected as capital of the Common Market much to everyone's surprise. They decided if they were to be the administrative center of Europe they needed to develop international understanding." The Belgians responded to the idea of action learning with enthusiasm. Top managers were exchanged between organizations to work on each other's problems. "I wasn't there to teach anyone anything. We got people talking to each other, asking questions. People from the airline business talked to people from chemical companies. People shared knowledge and experience," Revans explains. With minimal attention from the rest of the world, the Belgian economy enjoyed a spectacular renaissance— during the 1970s Belgian industrial productivity rose by 102 percent, compared with 28 percent in the United Kingdom. (This is potent proof that management ideas can and do make a difference. Interestingly, Belgium still performs rather well if you measure national performance by GDP per hour of work rather than per person. The United States leads the rankings in terms of GDP per person, but plummets to ninth if measured by GDP per hour. Japan similarly drops—from third to eighteenth. Meanwhile, Belgium moves from tenth to first.)

British coal miners were the font of a large amount of interesting insight that only struck a chord with executives elsewhere in the world in the 1970s. There was Revans and then there was E.F. Schumacher.

Schumacher's *Small Is Beautiful* was the antidote to corporatism 1970s-style. It was a cause supported by the likes of President Jimmy Carter.

And then there were experiments carried out by the highly influential Tavistock Institute of Human Relations in the United Kingdom during the 1950s. Theoretically, the Tavistock was a sister organization to the National Training Laboratories (NTL) for Group Dynamics based in Bethel, Maine. (The driving force behind NTL was the psychologist Kurt Lewin [1890–1947].)

Typical of the Tavistock's work was that with the British coal mines, which had introduced a more automated approach to mining. This, they expected, would increase productivity. It did not. The Tavistock researchers were called in to establish if there was something wrong with the new methods, as they now suspected, and what was the best way for the miners to work. The research team found that previously the miners had worked in interdependent pairs or groups and they were completely responsible for extracting the coal. The groups negotiated their own contracts with management and there were few status problems.

The new methods attempted to bring mass production techniques to mining. The result was declining working relationships, poor communication, increasing absenteeism and injuries. The miners returned to working as small teams.

In 1959 a Tavistock researcher, Fred Emery, reported on what had been named *sociotechnical systems* (STS). This was really a descendant of the Hawthorne research—with added psychological sensibilities. Emery contended that organizations are made up of a social and a technical system. The social system is made up of the division of labor, how work is coordinated, and issues such as job satisfaction. The technical system is made up of the tools and techniques required for the conversion process to transfer inputs into outputs. The Tavistock research suggested that the relationship between the two systems was key to success. Greater effectiveness and improved working lives required a balance.

The concepts of teamworking and industrial democracy found fertile ground in Scandinavia—as Tom Peters found. Work teams succeeded in Norway and then spread to Sweden—by 1973 there were seven hundred teamworking projects under way in Swedish factories.

More research into the nature of teamworking followed. In 1967 Henley Management College introduced a computer-based business game into one of its courses. In this game, known as the Executive Management Exercise, "company" teams of members competed to achieve the best score, according to the criteria laid down in the exercise. Henley arranged to collaborate with Meredith Belbin (born 1926), then with the Industrial Training Research Unit at University College, London.

Belbin was interested in group performance and how it might be influenced by the kinds of people making up a group. Members engaging in the exercise were asked, voluntarily and confidentially, to undertake a personality and critical-thinking test. From his observations, based on the test results, Belbin discovered that certain combinations of personality types performed more successfully than others. Belbin began to be able to predict the winner of the game and realized that given adequate knowledge of the personal characteristics and abilities of team members through psychometric testing, he could forecast the likely success or failure of particular teams. As a result, unsuccessful teams can be improved by analyzing their team design shortcomings and making appropriate changes.

Belbin's first practical application of this work involved a questionnaire that managers filled out for themselves. The questionnaire was then analyzed to show the function roles the managers thought they performed in a team. This had one drawback: what *you* think you do is not of much value if the people with whom you work think differently. Belbin refined his methods and worked with others to design a computer program to do the job.

From his firsthand observation at Henley's unique "laboratory," Belbin identified nine archetypal functions that go to make up an ideal team:

- *Plant:* creative, imaginative, unorthodox; solves difficult problems. Allowable weakness: bad at dealing with ordinary people.
- *Coordinator:* mature, confident, trusting; a good chairman; clarifies goals, promotes decision making. Not necessarily the cleverest.
- *Shaper:* dynamic, outgoing, highly strung; challenges, pressurizes, finds ways round obstacles. Prone to bursts of temper.

- *Teamworker:* social, mild, perceptive, accommodating; listens, builds, averts friction. Indecisive in crunch situations.
- *Completer:* painstaking, conscientious, anxious; searches out errors; delivers on time. May worry unduly; reluctant to delegate.
- *Implementer:* disciplined, reliable, conservative, efficient; turns ideas into actions. Somewhat inflexible.
- *Resource investigator:* extrovert, enthusiastic, communicative; explores opportunities. Loses interest after initial enthusiasm.
- *Specialist:* single-minded, self-starting, dedicated; brings knowledge or skills in rare supply. Contributes only on narrow front.
- *Monitor and evaluator:* sober, strategic, discerning. Sees all options, makes judgments. Lacks drive and ability to inspire others.

The Volvo Way

Meanwhile, the search for new approaches became more pressing by the day. Most notably, the once-mighty car industry was stopped in its tracks.

Over the decades cars had become gradually smaller. But in the gas-guzzling United States, not much smaller. New regulations in 1971 required cars to use unleaded fuel. The oil embargo of 1974 increased demands for greater efficiency and smaller vehicles. Unfortunately for most U.S. manufacturers, their competitors were already producing smaller, more fuel-efficient cars in abundant numbers. The number of foreign cars imported into the United States reached two million in 1977—having been a minuscule twenty-one thousand in 1950.

Particularly desperate was General Motors. "I was a consultant to GM for many years and I constantly heard about their various attempts to head off the energy crisis that they knew loomed ahead," says William Halal of George Washington University, author of *The Infinite Resource.* "They convened task forces to study it many times during the sixties and seventies, introduced two or three small cars that bombed, looked into alternative fuels, and so on. But when the OPEC oil embargo hit they bit the bullet and decided to reduce the entire line of GM cars by a thousand pounds each. Because GM was the powerhouse of the Industrial Age, this decision changed the entire American view of the auto and ended the age of innocence when we had heretofore disregarded the environment and its limitations."[11]

GM pulled out all the stops. A new fuel-efficient Chevy Chevette was launched; Cadillac moved into "small" cars with the 1975 Seville, having previously ignored changes in demand. But, like many others, GM increasingly looked elsewhere for inspiration. In the car industry, too, inspiration could be found in Scandinavia—this time at the carmaker Volvo.

The 1970s were generally good to Volvo. In 1970 it passed the two-million-car production mark and the following year it recorded its twentieth successive year of increased sales. When the first oil crisis hit, in 1973, Volvo's production rate was the highest in the company's history.

Under new company president Pehr Gyllenhammar, Volvo began to experiment with its working practices. Volvo already had a greater level of industrial democracy than most of its competitors—employees were represented on the board of the company. Its new car plant in Kalmar used innovative production processes, including automatic carriers that transported the car bodies. The plant was also designed so that workers could work together in small teams.

Volvo's interest in teamworking had been encouraged by its experiences at its Lundby truck plant. By 1974 this plant was working at full capacity. Volvo, however, needed to produce another four hundred trucks per year. To do so it set up a temporary plant at Arendal in Göteborg. Volvo was unwilling to invest heavily in what was likely to be a temporary facility. As a result, it decided to experiment with a new production method. This involved assigning a group of twelve the job of producing two trucks a day. This was thought to be ambitious. The group was given responsibility for assembly, materials handling, quality control, and correcting defects.

The experiment was an immediate success. The group produced two trucks a day with ease. Within four months assembly time was significantly reduced. The group spent their spare time examining what they had done and planning for the next day.

There were many skeptics. Volvo examined the quality of the trucks produced by the group. They found that they were of higher quality than those produced by conventional means. But still the skeptics won the day and the temporary plant remained just that—it was closed in 1977.

Volvo's experiences came to the attention of General Motors. It began experimenting with sociotechnical systems around the time of the 1973 oil crisis.

It announced cooperation with the United Auto Workers to improve the quality of working life. The sociotechnical approach was piloted at a number of GM companies. Between 1974 and 1980 two Delco Battery plants (one in Canada) and two Packard Electric wire-harness plants were designed by GM consultants using STS principles. These were highly successful with lower staff turnover and higher than average performance. The example was not followed elsewhere in the company. Another opportunity to escape the legacy of scientific management and Henry Ford was missed.

The Dow Jones Industrial Average Companies as of January 1, 1979

Allied Chemical	Procter & Gamble
American Can	Johns-Manville
Minnesota Mining & Manufacturing	International Paper
DuPont	General Foods
Eastman Kodak	United Technologies
Goodyear	Sears, Roebuck
Bethlehem Steel	Exxon
Chrysler	Texas Corporation
General Electric	Owens-Illinois Glass
General Motors	Union Carbide
American Tobacco B	U.S. Steel
Standard Oil of California	American Telephone & Telegraph
International Harvester	Westinghouse Electric
Inco	Woolworth
Esmark	Aluminum Co.

The Management Century: Tale of the Tape

	Average Working Hours (per week)	
	1900	*1998*
Germany	51.6	29.0
France	51.7	31.7
Japan	51.7	38.3
Netherlands	52.0	30.8
United States	52.0	37.9
Britain	52.4	35.6

Source: Time, April 13, 1998.

The Harvard 100

Top Five HBR *Articles Published in the 1970s*	Ranking in Top 100
"Management Time: Who's Got the Monkey?" William Oncken and Donald Wass—November-December 1974	2
"How Competitive Forces Shape Strategy," Michael E. Porter—March-April 1979	10
"The Manager's Job: Folklore and Fact," Henry Mintzberg—July-August 1975	12
"Managing the Crisis in Data Processing," Richard L. Nolan—March-April 1979	20
"How to Run a Meeting," Antony Jay—March-April 1976	22

Source: "The 100 Best-Selling Articles."

The Management Century Timeline

1971

Cigarette advertising is banned from American television.

The NASDAQ is introduced.

Intel develops the microchip and the world's first microprocessor, the 4004. Just as well. "In the mid–1970s, someone came to me with an idea for what was basically the PC," Gordon Moore recalled. "I personally didn't see anything useful in it, so we never gave it another thought."

First color video cassette.

1972

The Dow closes above 1,000 for the first time on November 14— recession soon followed, pushing the Index down to 577.60 by the end of 1974. It was not until late 1982 that the Dow returned to the 1,000 mark.

Nike shoes and Atari's Pong game are introduced.

1973

Federal Express founded.

Henry Mintzberg describes what managers actually do in *The Nature of Managerial Work*.

United Farm Workers, led by César Chávez, is chartered by the AFL-CIO.

AT&T agrees to pay $15 million to women and minority employees after a job-discrimination lawsuit.

1975

Home computers are introduced.

Betamax VCR—first home use video system.

1977

Steve Jobs and Steve Wozniak found Apple Computer in a garage and go on to build the Apple 1, regarded by many as the first true personal computer.

Apple introduces Apple 2, the first fully assembled personal computer.

1978

President Jimmy Carter raises mandatory retirement age from sixty-five to seventy.

Microwave ovens are found in 7.2 percent of U.S. households.

Chris Argyris and Donald Schön's *Organizational Learning* is published.

1979

Sony Walkman is introduced.

1980

Michael Porter's *Competitive Strategy* is published.

Ted Turner introduces Cable News Network (CNN).

The U.S. federal government bails out Chrysler Corporation.

Apple goes public on the strength of the success of the Apple 1 and Apple 2.

Alvin Toffler invents the future in *The Third Wave*.

Chapter 9
1981–1990: An Excellent Adventure

Everyone doing his best is not the answer. It is first necessary that people know what to do. Drastic changes are required. The first step in the transformation is to learn how to change. . . . Long term commitment to new learning and new philosophy is required of any management that seeks transformation. The timid and the faint-hearted, and people that expect quick results, are doomed to disappointment.
        —W. EDWARDS DEMING[1]

How the West Woke Up

In 1979 NBC was fishing around for subjects for a documentary. The basic idea was for a program on the decline of American business— executive producer Reuven Frank had begun with the far from populist working title of "What to Do About America's Falling Productivity?"— which had metamorphosed into "What Ever Happened to Good Old Yankee Ingenuity?" Neither seemed likely to set the world alight. Then it was suggested to Frank that he send someone along to see an elderly NYU academic who lived in Washington, D.C.

Clare Crawford-Mason was working on the project with Frank and was assigned to pay the mysterious old man a visit. Later Crawford-Mason recalled: "I called the man's office and set up an appointment. It wasn't difficult; his schedule was open. I recall postponing the first meeting. I was directed to go to the side of a residential house and come down the basement steps. I did. I knocked on the cellar door and walked into a two-room, below-ground office, filled with books and papers and overflowing desks and a blackboard covered with mathematical formulas." She found "the old gentleman . . . pleasant, courtly and vehement."[2]

The man was W. Edwards Deming. To the outside observer, Deming matched the stereotype of the academic eccentric. He eschewed luxury and wrote the date of purchase on his eggs with felt-tip pen. (Later, when he was wealthy, Deming continued to drive a 1969 Lincoln Continental and to use public transport.) His staff comprised a single assistant—Cecilia "Ceil" Kilian, who eventually worked with him for thirty-nine years—and he worked six days a week for twelve hours.

Deming told the NBC team that he had played a central part in the renaissance of the Japanese economy in the postwar years. This was news to virtually everyone in the Western world. Deming was unheard-of, an obscure statistician. But he was persuasive and impressive. The facts checked out. Deming was well known and honored in Japan. An NBC program evolved from that mysterious first meeting. It was broadcast on June 26, 1980, with its final title: "If Japan Can, Why Can't We?"

The NBC program was a seminal moment in the development of Western management theory and practice. It was also a late and long-delayed recognition of W. Edwards Deming. (There was some irony in the fact that, at that point, Deming didn't own a television set and had watched TV only once—to see the 1969 moon landing.) Deming gave American businesspeople a lecture in the quality basics. "Inspection does not build quality, the quality is already made before you inspect it. It's far better to make it right in the first place," he intoned. "Statistical methods help you to make it right in the first place so that you don't need to test it. You don't get ahead by making product and then separating the good from the bad, because it's wasteful. It wastes time of men, who are paid wages; it wastes time of machines, if there are machines; it wastes materials."

After the program, NBC was inundated with phone calls. The executives of the Fortune 500 woke up in front of their TV sets.

The program's message was simple but stark. "It was the first time anyone had said that if America did not improve its productivity our children would be the first generation of Americans who could not expect to live better than their parents," says Clare Crawford-Mason.[3]

The early 1980s provided wake-up calls aplenty. The alarm bells became louder and louder. Bad news stalked every corner. Western industry was, by common consensus, held to be on its knees. The oil crisis of the mid-seventies was the portent of a period of navel-examination, self-analysis. Businesspeople contemplated their poorly performing companies and their underproductive workforces with bemusement. During the early 1980s, Western industrialists were willing to raise their hands and admit, "We've screwed up." They would also have quickly moved on to blaming irresponsible unions and greedy sheiks for this sad situation before desperately professing that they had little clue as to what to do next. The death knell of postwar industrial optimism and unquestioning faith in the mighty corporation was sounding. Only the profoundly deaf carried on regardless—and there were many who chose to ignore the signals.

As the death knell rang out, there was no shortage of obituary notices. A few days after the Deming TV program, two Harvard Business School academics, Robert Hayes and Bill Abernathy, had an article titled "Managing Our Way to Economic Decline" published in the July/August 1980 issue of the *Harvard Business Review*. It proved grim and highly influential reading.

Hayes and Abernathy had wrestled with the demons of decline and emerged dismayed. "Our experience suggests that, to an unprecedented degree, success in most industries today requires an organizational commitment to compete in the marketplace on technological grounds— that is, to compete over the long run by offering superior products," wrote Hayes and Abernathy. (It is astounding in retrospect that such commercial facts of life needed restating.) "Yet, guided by what they took to be the newest and best principles of management, American managers have increasingly directed their attention elsewhere. These new principles, despite their sophistication and widespread usefulness, encourage a preference for (1) analytic detachment rather than the insight that comes from 'hands on' experience and (2) short-term cost reduction rather than long-term development of technological competitiveness. It is this new managerial gospel, we feel, that has played a major role in undermining the vigor of American industry."[4] Hayes and Abernathy went on to champion customer orientation as a vital ingredient in reversing the apparently irreversible trend. Their message was that management was the problem. Forget about union militancy, forget about foreign competition, look upstairs to the boardroom.

The popularity of Hayes and Abernathy's article was the signal for a sea change. An article buried in the *Harvard Business Review* does not usually excite or ignite debate. This one did. Hayes and Abernathy announced that the Western corporate postwar dream was approaching its final hours. People asked: What next?

Turning Japanese

One answer was to take Deming's advice and look to the East. This was a new experience. The ability—not to mention the arrogance and torpor—to ignore the rise of Japan was truly astonishing. The emergence of Japanese competitors had been generously signaled by the media.

As early as 1964, *Fortune* noted: "American manufacturers of radios, television sets and other consumer electronic equipment have been repeatedly confounded by the agile competitiveness of Japan's Sony Corp. A small company even by Japanese standards—its sales last year amounted to $77 million—Sony has astutely used its limited capital to concentrate on a few unusually designed products beamed to a great extent at export markets, particularly the U.S."[5] In the very same article, it was noted that Sony founder Akio Morita had been based in New York rather than Tokyo since 1963. The other founder of the company, Masaru Ibuka, visited the United States in 1952—by 1958 Sony's export sales totaled $2.6 billion.[6]

The *Fortune* article went on to cite a 1960s survey that had asked American radio dealers whether they had ever handled Japanese radios. Most dealers said no. The next question asked whether they had ever handled Sony radios. The majority said yes.[7] *Fortune* concluded that Sony's "well made products are usually priced a notch or so above competitive U.S. made equipment and well above the normal run of imports from Japan."[8]

The warnings were ignored. Suddenly, however, the appetite for knowledge was enormous. A succession of books examined the secrets behind the perceived success of Japan.[9]

William Ouchi's 1981 *Theory Z* venerated Japan's employment and managerial practices. Theory Z was the natural development of McGregor's Theories X and Y. Richard Pascale and Anthony Athos also published the best-selling *Art of Japanese Management*. It played a crucial role in the discovery of Japanese management techniques as Pascale and Athos considered how a country the same size as Montana could be outstripping the American industrial juggernaut. "In 1980, Japan's GNP was third highest in the world and, if we extrapolate current trends, it would be number one by the year 2000," warned Pascale and Athos.[10]

Harsh home truths lurked on every page of *The Art of Japanese Management*. "If anything, the extent of Japanese superiority over the United States in industrial competitiveness is underestimated," wrote Pascale and Athos, observing that "a major reason for the superiority of the Japanese is their managerial skill." In its comparisons of U.S. and Japanese companies, *The Art of Japanese Management* provided rare insights into the truth behind the mythology of Japanese management and the inadequacy of much Western practice.

Among the key components of Japanese management identified by Pascale and Athos was that of vision, something they found to be notably lacking in the West. "Our problem today is that the tools are there but our 'vision' is limited. A great many American managers are influenced by beliefs, assumptions, and perceptions about management that unduly constrain them," wrote Pascale and Athos. The book, they said, was "not an assault on the existing tools of management, but upon the Western vision of management which circumscribes our effectiveness."[11]

Adding his voice to the argument was the Japanese consultant Kenichi Ohmae. Ohmae (born 1943) did much to reveal the truth behind Japanese strategy-making practices to an expectant Western audience. He demonstrated that the Japanese were human after all—at the time, Western managers were beginning to wonder. Ohmae explored—and largely exploded—simplistic Western myths about Japanese management. Forget company songs and lifetime employment, there was more to Japanese management than that. Most notably there was the Japanese art of strategic thinking. This, said Ohmae, is "basically creative and intuitive and rational." Japanese companies weren't mired in endless analysis or pointless hierarchies. "Most Japanese companies don't even have a reasonable organization chart," Ohmae told Peters and Waterman, authors of *In Search of Excellence.* "Nobody knows how Honda is organized, except that it uses lots of project teams and is quite flexible. . . . Innovation typically occurs at the interface, requiring multiple disciplines. Thus, the flexible Japanese organization has now, especially, become an asset."[12]

Ohmae's *Mind of the Strategist* reached America in 1982. It had been published in Japan in 1975, though at that time there was no interest in the West in how Japan did anything. Ohmae pointed out that unlike large U.S. corporations, Japanese businesses tend not to have massive strategic planning staffs. Instead they often have a single, naturally talented strategist with "an idiosyncratic mode of thinking in which company, customers, and competition merge in a dynamic interaction out of which a comprehensive set of objectives and plans for action eventually crystallizes."

Ohmae also noted that the customer was at the heart of the Japanese approach to strategy and key to corporate values. "In the construction of any business strategy, three main players must be taken into account: the corporation itself, the customer, and the competition. Each of these 'strategic three Cs' is a living entity with its own interests and objectives. We shall call them, collectively, the 'strategic triangle,'" Ohmae wrote. "Seen in the context of the strategic triangle, the job of the strategist is to achieve superior performance, relative to competition, in the key factors for success of the business. At the same time, the strategist must be sure that his strategy properly matches the strengths of the corporation with the needs of a clearly defined market. Positive matching of the needs and objectives of the two parties involved is required for a lasting good relationship; without it, the corporation's long-term viability may be at stake."

The central thrust of Ohmae's arguments was that strategy as epitomized by the Japanese approach is irrational and nonlinear. (Previously, the Japanese had been feted in the West for the brilliance of their rationality and the far-sighted remorselessness of their thinking.) "Phenomena and events in the real world do not always fit a linear model," wrote Ohmae. "Hence the most reliable means of dissecting a situation into its constituent parts and reassembling them in the desired pattern is not a step-by-step methodology such as systems analysis. Rather, it is that ultimate nonlinear thinking tool, the human brain. True strategic thinking thus contrasts sharply with the conventional mechanical systems approach based on linear thinking. But it also contrasts with the approach that stakes everything on intuition, reaching conclusions without any real breakdown or analysis."

Unfortunately, faith in the linear model remained strong. (Managers had been ignoring Henry Mintzberg's similar exhortations to increase the level of creativity in strategy formulation for years.) Western managers weren't ready for the ultimate nonlinear thinking tool, they wanted something to measure, something to do, something to get hold of.

The Quality Gospel

And they found it in the notion of "quality." Western managers grabbed hold of quality with the enthusiasm of the truly desperate. "I think people here expect miracles. American management thinks that they can just copy from Japan. But they don't know what to copy," Deming said on the famous NBC broadcast. He became the great deliverer, the aging sage from Sioux City, Iowa, the miracle worker.

Deming's impact was huge. Ignored for five decades—though feted and celebrated in Japan—Deming made up for lost time. In 1991 *U.S. News & World Report* identified nine people or events that had changed the world. The Apostle Paul was the first identified; W. Edwards Deming was the most recent.

Deming's message remained remarkably similar to that delivered in Japan in 1950.

First, management was responsible for the mess. "Failure of management to plan for the future and to foresee problems have brought about waste of manpower, of materials, and of machine-time, all of which raise the manufacturer's cost and price that the purchaser must pay. The consumer is not always willing to subsidize this waste. The inevitable result is loss of market," he wrote.[13] Quality must be led from the top. Exhortations to work harder do not lead to quality.

Second, the customer was king, emperor, CEO, and dictator. Or, as Deming phrased it, "the consumer is the most important part of the production line." Quality is defined by the customer.

Third, the old Shewhart mantra: understand and reduce variation in every process. The process is the thing, not the product (by the time the inspector has a product in hand it is too late).

Four, never stop—apply quality to everything. Change and improvement affect and must involve everyone in the organization (as well as suppliers) and must be continuous and all-encompassing.

Five, train people. Deming's faith in the willingness of people to do a good job was undimmed by seven decades on earth.

Deming's call to arms was most powerfully put in his well-known Fourteen Points:

1. Create constancy of purpose for improvement of product and service.
2. Adopt the new philosophy.
3. Cease depending on inspection to achieve quality.
4. End the practice of awarding business on the basis of price tag alone. Instead, minimize total cost by working with a single supplier.
5. Improve constantly and forever every process for planning, production, and service.
6. Institute training on the job.
7. Adopt and institute leadership.
8. Drive out fear.
9. Break down barriers between staff areas.
10. Eliminate slogans, exhortations, and targets for the workforce.
11. Eliminate numerical quotas for the workforce and numerical goals for management.

12. Remove barriers that rob people of pride of workmanship. Eliminate the annual rating or merit system.
13. Institute a vigorous program of education and self-improvement for everyone.
14. Put everybody in the company to work to accomplish the transformation.

For some Deming's Fourteen Points became the commandments of the quality movement. In his efforts to move quality out of the factory floor and onto the desk of every single executive, Deming re-created it as a philosophy of business and, for some, of life. "Unfortunately, a system of totality insists, by definition, that it will solve everything," noted one obituary to Deming.[14]

Deming did not have a monopoly on quality. A procession of other quality gurus emerged from the shadows with varying degrees of credibility. The career of the most notable, Joseph Juran (born 1904) bore a resemblance to that of Deming. Trained as an electrical engineer, Juran worked for Western Electric in the 1920s and then AT&T. In 1953 he made his first visit to Japan on the invitation of the Japanese Federation of Economic Associations and the Japanese Union of Scientists and Engineers. For two months Juran observed Japanese practices and trained managers and engineers in what he called "managing for quality."

Juran's weighty *Quality Control Handbook* was published in 1951. Juran was later awarded the Second Class Order of the Sacred Treasure by the Emperor of Japan—the highest honor for a non-Japanese citizen—for "the development of quality control in Japan and the facilitation of US and Japanese friendship."

Juran argued there was a blessed quality trinity of planning, control, and improvement. In keeping with the desire for simplification and checklists, Juran produced his "Quality Planning Road Map," which advocated nine steps to quality nirvana:

1. Identify who are the customers.
2. Determine the needs of those customers.
3. Translate those needs into our language.
4. Develop a product that can respond to those needs.
5. Optimize the product features so as to meet our needs as well as customer needs.

6. Develop a process that is able to produce the product.
7. Optimize the process.
8. Prove that the process can produce the product under operating conditions.
9. Transfer the process to Operations.

Such neat prescriptions helped the quality gospel spread throughout the world. Deming and Juran criss-crossed time zones with the enthusiasm of rock stars whose breakthrough album has just topped the *Billboard* chart. The quality concept—though not necessarily the practice—carried all before it. Deming Associations appeared in France, the United Kingdom, and other countries. Total Quality Management Institutes were launched—though without Deming's blessing as he didn't like the phrase.

Deming, Juran, and the other quality gurus went out of their way to stress that miracles simply did not happen. Their audience continued to believe in miracles. "Solving problems, big problems and little problems, will not halt the decline of American industry, nor will expansion in use of computers, gadgets, and robotic machinery," wrote Deming. "Benefits from massive expansion of new machinery also constitute a vain hope. Massive immediate expansion in the teaching of statistical methods to production workers is not the answer either, nor wholesale flashes of quality control circles. All these activities make their contribution, but they only prolong the life of the patient, they can not halt the decline."[15]

Changes in management were the key to halting the decline. Deming's audience, however, preferred to introduce quality circles and to publish quality newsletters.

Some companies did embrace the quality gospel with genuine vigor and commitment. The Nashua Corporation was the first U.S. company to adopt Deming's quality management principles. Other well-known converts included the Ford Motor Company and Florida Power & Light (the first U.S. winner of the Deming Prize and advised by Asaka Tetsuichi). Ford initially called on Japanese quality guru Ishikawa Kaoru for guidance but found his lectures too complex—and anyway, Ford managers were tired of having Japan's virtues thrust down their throats at every opportunity. Ford turned to Deming, acknowledging that he was opinionated and abrasive but reassuringly American.

Others embraced the idea and then failed to reap the expected dividends. Typical of this group was Kodak, which introduced a company-wide quality campaign in the early 1980s. Its "corporate policy quality statement" committed Kodak "to be world leader in the quality of its products and services. We will judge this quality by how well we anticipate and satisfy customer needs."[16] Kodak seemed to do everything prescribed—employees were trained in statistical techniques, annual worldwide quality conferences were held, top managers were actively involved, and so on. None of this got the company very far. In 1991 Kodak announced a $1.6 billion restructuring of the company and contemplated whether stronger medicine would do the trick.

Back to Basics

While some companies in the West desperately embraced Japanese techniques, others contemplated a more fundamental re-think. They returned to the basics. Hardy perennials of management were redis-covered, brushed down, reevaluated, and reapplied. This happened in four key areas: competitiveness, customer service, human resource management, and leadership.

Leading the intellectual charge was Harvard Business School's Michael Porter (born 1947). Porter encouraged a complete reevaluation of the nature of competitiveness.

While completing his Ph.D. at Harvard Porter came under the in-fluence of economist Richard Caves, who became his mentor. He joined the Harvard faculty at the age of twenty-six—one of the youngest tenured professors in the school's august history. Porter's genius lay in producing brilliantly researched and cogent models of competitiveness at a corpo-rate, industry-wide, and national level. For example, Porter took an in-dustrial economics framework—the structure-conduct performance paradigm (SCP)—and translated it into the context of business strategy.

From this emerged his best-known model, the five forces framework, which states that "in any industry, whether it is domestic or international or produces a product or a service, the rules of competition are embodied in five competitive forces." These five competitive forces are

- *The entry of new competitors.* New competitors necessitate some competitive response that will inevitably use some of your resources, thus reducing profits.
- *The threat of substitutes.* If there are viable alternatives to your product or service in the marketplace, the prices you can charge will be limited.
- *The bargaining power of buyers.* If customers have bargaining power they will use it. This will reduce profit margins and, as a result, affect profitability.
- *The bargaining power of suppliers.* Given power over you, suppliers will increase their prices and adversely affect your profitability.
- *The rivalry among existing competitors.* Competition leads to the need to invest in marketing, R&D, or price reductions that will reduce your profits.

"The collective strength of these five competitive forces determines the ability of firms in an industry to earn, on average, rates of return on investment in excess of the cost of capital. The strength of the five forces varies from industry to industry, and can change as an industry evolves," Porter observed.

The five forces (outlined in Porter's best-selling *Competitive Strategy*) were a means by which a company could begin to understand its particular industry. Initially, they were passively interpreted as valid statements of the facts of competitive life. Now, however, they are more regularly interpreted as the rules of the game that have to be changed and challenged if an organization is to achieve any impact in a particular market. "Porter's translation did not resolve, and could not resolve, the fundamental weakness of the SCP approach. Why did some companies manage the five forces better than others?" notes leading British economist John Kay.[17] The five forces framework was once seen as providing all the answers. Now the suggestion is that it actually is better used as a means of provoking questions.

Having mapped out the facts of competitive life, Porter nearly left the obvious next question—What can we do about it?—unanswered. A late addition to his book was the concept of generic strategies. Porter argued that there were three "generic strategies," "viable approaches to dealing with . . . competitive forces." Strategy, in Porter's eyes, was a matter of *how* to compete.

The first of Porter's generic strategies was *differentiation,* competing on the basis of value added to customers (such as through quality and service) so that customers will pay a premium to cover higher costs. The second was *cost-based leadership,* offering products or services at the lowest cost. Quality and service are not unimportant, but cost reduction provides focus to the organization. *Focus* was the third generic strategy identified by Porter. Companies with a clear strategy outperform those whose strategy is unclear or those that attempt to achieve both differentiation and cost leadership. "Sometimes the firm can successfully pursue more than one approach as its primary target, though this is rarely possible," he said. "Effectively implementing any of these generic strategies usually requires total commitment, and organizational arrangements are diluted if there's more than one primary target."

If a company failed to focus on any of the three generic strategies it was liable to encounter problems. "The firm failing to develop its strategy in at least one of the three directions—a firm that is *stuck in the middle*—is in an extremely poor strategic situation," Porter wrote. "The firm lacks the market share, capital investment, and resolve to play the low-cost game, the industry-wide differentiation necessary to obviate the need for a low-cost position, or the focus to create differentiation or low cost in a more limited sphere. The firm stuck in the middle is almost guaranteed low profitability. It either loses the high-volume customers who demand low prices or must bid away its profits to get this business away from low-cost firms. Yet it also loses high-margin business—the cream—to the firms who are focused on high-margin targets or have achieved differentiation overall. The firm stuck in the middle also probably suffers from a blurred corporate culture and a conflicting set of organizational arrangements and motivation system."

When *Competitive Strategy* was published in 1980, Porter's generic strategies offered a rational and straightforward method for companies to extricate themselves from strategic confusion. The reassurance proved short-lived. Less than a decade later, companies were having to compete on all fronts. They had to be differentiated, through improved service or speedier development, and be cost leaders, cheaper than their competitors.

Rediscovering People

The other areas of rediscovery were concerned with injecting humanity back into management. Western companies had become disengaged from their customers and from their employees. A variety of thinkers and books promised to bring them back together again.

The most powerful of these was *In Search of Excellence* by Tom Peters and Robert Waterman, which appeared before an apparently uninterested public in October 1982. *In Search of Excellence* was a book with a simple formula and even simpler intention. The subtitle is straightforward: "Lessons from America's Best-Run Companies." Here is what works; here are successful companies, and this is why they are successful. "In a way, the whole notion behind our excellent company research is: If you really want to learn, watch the best. Watch what they're doing," said Waterman. "It's done all the time in sports, but to our minds it's done very little in business. In business—so far at least—it's been as if, in order to learn how to succeed, you went out and looked at everybody else's mistakes and told yourself, 'Don't do that.' "[18]

In Search of Excellence was enticing. "Let us never underestimate the market for hope. *In Search of Excellence* appeared when the industrial self-confidence of the West was at its lowest ebb ever. You, too, can be great was the message. No surprise then, that it found a mass audience," says Gary Hamel, coauthor of *Competing for the Future.* "The dividing line between simple truths and simplistic prescription is always a thin one. For the most part, Peters and Waterman avoided the facile and the tautological. Indeed, the focus on operations research, elaborate planning systems, and (supposedly) rigorous financial analysis had, in many companies, robbed management of its soul—and certainly had taken the focus off the customer. Peters and Waterman reminded managers that success often comes from doing common things uncommonly well."[19]

As Hamel observes, people like good news. *In Search of Excellence* glowed with good tidings. It radiated bonhomie. "The findings from the excellent companies amount to an upbeat message. There is good news from America. Good management practice today is not resident only in Japan," proclaimed Peters and Waterman. "But, more important, the good news comes from treating people decently and asking them to shine, and from producing things that work."[20]

The book's timing was perfect. "By 1982, people were prepared to listen. There was a whole new readiness to accept that Americans don't walk on water. The economy went deep south and people were ready to listen in a way they hadn't been earlier," says Peters. "The handbook/MBA logic was the logic of world management. That's not a grotesque exaggeration. Hayes and Abernathy trashed American management and wrote it in the Harvard manual. They could say we piggybacked on their work, but they put a shot across the bows of received wisdom and we continued with it."[21] Received wisdom was being rewritten and, somewhat ironically, the purveyor of much of the rewriting was Harvard Business School, which had done so much to create what its best minds were now set on undermining.

Peters and Waterman largely ignored Japan—it rates only ten index references in *In Search of Excellence.* Peters and Waterman directed their fire closer to home. Western management was in gridlock headed down a dead-end road. "The problem in America is that our fascination with the tools of management obscures our apparent ignorance of the art," they wrote. "Our tools are biased toward measurement and analysis. We can measure the costs. But with these tools alone we can't really elaborate on the value of a turned on . . . workforce churning out quality products."[22]

You could churn things out and they could still be good. Common people could do uncommon things—even if they weren't Japanese. There was room for optimism and in this positive message lies the secret of the book's long-lasting success. *In Search of Excellence* was homemade apple pie after a diet of humble pie. It was common sense—at a time when common sense appeared a radical alternative.

Hayes and Abernathy's article identified the malaise in America's corporate world. But the last thing a sick person wants to be told is that they are sick. They want to know how and when they will get better. This is exactly what *In Search of Excellence* provided.

Peters and Waterman's conclusions were distilled down into eight crucial characteristics. These have largely stood the test of time:

- Bias for action
- Close to the customer
- Autonomy and entrepreneurship
- Productivity through people
- Hands-on values driven
- Stick to the knitting
- Simple form, lean staff
- Simultaneous loose-tight properties

There was an air of back-to-basics zeal to *In Search of Excellence.* It offered to transport managers back to simpler times, when they knew what mattered without thinking about it. The thing that was picked upon from the book was its selection of excellent companies—largely predictable, uninspired, and nationalistic as it turned out. The fact that some of the companies didn't perform very well in the years following publication created a constant stream of articles. This missed the point. Peters and Waterman struck back against the analysts. They espoused management as art as well as science. They espoused people before data.

In doing so, Peters and Waterman were picking up the baton that had been dropped after the end of the 1950s. They rediscovered the humanistic counter to corporate dominance. They were joined by a number of other important thinkers. Most notable among these was Rosabeth Moss Kanter (born 1943) of Harvard Business School.

Kanter began her career as a sociologist examining utopian communities. "Most management gurus learn their craft by taking MBAs and serving time in business schools or consultancies. Rosabeth Moss Kanter learnt hers hanging around in the counter-culture, rubbing shoulders with the sort of gurus who believe in founding communes rather than re-inventing corporations," observed the *Economist.*[23]

Her first book, *Men and Women of the Corporation* (1977), looked at the innermost working of an organization. The sociologist within Kanter remains strong. "Kanter-the-guru still studies her subject with a sociologist's eye, treating the corporation not so much as a micro-economy, concerned with turning inputs into outputs, but as a mini-society, bent on shaping individuals to collective ends," the *Economist* pointed out.[24]

Moving on from her intricate examination of corporate life, Kanter mapped out the potential for a more people-based corporate world. This is driven by smaller organizations, or at least less monolithic organizations. She introduced the concept of the post-entrepreneurial firm that manages to combine the traditional strengths of a large organization with the flexible speed of a smaller organization.

Key to this is the entire idea of innovation. This has been a recurrent theme of Kanter's since her 1983 book, *Change Masters*—subtitled "Innovation and Entrepreneurship in the American Corporation." She defined *change masters* as "those people and organizations adept at the art of anticipating the need for, and of leading, productive change." At the opposite end to the change masters are the *change resisters,* intent on reining in innovation.

Kanter argued that change is fundamentally concerned with innovation (or "newstreams" in Kanter-speak). The key to developing and sustaining innovation is an "integrative" approach rather than a "segmentalist" one. (This has distinct echoes of the theories of that other female management theorist, Mary Parker Follett, whose work Kanter admires.) American woes were firmly placed at the door of "the quiet suffocation of the entrepreneurial spirit in segmentalist companies."

"Three new sets of skills are required to manage effectively in such integrative, innovation-stimulating environments," wrote Kanter. "First are 'power skills'—skills in persuading others to invest information, support, and resources in new initiatives driven by an 'entrepreneur.' Second is the ability to manage the problems associated with the greater use of teams and employee participation. And third is an understanding of how change is designed and constructed in an organization— how the microchanges introduced by individual innovators relate to macrochanges or strategic reorientations."

Kanter was partly responsible for the rise in interest in—if not the practice of—empowerment. "The degree to which the opportunity to use power effectively is granted to or withheld from individuals is one operative difference between those companies which stagnate and those which innovate," she wrote. (She later expressed grave doubts about whether the corporate hype about the subject goes anywhere near matching reality—"Managers may say they're empowering employees, for instance, but how many are really doing it?"[25])

Kanter's work pointed to the final strand in the move back to basics: leadership. People made the difference; leaders could not only help people make a difference, they could ignite large-scale processes of change. The only trouble was that as managers looked around, leaders were thin on the ground.

In the study of leadership a direct link was made between the human relations school of the 1950s and the reality of the 1980s. The link was made all the more real by the involvement of Warren Bennis (born 1925). Bennis served in the Second World War before studying at Antioch College, where he fell under the influence of his mentor, Douglas McGregor, creator of the motivational Theories X and Y. Later, Bennis followed McGregor to MIT.

From being an early student of group dynamics in the 1950s, Bennis became a futurologist in the 1960s. His work—particularly *The Temporary Society* (1968)—explored new organizational forms. Bennis envisaged organizations as *ad-hocracies*—roughly the direct opposite of bureaucracies—freed from the shackles of hierarchy and meaningless paperwork.

While Bennis was mapping out potential futures for the business world, he was confronting realities as a university administrator at the State University of New York at Buffalo and as president of the University of Cincinnati. He found that his practice disappointed his theory—a rare example of an academic putting his reputation where his ideas are. "When I was at the University of Cincinnati I realized that I was seeking power through position, by being President of the university. I wanted to *be* a university president but I didn't want to *do* it. I wanted the influence," says Bennis. "In the end I wasn't very good at being a president. I looked out of the window and thought that the man cutting the lawn actually seemed to have more control over what he was doing."

Bennis returned to the other side of the academic fence and became the doyen of leadership studies. "I have been thinking about leadership almost as long as I have been thinking," he says in the autobiographical collection, *An Invented Life.*[26] "It is probably a trap of my own making," he admits. "My first major article came out in 1959 and was on leadership. Since 1985 most of my work has been in that area. You build up some sort of brand equity and there is a degree of collusion between that and the marketplace—people say leadership that's Bennis. It makes life a little simpler."[27]

With the torrent of publications and executive programs on the subject, it is easy to forget that leadership had been largely forgotten as a topic worthy of serious academic interest until it was revived by Bennis and others in the 1980s. Since then, Bennis admits, "leadership has become a heavy industry. Concern and interest about leadership development is no longer an American phenomenon. It is truly global."

Bennis's work stands as a humane counter to much of the military-based hero worship that dogs the subject. Bennis argues that leadership is not a rare skill; leaders are made rather than born; leaders are usually ordinary people—or apparently ordinary—rather than charismatic; leadership is not solely the preserve of those at the top of the organization—it is relevant at all levels; and, finally, leadership is not about control, direction, and manipulation.

Bennis's best-known leadership research involved ninety of America's leaders. These included Neil Armstrong as well as the coach of the L.A. Rams, orchestral conductors, and businessmen such as Ray Kroc of McDonald's. "They were right-brained and left-brained, tall and short, fat and thin, articulate and inarticulate, assertive and retiring, dressed for success and dressed for failure, participative and autocratic," said Bennis.[28] The link between them was that they had all shown "mastery over present confusion." Bennis's message was that leadership is all-encompassing and open to all.

From the ninety leaders, four common abilities were identified: management of attention, of meaning, of trust, and of self. Management of attention is, said Bennis, a question of vision. Indeed, he defines leadership as "The capacity to create a compelling vision and translate it into action and sustain it." Successful leaders have a vision that other people believe in and treat as their own.

Having a vision is one thing, converting it into successful action is another. The second skill shared by Bennis's selection of leaders is management of meaning—communications. A vision is of limited practical use if it is encased in four hundred pages of wordy text or mumbled from behind a paper-packed desk. Bennis believes effective communication relies on use of analogy, metaphor, and vivid illustration as well as emotion, trust, optimism, and hope.

The third aspect of leadership identified by Bennis is trust, which he describes as "the emotional glue that binds followers and leaders together." Leaders have to be seen to be consistent.

The final common bond among the ninety leaders studied by Bennis is "deployment of self." The leaders do not glibly present charisma or time management as the essence of their success. Instead, the emphasis is on persistence and self-knowledge, taking risks, commitment and challenge, but, above all, learning. "The learning person looks forward to failure or mistakes," says Bennis. "The worst problem in leadership is basically early success. There's no opportunity to learn from adversity and problems."

The leaders have a positive self-regard, what Bennis labels "emotional wisdom." This is characterized by an ability to accept people as they are; a capacity to approach things in terms of only the present; an ability to treat everyone, even close contacts, with courteous attention; an ability to trust others even when this seems risky; and an ability to do without constant approval and recognition.

Leaders were the final bastions. As Western managers scratched their heads in bemusement, leaders offered hope; they offered clarity and optimism in a world befuddled with pessimism and confusion. They were a human way out rather than one that required a framework or matrix.

The Dow Jones Industrial Average Companies as of January 1, 1989

AlliedSignal Inc.	Procter & Gamble
Primerica	American Express
Minnesota Mining & Manufacturing	International Paper
DuPont	Philip Morris
Eastman Kodak	United Technologies
Goodyear	Sears, Roebuck
Bethlehem Steel	Exxon
International Business Machines	Texas Corporation
General Electric	Coca-Cola
General Motors	Union Carbide
McDonald's	USX Co.
Chevron	American Telephone & Telegraph
Navistar International Corporation	Westinghouse Electric
Boeing	Woolworth
Merck	Aluminum Co.

The Harvard 100

Top Five HBR *Articles Published in the 1980s*	Ranking in Top 100
"Managing Your Boss," John J. Gabarro and John P. Kotter—January-February 1980	8
"Quality on the Line," David A. Garvin—September-October 1983	17
"Information Technology Changes the Way You Compete," F. Warren McFarlan—May-June 1984	19
"Strategic Intent," Gary Hamel and C.K. Prahalad—May-June 1989	26
"How Information Gives You Competitive Advantage," Michael E. Porter and Victor E. Millar—July-August 1985	34

Source: "The 100 Best-Selling Articles."

The Management Century Timeline

1981

Richard Pascale and Anthony Athos seek out the secrets behind Japanese success with *The Art of Japanese Management* and introduce the Seven S framework.

In April, Adam Osborne shows off the Osborne 1 computer for the first time. Orders flood in and, by September, his company is recording monthly sales of over $1 million. The Osborne 1 and Adam Osborne seem to be at the forefront of the technological revolution. The confident and cheerfully opinionated Osborne appears to be the man for the times. "From Brags to Riches" reads one magazine headline. It proves a fleeting glimpse of what might have been. During 1982 Osborne Computer re-ports losses of $8 million. It is soon bankrupt, a historical footnote.

Pac-Man video game makes its debut.

1982

A psychopath puts cyanide into some Tylenol capsules. Eight people die. In response, Johnson & Johnson withdraws the product in its entirety from store shelves. A total of thirty-one million bottles were returned to J&J. This cost J&J $100 million.

"Ma Bell" is broken up into seven U.S. regional telephone companies.

Tom Peters and Robert Waterman ignite the business book market thanks to their human and optimistic blockbuster *In Search of Excellence.*

Bill Gates and his long-time friend Paul Allen found a company together.

After selling billions of hamburgers, McDonald's joins the Dow.

Kenichi Ohmae's *Mind of the Strategist* is published in the West.

Disaster hits the Union Carbide plant in Bhopal, India.

1983

IBM offers the first PC with a built-in hard disk.

Rosabeth Moss Kanter's *Change Masters* published.

1984

Apple introduces the Macintosh.

Michael Eisner and Frank Wells join Disney and begin the process of turning it around. Disney is in poor shape—in 1983 its studios recorded losses of $30 million as excessively high costs took their toll. Attendances at Disney's theme parks are also on a downward slope.

Meredith Belbin's *Management Teams* reintroduces management to teamworking.

1985

Ed Schein's *Organizational Culture and Leadership* is published.

New Coke introduced—briefly.

1986

The use of affirmative action to remedy job discrimination is upheld by the U.S. Supreme Court.

1987

The Dow first closes above 2,000 on January 8 then records its biggest one-day percentage loss of 22.6 percent on October 19.

1988

Joseph Juran lays down his quality gospel in *Planning for Quality*.

Sony buys CBS Records to form Sony Music Entertainment and then, in 1989, acquires Columbia Pictures to form Sony Pictures Entertainment as well as launching the 3.5-inch micro floppy disk.

1989

Charles Handy's *Age of Unreason* and Sumantra Ghoshal and Christopher Bartlett's *Managing Across Borders* unveil the emergent corporate realities.

The *Exxon Valdez* spills eleven million gallons of crude oil off Alaska.

1990

Michael Porter sweeps the world with *The Competitive Advantage of Nations* while Kenichi Ohmae envisages *The Borderless World*.

Perrier recalls its bottled water after traces of benzene are discovered.

McDonald's conquers Moscow.

Richard Pascale's *Managing on the Edge* is published.

Chapter 10

1991–2000: The New Balance of Power

Tomorrow's effective "organization" will be conjured up anew each day.
—TOM PETERS[1]

Functional Death

Research at the Massachusetts Institute of Technology suggests that management fads follow a regular life cycle. This starts with academic discovery. The new idea is then formulated into a technique and published in an academic publication. It is then more widely promoted as a means of increasing productivity, reducing costs, or whatever is currently exercising managerial minds. Consultants then pick the idea up and treat it as the universal panacea. After practical attempts fail to deliver the impressive results promised, there is realization of how difficult it is to convert the bright idea into sustainable practice. Finally, there follows committed exploitation by a small number of companies.

Nothing better exemplifies this pattern than the rise to global prominence and inevitable fall of business process reengineering. The idea of reengineering was brought to the fore in the early 1990s by James Champy, cofounder of the consultancy company CSC Index, and

Michael Hammer, an electrical engineer and former computer science professor at MIT. The roots of the idea lay in the research carried out by MIT from 1984 to 1989 on "Management in the 1990s."

Champy and Hammer's book, *Reengineering the Corporation,* was a best-seller that produced a plethora of reengineering programs at companies throughout the world, the creation of many consulting companies, and a deluge of books promoting alternative approaches to reengineering. (Thanks to the popularity of reengineering, CSC became one of the largest consultancy companies in the world.)

The basic idea behind reengineering is that organizations need to identify their key processes and make them as lean and efficient as possible. Peripheral processes (and, therefore, peripheral people) need to be discarded. "Don't automate; obliterate," Hammer proclaimed. Champy and Hammer defined reengineering as "the fundamental rethinking and radical redesign of business processes to achieve dramatic improvements in critical measures of performance such as cost, quality, service and speed."

As can be seen, the beauty of reengineering was that it embraced many of the fashionable business ideas of recent years and nudged them forward into a tidy philosophy. There were strains of total quality management, just-in-time manufacturing, customer service, time-based competition, and lean manufacturing in the reengineering concept. Big name corporations jumped on the bandwagon and Champy and Hammer's book was endorsed, somewhat surprisingly, by no less a figure than Peter Drucker.

To Champy and Hammer, reengineering was more than dealing with mere processes. They eschewed the phrase "business process reengineering," regarding it as too limiting. In their view the scope and scale of reengineering went far beyond simply altering and refining processes. True reengineering was all-embracing, a recipe for a corporate revolution.

To start the revolution, it was suggested that companies equip themselves with a blank piece of paper and map out their processes. This was undoubtedly a useful exercise. It encouraged companies to consider exactly what their core activities were—and what processes were in place, and needed to be in place, to deliver them efficiently. It also encouraged companies to move beyond strict functional demarcations to more free-flowing corporate forms governed by key processes rather than fiefdoms.

Inevitably, the optimal processes involved more effective utilization of resources. Functional organizations (as opposed to process-based ones) tend to contain elements of self-serving protectionism. Different functions do not necessarily share knowledge or work toward the same objectives. Clearly this is at best inefficient. As a result, some stages in processes were eliminated completely. Others were streamlined or made more effective through use of information technology. Having come up with a neatly engineered map of how their business should operate, companies could then attempt to translate the paper theory into concrete reality.

The concept was simple. Indeed, it contained strong echoes of Frederick Taylor's scientific management, with its concentration on processes and efficiency. Nearing the end of the twentieth century, efficiency was still the mantra.

While its relative simplicity made it alluring, actually turning reengineering into reality proved immensely more difficult than its proponents suggested. The revolution has largely been a damp squib.

The first problem was that the blank piece of paper ignored the years, often decades, of cultural evolution that led to an organization's doing something in a certain way. Such preconceptions and often justifiable habits were not easily discarded. Functional fiefdoms may be inefficient, but they are difficult to break down.

The second problem was that reengineering appeared inhumane—another echo of Frederick Taylor. In some cases, people were treated appallingly in the name of reengineering. Reengineering, as the name suggests, owed more to visions of the corporation as a machine than as a human, or humane, system. The human side of reengineering has proved its greatest stumbling block. To reengineering purists, people were objects who handle processes. Depersonalization was the route to efficiency. Here, the similarities with Taylor's management by scientific dictatorship are most obvious.

Reengineering became a synonym for redundancy and downsizing. For this the gurus and consultants could not be entirely blamed. Often, companies that claimed to be reengineering—and there were plenty—were simply engaging in cost-cutting under the convenient guise of the fashionable theory. Downsizing appeared more publicly palatable if it was presented as implementing a leading-edge concept.

The third obstacle was that corporations are not natural nor even willing revolutionaries. Instead of casting the reengineering net widely they tended to reengineer the most readily accessible process and then leave it at that. Related to this, and the subject of Champy's sequel, *Reengineering Management,* reengineering usually failed to impinge on management. Not surprisingly, managers were all too willing to impose the rigors of a process-based view of the business on others, but often unwilling to inflict it upon themselves. "Senior managers have been reengineering business processes with a passion, tearing down corporate structures that no longer can support the organization. Yet the practice of management has largely escaped demolition. If their jobs and styles are left largely intact, managers will eventually undermine the very structure of their rebuilt enterprises," Champy noted in 1994, at the height of reengineering's popularity. In response, he suggested reengineering management should tackle three key areas: managerial roles, managerial styles, and managerial systems. In retrospect, the mistake of reengineering was not to tackle reengineering management first.

Organizational Models

The achievements of reengineering, however, were twofold. First, it encouraged managers to consider once again the thorny issue of how best to organize their companies. Second, it promoted organization along process rather than functional lines. This was significant in that it broke free from the organizational rigidity inherent in functional organization. The trouble was that reengineering replaced one form of organizational rigidity with another.

With rapid advances in technology, the 1990s were dominated by organizational issues. The book that set the agenda—despite being greatly maligned—was Tom Peters's *Liberation Management* (1992). It was, observed Karl Weick, written in "hyper-text."

In *Liberation Management,* Peters broke free from traditional and functional notions of corporate structure. His exemplars of the new organizational structure were notable for their apparent lack of structure. And herein lay Peters's point. Companies such as CNN, Asea Brown Boveri (ABB), and Body Shop thrived through having highly flexible structures able to change to meet the business needs of the moment. Free-flowing, impossible to pin down, unchartable, simple yet complex, these were the paradoxical structures of the future.

Key to the new corporate structures envisaged by Peters were networks with customers, with suppliers, and, indeed, with anyone else who can help the business deliver. "Old ideas about size must be scuttled. 'New big,' which can be very big indeed, is 'network big.' That is, size measured by market power, say, is a function of the firm's extended family of fleeting and semi-permanent cohorts, not so much a matter of what it owns and directly controls," he wrote.

And networks must move quickly. The book's central refrain was that of fashion—"We're all in Milan's haute couture business and Hollywood's movie business," wrote Peters. "This book is animated by a single word: fashion. Life cycles of computers and microprocessors have shrunk from years to months." The new model organization moved fast and did so continually, seeking out new areas that make it unique in its markets.

Clearly, this required quite different managerial skills from those traditionally needed by managers. Indeed, Peters said that the new organizational forms he depicted were "troublesome to conceive—and a downright pain to manage." The new skills are now familiar. Peters bade farewell to command and control, ushered in a new era characterized by "curiosity, initiative, and the exercise of imagination." It was, he argued, a step into the unknown for most organizations but also a return to first principles: "For the last 100 years or so . . . we've assumed that there is one place where expertise should reside: with 'expert' staffs at division, group, sector, or corporate. And another, very different, place where the (mere) work gets done. The new organization regimen puts expertise back, close to the action—as it was in craft-oriented, pre-industrial revolution days. . . . We are not, then, ignoring 'expertise' at all. We are simply shifting its locus, expanding its reach, giving it new respect—and acknowledging that everyone must be an expert in a fast-paced, fashionized world."

Peters's view of the need for organizational change was followed by a welter of new organizational models—virtual organizations, network organizations, and the like.

Among the most considered participants in this debate was the British thinker Charles Handy (born 1932). Handy anticipated that certain forms of organization would become dominant. These were the type of organization most readily associated with service industries. First and most famously, what he called "the shamrock organization"—"a form of organization based around a core of essential executives and workers supported by outside contractors and part-time help." The consequence of such an organizational form was that organizations in the future are likely to resemble the way consultancy firms, advertising agencies, and professional partnerships are currently structured.

The second emergent structure identified by Handy was the *federal* one—not, he pointed out, another word for decentralization. He provided a blueprint for federal organizations in which the central function coordinates, influences, advises, and suggests. It does not dictate terms or short-term decisions. The center is, however, concerned with long-term strategy. It is "at the middle of things and is not a polite word for the top or even for head office."

The third type of organization Handy anticipated is what he called "the Triple I"—Information, Intelligence, and Ideas. In such organizations the demands on personnel management are large. Handy explained: "The wise organization already knows that their smart people are not to be easily defined as workers or as managers but as individuals, as specialists, as professionals or executives, or as leader (the older terms of manager and worker are dropping out of use), and that they and it need also to be obsessed with the pursuit of learning if they are going to keep up with the pace of change."

The debate about organizational structures is continuing. In practice, however, the 1990s have seen the emergence of a distinctly new breed of corporation. The exemplars of his new generation are, among others, ABB, Toyota, GE, and Dell.

The Matrix Model

Asea Brown Boveri (ABB) is one of the most lauded and reported on companies of our time. Case studies abound. Those paying homage include Tom Peters, London Business School's Sumantra Ghoshal, and Harvard's Christopher Bartlett (authors of *The Individualized Corporation*), and virtually every other management thinker you care to mention. ABB is routinely decorated with corporate baubles as Europe's most admired company. Commentators praise, analysts purr.

First the facts. Headquartered in Zurich, Switzerland, ABB is the world's leading power engineering company, employing over 213,000 people in fifty countries. A $31 billion company, it is broken down into thirty-five business areas with five thousand profit centers. ("Five thousand perceived companies," says chief executive officer Göran Lindahl.)

ABB came about from the merger of the Swedish company Asea, then led by the redoubtable Percy Barnevik, and the Swiss company Brown Boveri. It was the biggest cross-border merger since Royal Dutch Shell's oily coupling. Barnevik became the CEO of the resulting ABB and revolutionized its organization and performance until being succeeded by Lindahl in 1997.

Along the way, Barnevik has been portrayed as a kind of European Jack Welch. There are similarities. Both men have a long-held and passionate disdain for bureaucracy. Barnevik is famous for his 30 percent rule—on taking over a company 30 percent of headquarters staff are fired, 30 percent moved to other companies in the group, and 30 percent spun off into separate profit centers, leaving 10 percent to get on with the work. Both Barnevik and Welch are inveterate and powerful communicators who have managed to maintain a heady tempo of change. They have changed then changed again.

The story of the Asea–Brown Boveri merger is a riveting one. Negotiations were conducted in secret. When the boards were shown the draft agreement for the first time, some directors had no idea a merger was afoot. They had an hour to read the papers. The entire process was extraordinarily quick. Due diligence was notable for its absence as Barnevik pushed to clinch the deal. When a draft agreement was generated, Barnevik read it out line by line in front of both negotiating teams. Objections were ironed out on the spot. If voices weren't raised, it was taken as agreed. "We had to be fast; there could be no leakage; we could not have lawyers around; we had to trust each other," Barnevik reflected.[2]

The level of trust is perhaps the most striking thing about the merger. Both sets of management recognized that it was a good idea. There was no political maneuvering. Secret discussions remained secret. Decisions were made and kept to. This atmosphere of mutual respect and trust was probably helped by the fact that it was a merger rather than a takeover—"A takeover would have destroyed a lot, psychologically, politically and commercially," says Barnevik.[3]

The merger was announced on August 10, 1987. The corporate world was stunned by its suddenness. The *Wall Street Journal* said that it was a merger "born of necessity, not of love." This overlooked the uncanny fit between the two companies. It was truly a marriage made in corporate heaven. Brown Boveri was international, Asea was not. Asea excelled at management, Brown Boveri did not. Technology, markets, and cultures fitted together. Of course, whether this was luck or strategic insight is a matter of continuing discussion.

Then, quite simply, Barnevik made it work. "The challenge set by Barnevik was to create—out of a group of 1,300 companies employing 210,000 people in 150 countries—a streamlined, entrepreneurial organization with as few management layers as possible," wrote Kevin Barham and Claudia Heimer in their book examining the company, *ABB: The Dancing Giant.*[4] To enable this to happen, Barnevik introduced a complex matrix structure—what Lindahl has called "decentralization under central conditions." The company is run by an Executive Committee with the organization below divided by business areas, company and profit centers, and country organizations. The aim is to reap the advantages of being a large organization while also having the advantages of smallness.

ABB's matrix structure has been the source of much debate. It has been hailed as a new organizational model and Barnevik as GM's Alfred P. Sloan reincarnated. (Perhaps this is what GM had in mind when it appointed Barnevik as a non-executive director.) Barnevik argues that the matrix system is simply a formal means of recording and understanding what happens informally in any large organization. The spider's web of the matrix is a fact of life.

Natural or not, the truth is that ABB's structure is complex, paradoxical, and ambiguous. As a corporate role model ABB is a complete nonstarter. ("I do not believe that you can mechanically copy what another company has done," advises Barnevik.) As a sophisticated means of managing this particular organization it has proved highly effective. What holds this "globally connected" company together is deep-rooted local presence, global vision, cross-border understanding, global values and principles for managing creative tension, global connection at the top, and global ethics. In addition, it requires a CEO with the rare dynamism and intelligence of Barnevik. Imitators beware.

While it may prove unwise to slavishly copy ABB, the company is inspirational in other ways. You could summarize ABB's management style and philosophy as management for and by grown-ups. It is seemingly free of pointless infighting. Constructive debate is welcomed. Managers from different countries work together effectively. There is the impression that decisions are thought through, backed by analysis, then made and carried out. ABB is a ringing endorsement for professional management at the end of the twentieth century.

None of this happened overnight or easily. But it all happened deliberately. Throughout there is a keen sense of commonsensical managerial decisions leading to a greater corporate destiny. Certainty, clarity, and communication are key. These are the basic gifts of Percy Barnevik; the gifts he has liberally endowed ABB with. He possesses a rare certainty of judgment. He communicates constantly and brings absolute clarity to his decisions. ABB does much the same; the question must be whether it can continue to do so.

The Management Model

In December 1980 John Francis Welch Jr. (born 1935) was announced as the new CEO and chairman of General Electric. It was a record-breaking appointment. At forty-five, Welch was the youngest chief the company had ever appointed. Indeed, he was only the eighth CEO the company had appointed in ninety-two years.

He took over a company that was a model for American corporate might and for modern management techniques. GE had moved with the times—though usually more slowly. It got there eventually but was, even then, a sizeable juggernaut. Changing direction and learning new tricks weren't things that came naturally. GE was in the habit of weighing things up and then moving, minimizing risks but still progressing forward. It was highly focused but still managed to view the world more broadly than some other corporate giants.

When Jack Welch became top man GE's net income was $1.7 billion. By most measures, the company was growing at a healthy rate—by 9 percent in the preceding year. Everything seemed rosy. More plain sailing was anticipated as the new chief got used to the job. After all, Welch was an insider. He was hardly likely to turn on the organization that had nurtured him so carefully.

The company Welch took over was—and is—one of the great corporate stories. It has survived the vicissitudes of time with remarkable resilience.

In 1878, Thomas A. Edison set up the Edison Electric Light Company. The company evolved into the Edison General Electric Company and, in 1892, merged with Thomson-Houston Electric Company to form the General Electric Company. In 1896, when the Dow Jones Industrial Index was launched, General Electric was listed. It is the only one of the original companies still listed.

GE's progression has, indeed, been built on solid foundations. It earned $3 million in its first seven months of existence and has been run cautiously and prudently ever since. One generation has handed on to another seamlessly. All have been committed to change—to a greater or lesser extent. "GE's genius has been in its choice of successive CEOs each of whom tended to counter the extremes of his predecessors," concluded Richard Pascale after studying the company's history in *Managing on the Edge*.[5]

Indeed, GE's performance has been consistently good. In their book *Built to Last,* Jerry Porras and Jim Collins found that Welch's record in his first decade in charge wasn't the best in GE's history. In fact, the celebrated CEO came in fifth place out of seven when measured by return on equity. "To have a Welch-caliber CEO is impressive. To have a century of Welch-caliber CEOs all grown from inside—well, that is one key reason why GE is a visionary company," conclude Porras and Collins.[6] It is a formidable record. No other large organization has been so successful in recruiting from within or managed to sustain such consistent performance over such an extended period. General Electric is the greatest advertisement for management on planet Earth.

Another reason behind GE's success is that it has been built around a simple, commonsense culture. Nothing fancy has distracted it. No thrills. Nothing too smart. "Sure we have good people, but we were all taken from the same pool as the people of all other companies, and yet I think we have something unique," ex-CEO Fred Borch said in 1965. "And our uniqueness, I think, is due to this matter of climate; respect for one another and working at our jobs to have as much darn fun out of it as we possibly can."[7]

Keeping it simple means that GE gets through CEOs at a far slower rate than its rivals. As Don Hambrick and Greg Fukotoni pointed out in 1991, since 1960 some 19 percent of CEOs in Fortune 500s served less than three years.[8] GE, on the other hand, is rarely on the phone to headhunters. GE has long recognized that it is better and cheaper to nurture talent and promote from within. It is significant that GE executives are enthusiastically courted by other companies.

The roll call of GE CEOs is worth reading:

- *Charles Coffin:* Chairman and CEO 1892–1922. Coffin was the leader of the group that bought Edison's patents and began the serious development of the business.

- *Gerard Swope:* Swope (1872–1957) joined GE in 1919 as first president of International General Electric. He became president in 1922 with Owen Young as chairman. By the late 1920s the company had seventy-five thousand employees and sales of $300 million. The company moved into home appliances. Swope emphasized the company's heritage as an engineering and manufacturing company, and combined that with solid systems and—by the standards of the times—progressive human resources management. The Swope Plan of 1931 was one of the building blocks of the New Deal. Swope retired in 1939 but returned temporarily when his successor was appointed to wartime jobs.

• *Charles Wilson:* Wilson's tenure from 1940 until 1952 was interrupted by wartime work that made his impact and legacy less substantial than his predecessor's.

• *Ralph Cordiner:* Cordiner (1900–1973) was GE's CEO from 1950 until 1963. He was a robust champion of decentralization, which necessitated the creation of complex bureaucratic systems. His unsettling years in charge were notable for the introduction of management by objectives. Cordiner also launched GE Plastics and the company's aircraft engines business. He set up the company's Crotonville training center. Cordiner emphasized marketing and developed a new corporate slogan: "Progress is our most important product." His book, *New Frontiers for Professional Managers* (1956), summarized his managerial philosophy.

• *Fred Borch:* Borch introduced GE to strategic planning and calmed things down a little from the Cordiner years. His impact is favorably recalled by Jack Welch: "Borch let a thousand flowers bloom. He got us into modular housing and entertainment businesses, nurtured GE Credit through its infancy, embarked on ventures in Europe, and let Aircraft Engine and Plastics alone so they could really get started. It became evident after he stepped down that General Electric had once again established a foothold into some businesses with a future."[9] Borch ruled the GE roost from 1964 until 1972.

• *Reg Jones:* British-born Jones joined GE in 1939. In 1967 he became CFO and CEO in 1973. Jones developed GE's business in high-tech markets such as jet engines and nuclear reactors, as well as sharpening up its financial systems. He was voted the United States's most influential executive in 1979 and CEO of the year in 1980. A former GE executive later commented: "During Jones' tenure, GE was financially strong but it was a dull, unexciting company. We were an organization in decline—and that was not recognized."[10] Jones's diligent succession planning led to Jack Welch, CEO.

When he joined this small and illustrious list, Jack Welch did not plan on settling quietly into the executive suite. Plain sailing was not on Jack Welch's route map. Quiet, contented progress was not Jack Welch's plan. GE was shaken and then shaken again.

During the 1980s, Welch put his dynamic mark on GE and on corporate America. GE's businesses were overhauled. Some were cast out and hundreds of new businesses acquired. In 1984 *Fortune* called Welch the "toughest boss in America." GE's workforce bore the brunt of Welch's quest for competitiveness. GE virtually invented downsizing. Nearly 200,000 GE employees left the company. Over $6 billion was saved.

Welch was reincarnated—in the media at least—as *Neutron Jack*. He was the man who swept away people while leaving the buildings intact. Not surprisingly, he wasn't the most popular man in GE or the wider corporate world. For a while it seemed as though Welch could be bracketed alongside Al Dunlap as public enemy number one. Within GE there were grave concerns about what was happening. It was, Welch coolly reflected, part of the job. Not a nice part but one that was necessary. "I didn't start with a morale problem. I created it!" he told Richard Pascale with typical forceful candor. "The leader who tries to move a large organization counter to what his followers perceive to be necessary has a very difficult time. I had never had to do this before. I had always had the luxury of building a business and being the cheerleader. But it was clear that we had to reposition ourselves and put our chips on those businesses that could survive on a global scale."[11]

Stage One of life under Jack Welch was a brutal introduction to the new realities of business. Perhaps Welch was too brutal. But there is no denying that by the end of the 1980s GE was a leaner and fitter organization. Any complacency that might have existed had been eradicated. In retrospect, Welch's greatest decision may have been to go in with all guns blazing. Dramatic though relatively short-lived change was preferable to incremental change.

Having proved that he could tear the company apart, Welch had to move onto Stage Two: rebuilding a company fit for the twenty-first century. The hardware had been taken care of. Now came the software.

Central to this was the concept of Work-out, which was launched in 1989. This came about, it is reputed, after a chance question from

Professor Kirby Warren of Columbia University. Warren asked Welch: "Now that you have gotten so many people out of the organization, when are you going to get some of the work out?"[12] At this stage 100,000 people had left GE. Welch liked the idea of getting the work out. The idea turned into a reality. With typical gusto, Welch brought in twenty or so business school professors and consultants to help turn the emergent concept into reality. Welch has called Work-out "a relentless, endless company-wide search for a better way to do everything we do."[13]

Work-out was a communication tool that offered GE employees a dramatic opportunity to change their working lives. "The idea was to hold a three-day, informal town meeting with 40 to 100 employees from all ranks of GE. The boss kicked things off by reviewing the business and laying out the agenda, then he or she left. The employees broke into groups, and aided by a facilitator, attacked separate parts of the problem," explains Janet Lowe in *Jack Welch Speaks*. "At the end, the boss returned to hear the proposed solutions. The boss had only three options: The idea could be accepted on the spot; rejected on the spot; or more information could be requested. If the boss asked for more information, he had to name a team and set a deadline for making a decision."[14]

Work-out was astonishingly successful. It helped begin the process of rebuilding the bonds of trust between GE employees and management. It gave employees a channel through which they could talk about what concerned them at work and then actually change the way things were done. It broke down barriers.

Welch the destroyer became Welch the empowerer. Work-out was part of a systematic opening up of GE. Walls between departments and functions came tumbling down. Middle management layers had been stripped away in the 1980s. With Work-out, Welch was enabling and encouraging GE people to talk to each other, work together, and share information and experience. At first surprised, they soon reveled in the opportunity.

The next stage in Welch's revolution was the introduction of a wide-ranging quality program. Titled Six Sigma, it was launched at the end of 1995. "Six Sigma has spread like wildfire across the company, and it is transforming everything we do," the company reported two years on.[15]

Six Sigma basically spread the responsibility for quality. Instead of being a production issue it was recast as an issue for every single person in the company. "We blew up the old quality organization, because they were off to the side. Now, it's the job of the leader, the job of the manager, the job of the employee—everyone's job is quality," said Welch.[16]

The three stages of development—destruction, creation, and quality—have reshaped GE. The high-performing giant remains a high-performing giant—but one that is lean and nimble. The figures stack up nicely.

Back in 1981 as Jack Welch began life as CEO, GE had total assets of $20 billion and revenues of $27.24 billion. Its earnings were $1.65 billion. With 440,000 employees worldwide, GE had a market value of $12 billion.

By 1997, GE's total assets had mushroomed to $304 billion and total revenues to $90.84 billion. Around 270,000 employees—down a staggering 170,000—produced earnings of $8.2 billion and gave the company a market value of $300 billion, the highest in the world.

GE now operates in over a hundred countries—with 250 manufacturing plants in twenty-six countries. As a total entity, GE was ranked fifth in the most recent Fortune 500. Nine of GE's businesses would be in Fortune's top 50 if ranked independently. GE remains a corporate giant. And now it appears to be big in all the right places.

The broader lessons are equally significant. GE has succeeded because of a combination of professional management—driven by common sense rather than analysis—a strong culture (nurtured at Crotonville), and vigorous, thoughtful, leadership. It has refused to sit still.

The Lean Model

During the last forty years, Western carmakers have lurched from one crisis to another. They have always been a step behind. And the company they have been following is the Japanese giant, Toyota. The reason why is partly explained if you visit the Toyota headquarters building in Japan. There you will find three portraits. One is of the company's founder, the next of the company's current president, and the final one is a portrait of the American quality guru, W. Edwards Deming.

In the beginning—in 1918—the company was called the Toyoda Spinning & Weaving Co. In the 1930s the development of automatic looms convinced the company that its future lay elsewhere. Kiichiro Toyoda, the founder's son, had studied engineering and visited the United States and Europe. He decided the future lay in carmaking and changed the company's name to Toyota in 1936. In the aftermath of the Second World War, Toyoda announced his company's intention to "catch up with America in three years. Otherwise, the automobile industry of Japan will not survive." Toyoda remained as company president until 1950 and the company was run by a member of the Toyoda family until 1995.

The first Toyota car was the Model AA. (As something of an insurance policy, the company also continued in its old business—looms were still produced until the early 1950s.) In the 1950s Toyota established offices in Taiwan and Saudi Arabia. It began making forklift trucks (and is now the world number one in that market) and entered the American market (1958) and later the U.K. market (1965).

Its initial foray into the United States proved unsuccessful. Its Crown model was designed for the Japanese market and was ill suited to American freeways. Eventually Toyota got it right. In 1968 the success of the Corolla enabled it to make a great leap forward—by 1975 it had replaced Volkswagen in the United States as the number one auto importer. It got right in the heart of the American market in 1984, entering into a joint venture with General Motors to build Toyotas in California. (The joint venture also makes the GM Prizm.) It was this joint venture that led to a rise in Western interest in the company and its methods.

More successes have followed. The Camry was the best-selling car in the United States in 1997. Toyota is now the third biggest car maker in the world (behind GM and Ford). It sells 5 million vehicles a year (1.3 million in North America, 2 million in Japan and 0.5 million in Europe). In Japan it has nearly 40 percent of the market. Its 1998 sales were $88.5 billion with a net income of $3.5 billion.

Behind all this lurks the presence of Deming and the practical application of his ideas. Toyota's decision to follow Deming's quality philosophy was one of the most influential of the twentieth century. While

Western companies used costly, large, and unhappy workforces to produce gas-guzzling cars in the 1970s, Toyota was forging ahead with implementation of Deming's ideas. In the early eighties, Western companies finally woke up and began to implement Deming's quality gospel. By then it was too late. Toyota had moved on. (In fact, it didn't mind telling Western companies all about total quality management for this very reason.)

Toyota progressed to what became labeled *lean production,* or the Toyota Production System. (The architect of this is usually acknowledged as being Taichi Ohno, who wrote a short book on the Toyota approach and later became a consultant.) From Toyota's point of view, there was nothing revolutionary in lean production. In fact, lean production was an integral part of Toyota's commitment to quality and its roots can be traced back to the 1950s and Deming's ideas.

And the word was based on three simple principles. The first was that of just-in-time production. There is no point in producing cars, or anything else, in blind anticipation of someone's buying them. Waste is bad. Production has to be closely tied to the market's requirements. Second, responsibility for quality rests with everyone and any quality defects need to be rectified as soon as they are identified. The third, more elusive, concept was the "value stream." Instead of seeing the company as a series of unrelated products and processes, it should be seen as a continuous and uniform whole, a stream including suppliers as well as customers.

Toyota's production philosophy and the carefully developed strength of its brand reached its high point in 1990 with the launch of the Lexus. The Lexus was initially greeted as a triumph for Japanese imitation. Media pundits laughed at the company's effrontery—"If Toyota could have slapped a Mercedes star on the front of the Lexus, it would have fooled most of the people most of the time."

With the Lexus, Toyota moved the goalposts. It out-engineered Mercedes and BMW. Toyota is keen to tell you that the Lexus took seven years, $2 billion, 1,400 engineers, 2,300 technicians, and 450 prototypes to develop, and generated 200 patents. Its standard fittings include a satellite navigation system and much more. Toyota made great play of the fact that the car was tested in Japan on mile after mile of carefully built highways that exactly imitated roads in the United States, Germany, or the United Kingdom. Toyota even put in the right road signs.

But the Lexus, in typical Toyota style, was about more than mere engineering. There was the fabled Lexus ownership experience. When an early problem led to a product recall, Lexus had dealers call up people personally and immediately. Instead of having a negative effect it strengthened the product's position in the marketplace. Toyota screwed things up like everyone else, but then sorted the problem out in a friendly, human way. With the Lexus, Toyota proved that its capacity to stay ahead of the pack remains undiminished.

The New Model

Michael Dell made history when he became the youngest CEO ever to run a Fortune 500 company. Along the way, he has joined the ranks of the most revered entrepreneurs in America—as the man who took the direct-sales model and elevated it to an art form. (In 1999, Dell Computer came fourth in *Fortune*'s ranking of America's Most Admired Companies, behind GE, Coca-Cola, and Microsoft.)

The company Dell built is not the biggest in the world. Nor are its products the most innovative. Dell is that rarity: a corporate model, the benchmark for how companies can be organized and managed to reap the full potential of technology.

Dell started young. By the age of thirteen, he had become a dab hand at taking apart the motherboard of his Apple 2 computer. But his interest in business predated even that. "I first experienced the power— and rewards—of being direct when I was twelve years old," Dell says. "The father of my best friend in Houston was a pretty avid stamp collector, so naturally my friend and I wanted to get into stamp collecting, too. . . . I started reading stamp journals just for fun, and soon began noticing that stamp prices were rising. Before long, my interest in stamps began to shift from the joy of collecting to the idea that there was something here that my mother, a stockbroker, would have termed a 'commercial opportunity.'"

Dinnertime conversations in the Dell household reinforced his interest. The talk was about what the Federal Reserve was doing and how it affected the American economy, the oil crisis, and which company stocks to buy and sell. By the age of sixteen, young Michael was putting what he'd learned into practice.

He got a summer job selling newspaper subscriptions for the *Houston Post* and quickly realized that the list of phone numbers the company handed out was an inefficient way to drum up new business. Dell speedily identified a pattern for new subscribers. Feedback from potential customers convinced him that the best groups to target were newlyweds and people who had just bought new houses or apartments.

From the local courthouse he and his friends obtained lists of those who had applied for marriage licences. From another source he compiled a list of people who had recently applied for mortgages. He targeted the two groups with a personalized letter. Subscriptions poured in.

When the school term started, an assignment from his history and economics teacher asked students to complete a tax return. Dell calculated his income based on his successful newspaper subscriptions business at $18,000.

His teacher, assuming he had put the decimal point in the wrong place, corrected it. She was dismayed to learn that there was no mistake—her student had made more money than she had.

By then the fledgling entrepreneur had a new hobby—computers. While at the University of Texas, he rebuilt PCs and sold them. His business was kick-started with a $1,000 investment. Dell is living proof that having too little capital is better than too much. It forced him to reinvent the computer industry. Dell's 16 percent share of the company is now worth some $5 billion.

Dell's inspiration was to realize that PCs could be built to order and sold directly to customers. This had two clear advantages. First, it meant that the new company was not hostage to retailers intent on increasing their markups at its expense. Dell cut out the middlemen. By doing so, he reduced the company's selling costs from a typical 12 percent of revenue to a mere 4 percent to 6 percent of revenue.

Second, the company did not need to carry large stocks. It actually carries around eleven days of inventory. "The best indirect company has 38 days on inventory. The average channel has about 45 days of inventory. So if you put it together, you've got 80 days or so of inventory—a little less than eight times our inventory level," says Michael Dell.

In any language, high profit margins and low costs make business sense. In the fast-growing computer business they are nirvana. In its first eight years Dell grew at a steady rate of 80 percent. It then slowed down to a positively snail-like 55 percent. Its 1998 revenues were $12.3 billion.

Little wonder, perhaps, that Dell's competitors look pedestrian in comparison. While Dell has been growing explosively, Compaq has been growing at less than 20 percent. In terms of market share Dell is now closing in on Compaq in the United States (14.1 percent versus 15.8 percent in the third quarter of 1998) and is number two in worldwide share behind Compaq. Dell may well end up having the best-performing stock of the 1990s. Dell's market capitalization stands at $99 billion (compared with $75 billion and $169 billion for Compaq and IBM, respectively).

Inspired by such raw statistics emulators have come thick and fast. In an effort to keep ahead, Compaq has introduced programs that offer the ability to have PCs built to order. Crucially, they are still sold through intermediaries. The trouble for established companies like Compaq is that once the middlemen are in place it is very difficult to ease them out of the picture. Another Dell competitor, Gateway, has opted for a halfway house approach—it has introduced "Country Stores" to provide potential customers with a physical site to learn about products in person, the equivalent of a car showroom and test drive.

Emulation is the purest form of desperation as well as flattery. Dell's insight was, after all, blissfully simple. "There is a popular idea now that if you reduce your inventory and build to order, you'll be just like Dell. Well, that's one part of the puzzle, but there are other parts, too," Dell has said. He explains the company's success as "a disciplined approach to understanding how we create value in the PC industry, selecting the right markets, staying focused on a clear business model and just executing."

While the notion of selling direct is appealing, companies that do so are only as good as their ability to deliver. Dell's model creates a direct line to the customer, which the company has proved highly adept at maximizing. Direct knowledge of the end consumer builds a satisfied customer base—increasing Dell's brand strength, lowering customer acquisition costs, and boosting customer loyalty. The result is "mass customization" as opposed to the traditional method of broad market segmentation.

Dell, the interloper that has cut out the money-grabbing middleman, has a strong rapport with its customers—in a way that Microsoft, for example, has manifestly failed to achieve. "To all our nit-picky—over demanding—ask awkward questions customers. Thank you, and keep up the good work," read one Dell advertisement. "You actually get to have a relationship with the customer," explains Michael Dell. "And that creates valuable information, which in turn allows us to leverage our relationships with both suppliers and customers. Couple that information with technology and you have the infrastructure to revolutionize the fundamental business models of major global companies."

Dell has proved highly efficient in utilizing the full power of modern technology to create reliable logistic and distribution systems. It is among the pioneers of selling by the Internet. "The Internet for us is a dream come true," says Dell. "It's like zero-variable-cost transaction. The only thing better would be mental telepathy." Dell's online sales alone exceed $3 million a day and, during Christmas 1997, Dell was selling $6 million worth of products every day on-line.

The company's Web site is expected to handle half of Dell's transactions by the year 2000.

The beauty of the Dell model is that it can be applied to a range of industries where middlemen have creamed off profits. Its low overheads also mean that Michael Dell has no need to mortgage the business to expand. This year's model may be around for some time.

The Triumph of Marx

What links the stories of ABB, GE, Toyota, and Dell? The answer is that they are all thoroughly modern tales. The success of these companies is not based on what they make. Their products are important—but less important than how the companies are organized or managed. The success of ABB is attributable to its organizational model, which enables it to be strong globally and locally. The strength of GE increasingly lies in the lucrative services it bundles around its traditional products. Toyota's cars aren't exceptional, but how they are produced is. Dell's selling point is not the computers it makes but how it makes and delivers them.

How companies do things has never been more important and more integral to how successful they are. Essentially, this is a victory of intellect over substance. What sets ABB, GE, Toyota, and Dell apart is a matter of insight, management, and application. "The computer revolution by powerfully enhancing management's effectiveness in dealing with change should have the long-range effect of increasing demand for management men," *Fortune* accurately predicted over thirty years ago.[17]

Intellectual power is the new route to competitive advantage. This means that Karl Marx's objective of the workers controlling the means of production has been achieved. Our brains rule the corporate world. Capital used to be viewed in purely financial terms; now it must increasingly be seen in intellectual terms.

Intellectual capital can be crudely described as the collective brainpower of the organization. The concept is irrevocably bound up with the notion of the knowledge worker and knowledge management. In some hands, the terms are used virtually synonymously.

The root of the idea of intellectual capital, as with so many other ideas, lies in the work of Peter Drucker. His 1969 book, *The Age of Discontinuity,* introduced the term *knowledge worker* to describe the highly trained, intelligent managerial professional who realizes his or her own worth and contribution to the organization. The knowledge worker was the antidote to the previous model, corporate man and woman.

"The knowledge worker sees himself just as another *professional,* no different from the lawyer, the teacher, the preacher, the doctor or the government servant of yesterday," wrote Drucker in *The Age of Discontinuity.* "He has the same education. He has more income, he has probably greater opportunities as well. He may well realize that he depends on the organization for access to income and opportunity, and that without the investment the organization has made—and a high investment at that—there would be no job for him, but he also realizes, and rightly so, that the organization equally depends on him."

Drucker recognized the new breed, but key to his contribution was the realization that knowledge is both power *and* ownership. Intellectual capital is power. If knowledge rather than labor is the new measure of economic society, then the fabric of capitalist society must change: "The knowledge worker is both the true 'capitalist' in the knowledge society and dependent on his job. Collectively the knowledge workers, the employed educated middle-class of today's society, own the means of production through pension funds, investment trusts, and so on." Thinkers of the world unite.

Drucker later developed his thinking most notably in his 1992 book, *Managing for the Future,* in which he observes: "From now on the key is knowledge. The world is becoming not labor intensive, not materials intensive, not energy intensive, but knowledge intensive."

The information age places a premium on intellectual work. There is growing realization that recruiting, retaining, and nurturing talented people is crucial to competitiveness. The rise in interest is understandable and, perhaps, woefully late in the evolution of industrial life. "Of course, knowledge has always mattered, but two things have changed," argues Thomas Stewart, author of one of the major books on the subject. "First, as a percentage of the value added to a product it has grown to be the most important thing. Costs used to be 80 percent on material and 20 percent on knowledge—now it is split 70–30 the other way. Second, it is increasingly possible to manage knowledge."[18]

Intellectual capital is, in many ways, simply concerned with fully utilizing the intellects of those employed by an organization. "If Hewlett-Packard knew what it knows we'd be three times more productive," reflects Hewlett-Packard chief Lew Platt. In the year 2000, it is calculated that the United Kingdom will have ten million people who could be termed knowledge workers and seven million manual workers. In the United States, despite the downsizing epidemic, the numbers of managerial and professional workers *increased* by 37 percent from the beginning of the 1980s to the late 1990s.

Having identified intellectual capital as important, the next question is inevitable: How can it be measured? After all, what gets measured gets done. Intellectual capital is increasingly codified as part of corporate life. The Swedish company Skandia has a "director of intellectual capital" and others are following suit—with job titles at least. Skandia's Leif Edvinsson is one of the thought leaders in this field—he has developed a model for reporting on intellectual capital based around customers, processes, renewal and development, human factors, and finance.

The trouble is that turning bland statements about knowledge and intellectual capital into reality is a substantial challenge. Intellectual capital is good, but how do you create it? Here, companies can hit a wall. Research by Booz·Allen & Hamilton consultants Charles Lucier and Janet Torsilieri found that most knowledge management (or equivalent) programs have limited results. Indeed, they estimate that "about one-sixth of these programs achieve very significant impact within the first two years; half achieve small but important benefits; and the remaining third—the failures—have little business impact."

Amid the hype and hyperbole, as well as the plethora of conferences and publications, such research makes for salutary reading. For all the talk, successfully harnessing intellectual capital remains a formidable challenge—and one that few corporations can claim to have overcome.

The Dow Jones Industrial Average Companies as of January 1, 1999

AlliedSignal Inc.	Procter & Gamble
Citigroup Inc.	American Express
Minnesota Mining & Manufacturing	International Paper
DuPont	Philip Morris
Eastman Kodak	United Technologies
Goodyear	Sears, Roebuck
Johnson & Johnson	Exxon
IBM	J.P. Morgan
General Electric	Coca-Cola
General Motors	Union Carbide
McDonald's	Walt Disney Co.
Chevron	AT&T Co.
Caterpillar	Hewlett-Packard
Boeing	Wal-Mart Stores
Merck	Aluminum Co.

The Management Century: Tale of the Tape

	Life Expectancy	
	1900	*1998*
Mexico	33	74
Japan	44	80
Italy	44	78
United States	47	76

Source: Time, April 13, 1998.

The Harvard 100

Top Five HBR *Articles Published in the 1990s*	*Ranking in Top 100*
"The Core Competence of the Corporation," C.K. Prahalad and Gary Hamel—May-June 1990	15
"What Leaders Really Do," John P. Kotter—May-June 1990	24
"Reengineering Work: Don't Automate, Obliterate," Michael Hammer—July-August 1990	38
"The Discipline of Teams," Jon R. Katzenbach and Douglas K. Smith—March-April 1993	44
"From Affirming Action to Affirming Diversity," R. Roosevelt Thomas Jr.—March-April 1993	45

Source: "The 100 Best-Selling Articles."

The Five Worst Days

Largest One-Day Percentage Drops in the Dow Jones Industrial Average

Date	*Point Loss*	*Percentage Loss*
October 19, 1987	508.00	22.6
October 28, 1929	38.88	12.8
October 29, 1929	30.57	11.7
November 6, 1929	25.55	9.9
December 18, 1899	5.57	8.7

Where Are They Now?

The Fate of Original Dow 12

The Company	Its Fate
American Cotton Oil	Distant ancestor of Bestfoods
American Sugar	Evolved into Amstar Holdings
American Tobacco	Broken up in 1911 antitrust action
Chicago Gas	Absorbed by Peoples Gas, 1897
Distilling & Cattle Feeding	Whiskey trust evolved into Millennium Chemical
General Electric	Still in Dow
Laclede Gas	Still trading; removed from Dow in 1899
National Lead	Now NL Industries, removed from Dow in 1916
North American	Broken up in 1940s
Tennessee Coal & Iron	Absorbed by U.S. Steel in 1907
U.S. Leather (preferred)	Dissolved in 1952
U.S. Rubber	Became Uniroyal, today part of Michelin

The Management Century Timeline

1991

The Dow first closed above 3,000 on April 17—the first of many milestones to be passed in the dust as the decade progresses.

1992

Women's median hourly earnings are 79.4 percent of men's; women's median weekly earnings are 75.4 percent of men's.

Tom Peters's fulsome benchmark for the decade, *Liberation Management*, is published.

1993

Michael Eisner's total income from Disney Corporation in 1993 exceeds $200 million.

IBM posts a record loss of some $8 billion in the 1993 fiscal year. Former McKinsey consultant and turnaround master Lou Gerstner becomes CEO.

This calls to mind an old prediction: "I'm worried that IBM could become a big, inflexible organization which won't be able to change when the computer business goes through its next shift," Thomas Watson Jr. told Chris Argyris of Harvard in the 1950s when Argyris did some work for the company.

On April 2, the U.S. tobacco giant Philip Morris cuts the price of its branded cigarettes—including Marlboro—by 25 percent. A day earlier, people might have thought the company was joking, but this was deadly serious. The day became known as Marlboro Friday. The man behind the decision, Michael Miles, resigns as chairman and chief executive of Philip Morris just over a year later.

NAFTA ratified.

James Champy and Michael Hammer's *Reengineering the Corporation* is published and proclaims a revolution. It becomes the downsizer's bible.

1994

A flaw in Intel's new Pentium processor is a discovered by a math professor. Intel ends up writing off $475 million.

Henry Mintzberg sounds the death knell for traditional strategy with *The Rise and Fall of Strategic Planning.* The new generation of strategy is born with Gary Hamel and C.K. Prahalad's *Competing for the Future.*

1995

The Dow gains 33.5 percent, passing the 4,000 mark for the first time.

Sony Play Station launched.

Disney's *Toy Story* movie debuts—the first completely computer-animated feature film.

A fire rips through Malden Mills's factories leaving over a dozen people hospitalized and the company, it seemed, in ruins. CEO Aaron Feuerstein, the grandson of the company's founder, immediately announces that with no production capacity and no immediate hope of producing anything, he would continue to pay the company's 2,400 employees and pay their health insurance. It was estimated that the commitment to cover the payroll for 90 days and health insurance for 180 days would cost Feuerstein $10 million. Malden Mills is back to virtually full capacity within 90 days.

Disney buys ABC for $19 billion.

1996

The Dow reaches 6,000.

Archer Daniels Midland Co. announces it will pay a record $100 million fine for price fixing.

PC sales outpace the sale of TVs for the first time.

Time Warner acquires CNN, creating the world's largest media company.

The number one status symbol in America, according to a research poll, is . . . a long marriage.

1997

The Dow reaches 8,000.

IBM announces $10 billion in profits.

In largest Wall Street merger ever, Morgan Stanley Group merges with Dean Witter, Discover and Co.

1998

The Dow reaches 9,000.

The market valuation of Microsoft passes that of the mighty GE, to become America's biggest company with a market value of $262 billion.

1999

Dow closes above 10,000 points for first time.

Chapter 11
The State of Management

It is no longer sufficient to have one person learning for the organization, a Ford or a Sloan or a Watson. It's just not possible any longer to "figure it out" from the top, and have everybody else following the orders of the "grand strategist." The organizations that will truly excel in the future will be the organizations that discover how to tap people's commitment and capacity to learn at all levels in an organization.

—PETER SENGE[1]

Living and Dying by Ideas

As a profession management is uniquely placed. It is a profession driven by ideas. The emerging professional and practical agenda is as much set by business schools, consulting firms, and the array of gurus as by practitioners.

That there is skepticism about a great many of today's managerial ideas cannot be doubted. Managerial thinking is tainted with ever greater hype and hyperbole. The emerging agenda can be seen as driven by the media as much as by the research interests of academics or the needs of business. Depending on your perspective, this can be attributed to the substantial financial rewards available for those with the next bright idea to sweep the globe, or as a sign of ever-increasing desperation among managers to find ways in which they can make sense of the business world. Alternatively, and more positively, you can regard the merry-go-round of ideas as an indication of just how vital effective management is to the economies and people of the world.

Though there is clearly cynicism from executives who receive a deluge of material on how best to run their businesses, reading through the stream of management books you can detect some degree of consensus. No book is now complete without a fresh interpretation of ABB's remarkable performance under Percy Barnevik; GE's Jack Welch is feted and analyzed; Dell is examined and heads are shaken; Toyota's production methods are looked at in wonderment. At least when IBM was the premier corporate model you know where you stood. Now we have ABB, which has a structure that works exceptionally well but that few seem to understand—even if they work for ABB; GE, which appears to have been reinvented through the drive and imagination of a single individual (and one who has, against all the prevailing wisdom, spent decades with a single employer); Dell, which cuts out the middlemen while other e-businesses insert them; and Toyota, which manages to remain elusive, always one step ahead.

Managers yearn for clear, unequivocal messages, but that is no longer what they receive. They are saturated with reports and books on creating the global organization but are still asking, What does it mean? When it comes to the huge international corporations detailed in case study after case study our knowledge is extensive but highly fragmented.

There is a feeling that these companies possess something, but no one can quite encapsulate the entire message. There is no one great management book—though Peter Drucker has come pretty close to providing it. What one commentator pompously labeled "the over-arching meta-narrative" is usually notable by its absence. Management continues to defy the theorists who would like to guide it into a corner and nail it down. It continues to escape. It continues to slip though fingers.

The consequence of this is that managers are on a constant quest for new ideas, new interpretations, and new corporate cures. Inevitably, they consume a fair number of placebos along the way. Yet it is this quest for knowledge that marks management apart as a discipline. Fifty-year-old lawyers can afford to sit back and contemplate their bedrock of knowledge, knowing that updating it will be an occasional chore. Managers have no such luxury. Fifty-year-old managers *can* look back and contemplate their knowledge. If they do so, they will quickly find themselves out of a job. Management demands change and constant development. There is no hiding place. Updating knowledge is a continuing necessity.

Management, therefore, has become increasingly committed to the entire concept of learning. Albert Vicere and Robert Fulmer, two business professors from Penn State, calculate that businesses worldwide spend more than $100 billion on training their employees every year. Dauntingly, Vicere and Fulmer also estimate that over half of this is wasted as much is carried out with no objective. The global executive education market has been calculated to be worth in excess of $12 billion. Business schools are believed to account for approximately one-quarter of the total—about $3 billion.

If you add on all the many millions spent on management and business education at degree level, the figures become even more impressive—in 1995–96, 227,102 bachelor degrees in business were awarded in the United States. One survey, by management consultants Linkage Inc., concluded that $250 billion is spent annually on executive development. A McKinsey/Harvard report in 1995 found that the nondegree executive education market alone generated around $3.3 billion and was growing at 10 percent to 12 percent annually. Given the fragmented nature of the market this may well err on the conservative side.

The profusion of training and development is driven by a realization that companies must become "learning organizations" if they are to survive and prosper.

The roots of the concept of the learning organization can be traced to the work of Chris Argyris (born 1923) of Harvard Business School. Argyris was closely involved and greatly influenced by the human relations school of the late 1950s.

Argyris has examined learning processes, both in individual and corporate terms, in huge depth. "Most people define learning too narrowly as mere *problem solving,* so they focus on identifying and correcting errors in the external environment. Solving problems is important, but if learning is to persist managers and employees must also look inward. They need to reflect critically on their own behavior," he says.[2] Problems with learning, as Argyris has revealed, are not restricted to a particular social group. Indeed, it is the very people we expect to be good at learning—teachers, consultants, and other self-selected professionals—who often prove the most inadequate at actually doing so.

Argyris's most influential work was carried out with Donald Schön (most notably in their 1974 *Theory in Practice* and their 1978 *Organizational Learning*). Argyris and Schön originated two basic organizational models. The first was based on the premise that we seek to manipulate and form the world in accordance with our individual aspirations and wishes. In Model 1 managers concentrate on establishing individual goals. They keep to themselves and don't voice concerns or disagreements. The onus is on creating a conspiracy of silence in which everyone dutifully keeps their head down.

Defense is the prime activity in a Model 1 organization, though occasionally the best means of defense is attack. Model 1 managers are prepared to inflict change on others, but resist any attempt to change their own thinking and working practices. Model 1 organizations are characterized by what Argyris and Schön labeled "single-loop learning" ("when the detection and correction of organizational error permits the organization to carry on its present policies and achieve its current objectives").

In contrast, Model 2 organizations emphasized "double-loop learning," which Argyris and Schön described as "when organizational error is detected and corrected in ways that involve the modification of underlying norms, policies, and objectives." In Model 2 organizations, managers act on information. They debate issues and respond—and are prepared—to change. They learn from others. A virtuous circle emerges of learning and understanding. "Most organizations do quite well in single-loop learning but have great difficulties in double-loop learning," concluded Argyris and Schön.

In addition, Argyris and Schön proposed a final form of learning, which offered even greater challenges. This was "deutero-learning," "inquiring into the learning system by which an organization detects and corrects its errors."

While defensiveness has remained endemic, corporate fashions have moved Argyris's way. "Any company that aspires to succeed in the tougher business environment of the 1990s must first resolve a basic dilemma: success in the marketplace increasingly depends on learning, yet most people don't know how to learn. What's more, those members of the organization that many assume to be the best at learning are, in fact, not very good at it," he noted in a 1991 *Harvard Business Review* article.[3]

The entire concept of learning was brought back onto the agenda with the publication and success of the 1990 book, *The Fifth Discipline.* Written by MIT's Peter Senge (born 1947), it looked at how firms and other organizations can develop adaptive capabilities in a world of increasing complexity and rapid change. He argues that vision, purpose, alignment, and systems thinking are essential for organizations. Senge gave managers tools and conceptual archetypes to help them understand the structures and dynamics underlying their organizations' problems. "As the world becomes more interconnected and business becomes more complex and dynamic, work must become more *learningful,*" wrote Senge.

While the phrase "the learning organization" is used with great abandon by other theorists as well as executives, it is rarely fully understood—and it is even more rare to actually find a learning organization. "In the simplest sense, a learning organization is a group of people who are continually enhancing their capability to create their future," explains Senge. "The traditional meaning of the word *learning* is much deeper than just *taking information in.* It is about changing individuals so that they produce results they care about, accomplish things that are important to them."[4]

Senge suggests there are five components to a learning organization:

- Systems thinking
- Personal mastery
- Mental models
- Shared vision
- Team learning

The trouble, in practice, is that the learning organization is often regarded as an instant solution, yet another fad that can be implemented. Earnest attempts to turn it into reality have foundered and disappeared.

Even so, Senge argues that the interest in the concept of the learning organization is proof that institutions and people are ready for major change. Says Senge: "Our traditional ways of managing and governing are breaking down. The demise of General Motors and IBM has one thing in common with the crisis in America's schools and 'gridlock' in Washington—a wake-up call that the world we live in presents unprecedented challenges for which our institutions are ill prepared."[5]

In Search of Values

The quest for ideas and the rise of learning as an important ingredient of organizational life are only part of the changing face of management. Another aspect of this is the growing importance of values in both management thinking and practice. The issue of personal and corporate values is clearly related to that of motivation and loyalty.

If you believe everything you read in the business press, the business world is entirely populated by jargon-speaking free agents, flitting from project to project, from one interesting assignment to the next. According to the fashionable pundits, corporate loyalty is dead. Today's employees are loyal to no one but themselves.

Perhaps, for some, working life really is like that. Meanwhile, back in reality, many millions of people continue to work in much the same way, working much the same hours as they have done for decades.

The champions of free-agency would suggest that remaining with the same organization for ten, fifteen, maybe twenty years is mutually unsatisfactory. The employee becomes jaded, comfortable, and complacent—hardly good news for any organization. The bright and ambitious new arrival is surely preferable to the cynical long-term resident with an eye on retirement and a gift for corporate maneuvering.

The flip side of this is that an organization populated by people whose loyalty is at best fleeting and at worst elsewhere is hardly likely to take the world by storm. Indeed, it is more likely to be riven with political intrigue, uncertainty, and insecurity. Short-term employees have eyes only for the short term; free agents are set on their individual freedom and success rather than team goals. "Mercenaries tend to move on and not become marines. Can you build a company with a mercenary force?" asks Sumantra Ghoshal of London Business School, coauthor of *The Individualized Corporation.*

Luckily, perhaps, the talk of an army of mercenaries appears overblown. Research by Incomes Data Services found that in 1993, 36 percent of men had been with the same employer for ten years or more. This was at the peak of downsizing mania. Interestingly—and surprisingly given the hysterical talk of the emerging promiscuous workforce—in 1968 essentially the same proportion (37.7 percent) of men had been with the same employer for ten years or more.

More research from Business Strategies forecast that 79.2 percent of all employees would be in full-time permanent jobs in 2005—compared with 83.9 percent in 1986. The revolution has been postponed.

For better or worse, people stick around. Even after downsizing, the flurry of demographic time bombs, and talk of Generation X, working life retains a strong element of security. It may be unfashionable to spend thirty years working for a single employer but many people do. Some undoubtedly do so because they have limited opportunities elsewhere, limited ambition, or limited abilities. These are facts of life generally ignored by the free-agent propagandists.

But many choose to stay. They choose to do so presumably because they find their work and working environment stimulating, rewarding, or enjoyable. Indeed, some of the corporate titans of our age are devoted company loyalists. Perhaps the best known is GE's Jack Welch. Feted far and wide as the very model of the modern CEO, Welch joined the company in 1960. No one suggests that his loyalty has been misplaced.

With nearly forty years of service, people like Jack Welch may appear to some as throwbacks to a more naive, even simplistic age. It was never meant to be like that. In the 1970s pundits envisaged the leisure age; in the 1980s they talked of flexible working, a world of teleworkers. Well, the technology now exists and teleworking remains a decidedly minority pursuit. "The failure of teleworking to really catch on, despite the availability of the technology, demonstrates that some sort of a physical relationship is important to people at work. People want to feel part of a team and of something much bigger. They want to be connected," says

Gerry Griffin, director of global PR firm Burson-Marsteller and author of *The Power Game.*[6]

Corporate loyalty is engendered by the fact that conventional working life still holds a remarkable attraction. Its immediacy make business sense. In business, being there remains of crucial importance. The psychological dynamics of business means that conversations in corridors or over coffee actually move the business forward. Managers make an impact, make a difference, and get results by talking to people, walking around, and listening to people. They need to be there and for people to be there. The reality is that people are loyal to the environment they spend every day in and to their colleagues.

While the traditional attractions of office life remain, it is true that companies no longer have an aura of permanence. They change with accelerating regularity. The profusion of joint ventures, mergers, and acquisitions means that people's roles now change more regularly. In the past, people might have filled two or three roles in fifteen years with a company. Now, they are likely to change every three years or so. This, perversely perhaps, can actually encourage people to stay. If you want a fast-moving, stimulating, constantly changing environment, why move when it is happening all around you and you're a player in making it work? If you stay with a company for ten years or more, change will happen. You either develop your own skills and move forward with the organization or you leave.

All this is not to say that the corporate man of the 1950s and 1960s is alive and well. Blind loyalty is undoubtedly dead—and corporate man is now as likely to be corporate woman. Today's employees are more questioning and demanding. They are loyal but confident enough to air their concerns, grievances, and aspirations. If they were customers, we would call them sophisticated. (It is perhaps significant that we tend not to.) People are now more likely to question the action behind the corporate rhetoric. As a result the HR and internal communications functions are much more important than in decades past. Indeed, internal communications has emerged as an industry in its own right, reflecting the need for companies to create communication channels with their own people.

Central to the demanding nature of employees is the notion of values. In the past loyalty was basically bought. Job security, gradual progression up the hierarchy, and a decent salary were offered by the employer. In return, the employee offered unwavering loyalty and a hard day's work. Now, values determine loyalty. "Every organization needs values, but a lean organization needs them even more," GE's Jack Welch says. "When you strip away the support systems of staffs and layers, people have to change their habits and expectations, or else the stress will just overwhelm them."

A report produced by consultants Blessing/White, "Heart and Soul," studies the impact of corporate and individual values on business. "Values have two critical roles: a company that articulates its values enables potential recruits to apply a degree of self-selection. Values also provide a framework to match individual career goals with the organisation's objectives," it observed.

The challenge for organizations is that values are more complex than mere money. Values cannot be simplistically condensed into a mission statement or neatly printed onto an embossed card. In the past there was a belief in one set of values. Now, in more sophisticated companies, there is an awareness that the uniqueness of the firm comes from multiple values and cultures. Previously, people's needs were interpreted as being homogenous. Now there are flexible benefits and working arrangements and recognition that people are motivated by different things. Organizations have to understand what motivates individuals. Money and power don't work for everyone.

With values becoming an increasingly important aspect of loyalty and motivation, it is little wonder that companies are paying them more attention. Indeed, in the modern world, companies are crucial in identifying and developing the values that shape society. The corporation is a value creator in modern society. In our secular world, corporations create belief systems, values people buy into. Companies are the great institutions of our age. In the past, value systems were created by the church and the state. Now companies have distinct and strongly defined value systems that we may—or may not—buy into. The choice is ours.

"Companies increasingly resemble tribes," says Jonas Ridderstråle of the Stockholm School of Economics. "Companies have to find people who share their values. Recruiting is now about finding people with the right attitude, then training them in appropriate and useful skills—rather than the reverse. We can no longer believe in the idea of bringing in smart people and brainwashing them at training camps into believing what is right."[7]

For the better executives clearly there is a choice. They work for companies that are in accord with their own value systems. If they don't want to work for a polluter, they will not. After all, people want to hold their heads up when they are with their peers. They don't want an embarrassed silence when they announce who they work for. Who gets out of bed in the morning for a distant corporate objective? If a company gives its people real meaning to their work and the freedom and resources to pursue their ideas, then it's a good place to be. Values are the new route to developing loyalty among employees. Loyalty is not dead, it simply must be earned and, increasingly, earned in different ways.

Corporate Mortality

Implicit in all this is the notion that companies and individuals that fail to learn or identify appealing values will cease to exist. In the disposable society, companies and executives are more disposable than ever before.

This has led to a variety of lines of inquiry. First, there are those who argue that corporate mortality is a healthy thing. Over ten years, Andrew Campbell of the Ashridge Strategic Management Centre and his fellow U.K. researchers have exhaustively examined the role of corporate parents. (Work by Cynthia Montgomery and David Collins at Harvard Business School and C.K. Prahalad and Yves Doz of France's INSEAD has also pursued this line of research.) "Parent companies are competing with each other for the right to parent businesses. They need to offer parenting advantage for their existence to be justified. And parenting advantage can only come from doing things differently from other parents. Corporate parents, therefore, must offer unique and specialist skills and knowledge," says Campbell. The trouble is that the rise of the professional general manager encourages corporate parents, and corporate managers, to be alike rather than different. "The manager is a hero in the Western world, but an impostor," says Campbell. "The concept of management has proved a huge distraction. The management side of running a company is trivial compared to the importance of being commercial or entrepreneurial, or having a particular specialist skill. Any organization needs to have people with the skills relevant to its business rather than concentrating on turning the marketing director into a rounded general manager."[8]

Indeed, Campbell goes on to suggest that we have become preoccupied with creating immortal organizations rather than ones that work in the present. "Why do we want organizations to thrive for ever?" he asks. "On average organizations survive for less time than the working life of an individual. They become dysfunctional and, at that point, they should be killed off. What is encouraging is that, first through management buy-outs and now through demergers, we are becoming more adept at bringing an end to corporate lives which have run their course and creating new organizations in their place."

The second line of inquiry is to examine what leads to corporate longevity. The most notable works in this field are Arie de Geus's *Living Company* and Jerry Porras and Jim Collins's *Built to Last*.

Central to these books is the idea that the corporation is an important institution that needs to live for capitalist society to thrive. The trouble is that though companies may be legal entities, they are disturbingly mortal. "The natural average lifespan of a corporation should be as long as two or three centuries," writes de Geus, noting a few prospering relics such as the Sumitomo Group and the Scandinavian company, Stora.[9] But the reality is that companies do not head off into the Florida sunset to play bingo. They usually die young.

De Geus quotes a Dutch survey of corporate life expectancy in Japan and Europe that came up with 12.5 years as the average life expectancy of all firms. "The average life expectancy of a multinational corporation—Fortune 500 or its equivalent—is between 40 and 50 years," says de Geus, noting that one-third of 1970's Fortune 500 had disappeared by 1983. Such endemic failure is attributed by de Geus to the focus of managers on profits and the bottom line rather than the human community that makes up their organization.

In an attempt to get to the bottom of this mystery, de Geus and a number of his colleagues at the Shell Oil Company carried out some research to identify the characteristics of corporate longevity. As you would expect, the onus is on keeping excitement to a minimum. More Ronald Reagan than James Dean. The average human centenarian advocates a life of abstinence, caution, and moderation, and so it is with companies. The Royal Dutch–Shell team identified four key characteristics. The long-lived were "sensitive to their environment," "cohesive, with a strong sense of identity," "tolerant," and "conservative in financing." (These conclusions are echoed in *Built to Last*.)

Key to the entire argument that companies deserve and need to live is that there is more to them—and to their longevity—than mere money making. "The dichotomy between profits and longevity is false," says de Geus. The logic is impeccably straightforward. Capital is no longer king; the skills, capabilities, and knowledge of people are. The corollary of this is that "a successful company is one that can learn effectively." Learning is tomorrow's capital. In de Geus's eyes, learning means being prepared to accept continuous change.

Here, de Geus provides the new deal: contemporary corporate man or woman must understand that the corporation will, and must, change and it can only change if its community of people change also. "Built to last now means built to change," say Stan Davis and Christopher Meyer in their book, *Blur*. Individuals must change and the way they change is through learning. As a result, de Geus believes, senior executives must dedicate a great deal of time to nurturing their people. He recalls spending around a quarter of his time on the development and placement of people. Jack Welch claims to spend half of his time on such issues.

According to de Geus, all corporate activities are grounded in two hypotheses: "The company is a living being; and the decisions for action made by this living being result from a learning process." This faith in learning represents a considered and powerful riposte to the corporate nihilism of the early nineties. The wisdom of the past must be appreciated and utilized rather than cast out in some cultural revolution. Contrast this with reengineering, which (as practiced, if not necessarily preached) sought to dismiss the past so that the future could be begun anew with a fresh piece of paper. Thinkers like Arie de Geus suggest that the piece of paper already exists and notes are constantly being scrawled in the margins as new insights are added.

From Certainty to Chaos

A manager may have consumed the works of all the leading theorists and may have all the market information within easy reach. But what if the manager is charged with relaunching a product that previously failed; a product that costs the manager's company $7 to produce when its competitors produce it for a few cents? Such situations are now commonplace. Managers are surrounded by data and information, opinions and surefire solutions, time pressures and financial constraints. They consider various four- and nine-box models. They think of the long term and are under unrelenting short-term pressure. They decide whether something is strategic or tactical, a goal or an objective. It is intellectually stimulating and it fills flip charts, but it does not solve the problem.

What managers want—and believe they need if they are to keep their jobs—is to make the best decisions possible using the best data available and then to get others to put the solution into practice. In an earlier era this was achievable. Now complexity, choice, and confusion abound.

If the sanctity of corporate life is now open to debate it is just another sign that although management thinking once provided a healthy diet of answers, it now produces confusion and yet more questions. The debate about outsourcing, for example, is expanding from the simple cost benefits to contemplation of its repercussions for the nature of the organization—boundaryless and more abstract than ever before, it is difficult to determine where, why, and how the organization begins and ends.

Increasingly, attention is focusing on the nature of the questions rather than the pithiness of the answers. Indeed, many would argue that there are no longer any answers. Here, managers find themselves in the uncomfortable and discomfiting world of chaos and complexity theory. There is much talk of fractals and cognitive dissonance; uncertainty and ambiguity are the new realities. Organizational metaphors have metamorphosed. The organization was once talked of in mechanical terms. Now it is variously described through natural and scientific metaphors as an amoeba or a random pattern.

Is such theory mere metaphorical color or is it practically useful? Reaching a definitive conclusion on this is impossible—though, theorists suggest, that is just the sort of thing that managers will have to become used to. "Complexity theory is intriguing. Going beyond the metaphor is the trouble," observes Richard Pascale.[10] Others insist that complexity is not simply a metaphor. Ralph Stacey, author of *Complexity and Creativity*, says: "Complexity is an effective metaphor and practically useful. Everything's a metaphor. It's not possible to make sense of anything apart from through a paradigm. It is a different way of making sense of human systems and so it is more important than another recipe or technique. Some people are quite hostile because acceptance of complexity undermines their way of thinking. To others it is a release."[11]

Systems thinking, the concept that all the activities in an organization are interlinked, fits comfortably with other popular notions of global networks and transnational organizations. It all fits in some way, it's simply that we do not have a master plan to reassemble it in the right way.

Where this leaves aspiring or practicing managers is a matter of lively conjecture. They are, according to different commentators, fearful of the uncertainty now surrounding them or upbeat and set on making themselves indispensable in the managerial marketplace. In reality, there is no stereotypical situation or attitude. Instead, there are a bewildering array of options, tools, techniques, new ideas, and old ideas. Either/or questions have become either/and. The free-wheeling pragmatism offered by some offers all the answers and yet none at all. There is a thin line between order and chaos. That line is likely to become ever more blurred and indistinct in the years to come.

The Management Century: Tale of the Tape

Other Statistics

	1900	*1998*
World population	1.6 billion	5.9 billion
Worldwide car sales	4,000	54 million
Average U.S. earnings (weekly)	$9.70	$435

Source: Time, April 13, 1998.

A Century of Slogans

Coca-Cola Advertising Slogans Through the Twentieth Century

1904:   Delicious and refreshing
1905:   Coca-Cola Revives and Sustains
1906:   The Great National Temperance Drink
1917:   Three Million A Day
1922:   Thirst Knows No Season
1925:   Six Million A Day
1927:   Around the Corner From Everywhere
1929:   The Pause That Refreshes
1932.   Ice-cold Sunshine
1938:   The Best Friend Thirst Ever Had
1939:   Coca-Cola Goes Along
1942:   Wherever You Are, Whatever You Do, Wherever You May Be, When You
        Think of Refreshment, Think of Ice-Cold Coca-Cola
1942:   The Only Thing Like Coca-Cola Is Coca-Cola Itself. It's The Real Thing.
1948:   Where There's Coke, There's Hospitality
1949:   Coca-Cola . . . Along the Highway to Anywhere
1952:   What You Want Is A Coke
1956:   Coca-Cola . . . Making Good Things Taste Better
1957:   Sign of Good Taste
1958:   The Cold, Crisp Taste of Coke
1959:   Be Really Refreshed
1963:   Things Go Better With Coke
1970:   It's The Real Thing
1971:   I'd Like To Buy The World A Coke
1975:   Look Up America
1976:   Coke Adds Life
1979:   Have A Coke And Smile
1982:   Coke Is It!
1985:   We've Got A Taste For You
1986:   Catch The Wave
1989:   Can't Beat The Feeling
1990:   Can't Beat The Real Thing
1993:   Always Coca-Cola

Notes

Preface

1. Max Ways, "Tomorrow's management: A more adventurous life in a free-form corporation," *Fortune*, July 1966.
2. Peter Drucker, "Management's new paradigms," *Forbes*, October 5, 1998.
3. Lawrence A. Cunningham, *The Essays of Warren Buffett*, New York: Cardozo Law Review, 1998.
4. Sumantra Ghoshal, Christopher Bartlett, & Peter Moran, "A new manifesto for management," *Sloan Management Review*, Spring 1999.

Chapter 1

1. Frederick W. Taylor, *The Principles of Scientific Management*, New York: Harper Brothers, 1911, p. 70.
2. Warren Zimmermann, "Jingoes, goo-gooes, and the rise of America's empire," *Wilson Quarterly*, Spring 1998.
3. Grenville M. Dodge, *Report of the Commission Appointed by the President to Investigate the Conduct of the War Department in the War with Spain*, Washington, D.C.: Government Printing Office, 1899, p. 44.
4. Philip C. Jessup, *Elihu Root*, New York: Dodd, Mead, 1938, Vol. 1, p. 244; John L. Sutton, "The German general staff in U.S. defense policy," *Military Affairs*, Winter 1961–62, p. 197.
5. U.S. Congress, Senate, Committee on Military Affairs, "Efficiency of the Army," 57th Congress, 1st Session, 1902, 13, 17–18.

6. Peter Drucker, "Management's new paradigms," *Forbes,* October 5, 1998.

7. Dictionary definitions did not help a great deal. The *Concise Oxford Dictionary* of the time dismissed management as "trickery, deceitful contrivance."

8. Greenkeepers or unhappy putters may consult the full details of how this can be achieved by digging out Taylor's series of articles on the subject—"The making of a putting green"—published in 1915 issues of *Country Life.*

9. Memorial service for Frederick Taylor, Philadelphia, 1915.

10. Memorial service for Frederick Taylor.

11. Claude S. George, *History of Management Thought,* Upper Saddle River, N.J.: Prentice Hall, 1972.

12. Taylor was highly involved in the Society for the Promotion of Engineering Education and strongly supported the notion that college education should include a year's industrial experience.

13. The title of scientific management was reputedly decided on by a small group of engineers and thinkers who met in 1910 in New York. They included the lawyer Louis Brandeis (1856–1941) and Henry Gantt. Among the alternative titles considered were shop management, efficiency, functional management, and the Taylor system.

14. Alan Farnham, "The man who changed work forever," *Fortune,* July 21, 1997, p. 114.

15. Farnham, "The man who changed work forever."

16. T. P. Hughes, *American Genesis,* New York: Penguin Books, 1989, p. 190.

17. Taylor, *The Principles of Scientific Management,* p. 66.

18. John Dos Passos, *U.S.A. Book 3: Big Money,* New York: Harcourt, Brace, 1936, p. 24.

19. Peter Drucker, *The Effective Executive,* New York: Harper & Row, 1967.

20. Tom Lloyd, "Giant with feet of clay," *Financial Times,* December 5, 1994.

21. Charles Lucier & Janet Torsilieri, "The end of overhead," *Strategy & Business,* Second Quarter 1999.

22. Peter Drucker, "Knowledge-worker productivity: The biggest challenge," *California Management Review,* Winter 1999.

23. Taylor, *The Principles of Scientific Management,* pp. 5–29.

24. Taylor, *The Principles of Scientific Management,* p. 66.

25. Taylor, *The Principles of Scientific Management,* p. 69.

26. Wright's paper, originally given as an address before the American Social Science Association, bore the title "The Factory System as an Element in Civilization."

27. Antonio Gramsci, *Americanismo e Fordismo,* Milan: Universale Economica, 1949.

28. Taylor, *The Principles of Scientific Management.*

29. Taylor, *The Principles of Scientific Management,* pp. 52–53.

30. Memorial service for Frederick Taylor.

31. Ed Andrew, *Closing the Iron Cage: The Scientific Management of Work and Leisure,* Montreal: Black Rose, 1981, pp. 93–94.

32. Carl G. Barth, "Testimony of Carl G. Barth," Hearings of the U.S. Commissions on Industrial Relations, 64th Congress, 1st Session, Senate Doc. 26 (Ser. Vol. 6929), April 1914, p. 889.

Chapter 2

1. Henry Ford, *My Life and Work,* London: Heinemann, 1923, pp. 78–79.

2. Interestingly, Henry Ford's interest in production had first been ignited by watchmaking. In his teens his ambition was to make $1 watches.

3. Ford, *My Life and Work,* p. 80.

4. Ford, *My Life and Work.*

5. Ford, *My Life and Work.*

6. Ford, *My Life and Work,* p. 81.

7. William Abernathy, *The Productivity Dilemma: Roadblock to Innovation in the Automobile Industry,* Baltimore: Johns Hopkins University Press, 1978; David Hounshell, *From the American System to Mass Production, 1880–1932,* Baltimore: Johns Hopkins University Press, 1984.

8. Alfred P. Sloan, *Adventures of a White-Collar Man,* New York: Doubleday, Doran, 1941.

9. In *The Visible Hand: The Managerial Revolution in American Business* (Cambridge, Mass.: Belknap, 1977), Alfred Chandler argues that Ford vertically integrated for two reasons. First, it was the next logical step after mastering mass production. Doing it himself could reap economies of scale. Second, coordination was impossible unless Ford did it himself. He did not trust accountants nor managers to carry this out.

10. Ford, *My Life and Work,* p. 111.

11. Ford, *My Life and Work,* p. 128.

12. Ford, *My Life and Work,* p. 129.

13. These were the days when a car's name was of limited interest to makers. The Model A was a triumph of laziness over creativity.

14. Richard Grudens, "Industrialist Henry Ford helped lead American war production," www.thehistorynet.com/WorldWarII/articles/1997/01974_text.htm, accessed April 29, 1999.

15. B. Ramirez, *When Workers Fight: The Politics of Industrial Relations in the Progressive Era, 1898–1916,* Westport, Conn.: Greenwood Press, 1978.

16. Frank Gilbreth and Lilian Gilbreth, *Fatigue Study,* Easton, Md.: Hive, 1973, p. 149. (Originally published 1916.)

17. Alan Farnham, "The Man Who Changed Work Forever," *Fortune,* July 21, 1997.

Chapter 3

1. Alfred P. Sloan, *Adventures of a White-Collar Man,* New York: Doubleday Doran, 1941, pp. 132–133.
2. Max Weber, *The Theory of Social and Economic Organizations,* (transl. A. M. Henderson and Talcott Parsons), New York: Oxford University Press, 1947, p. 338.
3. Weber, *The Theory of Social and Economic Organizations.*
4. Russel Robb, *Lectures on Organization,* privately printed, 1910, p. 14.
5. Tom Peters & Robert Waterman, *In Search of Excellence,* New York: Harper & Row, 1982.
6. Chester Barnard, *The Functions of the Executive,* Cambridge, Mass.: Harvard University Press, 1938.
7. Buick's career plummeted. He eventually died, impoverished, working as a clerk in Detroit.
8. Sloan, *Adventures of a White-Collar Man,* p. 84.
9. Gilbert Burck, "DuPont under pressure," *Fortune,* November 1967.
10. The Buick City car plant in Flint closed in June 1999. Between 1906 and 1999, it produced nearly 16 million cars and once employed 28,000 people.
11. Sloan, *Adventures of a White-Collar Man,* p. 120.
12. Sloan, *Adventures of a White-Collar Man,* p. 85.
13. Sloan, *Adventures of a White-Collar Man,* p. 107.
14. In 1937 Sloan became chairman of General Motors. He continued as chief executive until 1946. He resigned from the chairmanship in 1956, and became honorary chairman until his death in 1966.
15. Peter Drucker, "Alfred P. Sloan's role," *Fortune,* July 1964.
16. Dan Cordtz, "The face in the mirror at General Motors," *Fortune,* August 1966.
17. "The changing nature of leadership," *Economist,* June 10, 1995.
18. Sumantra Ghoshal & Christopher Bartlett, *Financial Times Handbook of Management,* London: FT/Pitman, 1995.
19. *Fortune's Favorites,* New York: Knopf, 1931.
20. Alex Taylor, "Is Jack Smith the man to fix GM?" *Fortune,* August 3, 1998.
21. Peter Drucker, "Management's new paradigms," *Forbes,* October 5, 1998.

Chapter 4

1. Mary Parker Follett, *The New State,* New York: Longmans, Green, 1918, p. 230.
2. Wartime has provided a range of influences on management thinkers: Frederick Herzberg was deeply affected by the Dachau concentration camp, Edgar Schein studied the brainwashing of prisoners of war during the Korean War, Tom Peters served in Vietnam.

3. Fritz Roethlisberger, *The Elusive Phenomena* (edited by George Lombard), Cambridge, Mass.: Harvard University Press, 1977, p. 30.

4. Western Electric closed the Hawthorne Works in 1983.

5. Elton Mayo, *The Social Problems of an Industrial Civilization,* Cambridge, Mass.: Harvard University Press, 1945, p. 111.

6. The 1930s went some way to redressing the balance. The number of unionized companies in the United States grew fivefold between 1933 and 1945 and, by 1935, 64 percent of large companies had personnel practices in place.

7. Elton Mayo, *The Human Problems of an Industrial Civilization,* Cambridge, Mass.: Harvard University Press, 1933, p. 40.

8. Fritz Roethlisberger, "Introduction." In Mayo, *The Human Problems of an Industrial Civilization,* New York: Viking, 1960, p. xiii.

9. At the same time, it is worth noting that women's fortunes were on the rise in the 1930s. Frances Perkins was the first female member of the U.S. cabinet, Anna Rosenberg was the first senior woman manager at a U.S. corporation, R.H. Macy, and there were also Amelia Earhart and Eleanor Roosevelt.

10. Mary Parker Follett, *Dynamic Administration* (edited by Elliot Fox & Lyndall Urwick), New York: Harper Brothers, 1940.

11. Follett, *Dynamic Administration,* p. 235.

12. Richard Pascale, *Managing on the Edge,* London: Penguin Books, 1990.

13. Follett, *Dynamic Administration,* p. 304.

14. Follett, *Dynamic Administration,* p. 303.

15. Follett, *Dynamic Administration,* p. 255.

16. *Time,* "Man of the year," January 1, 1934.

17. *Time,* "Man of the year," January 1, 1934.

18. *Fortune's Favorites,* New York: Knopf, 1931.

Chapter 5

1. Nearly 40 percent of the debt was paid for by taxation and war bonds.

2. Report of the Secretary of the Treasury, 1954.

3. The involvement of carmakers in the war effort had a long-term legacy in terms of car design. The 1955 Chevy was designed by GM's chief World War Two tank engineer and GM designer Harley Earl was inspired by the tailfins of fighter planes. The result was the 1959 fin fiesta, the Cadillac Eldorado Seville.

4. The downside was, of course, that once the war finished, companies had to rethink their futures. At Hewlett-Packard, for example, the business flourished during wartime—employing 144 people at its height. Immediately after the war, sales fell off—by half in 1946 alone. Undaunted,

Hewlett and Packard hired technical talent. The business revived. By 1948 the company's sales were $2.1 million.

5. Likert later identified four main styles of management and categorized them as System 1, the exploitative-authoritative system, System 2, the benevolent-authoritative system, System 3, the consultative system, and System 4, the participative group system.

6. At times American soldiers were also walking advertisements—it helped Levi Strauss a great deal that American soldiers enjoyed their R&R in Europe wearing Levi's.

7. W. Edwards Deming, speech delivered in Tokyo, Japan, November 1985.

8. In 1993 Sony wrote off $3.2 billion for its movie operations—the major misadventure in its history.

9. Andrew Gordon, *Contests for the Workplace in Postwar Japan,* Princeton, N.J.: Princeton University Press, 1993, p. 378.

Chapter 6

1. Max Ways, "The postwar advance of the 500 million," *Fortune,* August 1964.

2. Michael T. Kaufman, "William H. Whyte obituary," *New York Times,* January 13, 1999.

3. Henry R. Luce, "The first thirty-five years of *Fortune,*" *Fortune,* February 1965.

4. Noel Tichy & Stratford Sherman, *Control Your Destiny or Someone Else Will,* New York: Currency Doubleday, 1993.

5. Tichy & Sherman, *Control Your Destiny or Someone Else Will.*

6. Interview with author.

7. The company had been known as IBM in Canada since 1917.

8. Thomas Watson, *A Business and Its Beliefs,* New York: McGraw-Hill, 1963.

9. Peter Drucker, *The Practice of Management,* New York: Harper & Row, 1954.

10. More recently, two academics have moved up the alphabet, suggesting the "RS-model" of content, context, and infrastructure.

11. Ted Levitt, "Marketing myopia 1975: Retrospective commentary," *Harvard Business Review,* September-October 1975.

12. In 1979, Wilson gave control of Holiday Inn to his two sons. Since then, Holiday Inn has been controlled by a number of corporate names. Holiday Inn is now part of the large U.K.-based leisure and entertainment group, Bass, which is owner or franchiser of over 2,600 Inter-Continental, Crowne Plaza, Holiday Inn, Holiday Inn Express, and Staybridge Suites.

Holiday Inn remains the most widely recognized lodging brand in the world. Bass is now building what it labels the "Holiday Inn of the Future."

13. Abraham Maslow, *Motivation and Personality,* New York: Harper & Row, 1954.

14. Abraham Maslow, *Eupsychian Management,* Homewood, Ill.: Irwin-Dorsey, 1965.

15. Abraham Maslow, *Eupsychian Management.*

16. Abraham Maslow, *Eupsychian Management.*

17. "An interview with Frederick Herzberg: Managers or animal trainers?" *Management Review,* 1971, pp. 2–5.

18. Abraham Maslow, *Eupsychian Management.*

Chapter 7

1. B. H. Liddell Hart, *Strategy,* New York: Praeger, 1967, pp. 343–344.

2. John Keegan, *The Mask of Command,* New York: Penguin Books, 1987, p. 149.

3. The authorship of *The Art of War* remains, perhaps understandably, clouded in mystery. It may have been written by Sun Wu, a military general who was alive around 500 B.C. His book is reputed to have led to a meeting between Sun Wu and King Ho-lü of Wu. The book's actual title is *Sun Tzu Ping Fa,* which can be literally translated as "The military method of venerable Mr. Sun."

4. Carl von Clausewitz, *On War,* Princeton, N.J.: Princeton University Press, 1984. (Originally published 1831.)

5. Von Clausewitz, *On War,* p. 182.

6. Tom Peters, *Liberation Management,* New York: Knopf, 1992.

7. Stuart Crainer, *The Ultimate Business Library,* Oxford, England: Capstone, 1996.

8. RAND, an acronym for Research and Development, was an American military think tank established after the war.

9. Max Ways, "Tomorrow's management: A more adventurous life in a free-form corporation," *Fortune,* July 1966.

10. Stanley H. Brown, "How one man can move a corporate mountain," *Fortune,* July 1966.

11. Brown, "How one man can move a corporate mountain."

12. Carol Loomis, "Harold Geneen's moneymaking machine is still humming," *Fortune,* September 1972.

13. Robert Lubar, "The Japanese giant that wouldn't stay dead," *Fortune,* November 1964.

14. "The massive statistics of General Motors," *Wall Street Journal,* July 15, 1966.

Chapter 8

1. Judson Gooding, "The fraying white collar," *Fortune,* December 1970.
2. Rowan Gibson (editor), *Rethinking the Future,* London: Brealey, 1997.
3. "Alvin Toffler: Still shocking after all these years," *New Scientist,* March 19, 1994.
4. Henry R. Luce, "The first thirty-five years of *Fortune,*" *Fortune,* February 1965.
5. Gooding, "The fraying white collar."
6. Michael Poole, *Industrial Relations: Origins and Patterns of National Diversity,* London: Routledge, 1986, pp. 129–130.
7. Interview with author.
8. Interview with author.
9. "Here Comes the Boss," BBC Radio Four, August 1, 1997.
10. Interview with author.
11. Correspondence with author.

Chapter 9

1. W. Edwards Deming, *Out of the Crisis,* London: Mercury, 1986.
2. Clare Crawford-Mason, "The discovery of the prophet of quality," *SPC INK* (newsletter published by Statistical Process Controls Inc., Knoxville, Tenn.), Fall 1992.
3. Crawford-Mason,"The discovery of the prophet of quality."
4. Robert Hayes & William Abernathy, "Managing our way to economic decline," *Harvard Business Review,* July/August 1980.
5. "Around the globe," *Fortune,* July 1964.
6. "Around the globe."
7. "Around the globe."
8. "Around the globe."
9. American companies had, to be fair, taken an interest in how the Japanese had managed to rebuild their economy. Shortly before Deming's TV appearance, teams from Ford and Pontiac visited Japan to see how Japanese carmakers organized themselves. They found exactly what they expected to find, and noticed none of the patterns Deming described.
10. Richard Pascale & Anthony Athos, *The Art of Japanese Management,* New York: Simon & Schuster, 1981.
11. Pascale & Athos, *The Art of Japanese Management.*
12. Tom Peters & Robert Waterman, *In Search of Excellence,* New York: Harper & Row, 1982.
13. Deming, *Out of the Crisis.*
14. Christopher Reed, "A profit in his own country," *Observer,* January 9, 1994.
15. Deming, *Out of the Crisis.*

16. Kodak Annual Report 1984.

17. John Kay, "Why gurus should cross the bridge into business," *Financial Times,* November 17, 1997.

18. Robert Waterman & Lewis Young, "Speaking of excellence," *McKinsey Quarterly,* Winter 1984.

19. Stuart Crainer, *The Ultimate Business Library,* Oxford, England: Capstone, 1996.

20. Peters & Waterman, *In Search of Excellence,* p. xxv.

21. Interview with author.

22. Peters & Waterman, *In Search of Excellence,* p. xxiv.

23. "Moss Kanter, corporate sociologist," *Economist,* October 15, 1994.

24. "Moss Kanter, corporate sociologist."

25. Victoria Griffith, "It's a people thing," *Financial Times,* July 24, 1997.

26. Warren Bennis, *An Invented Life,* Wokingham, England: Addison Wesley, 1993.

27. Interview with author, December 1997.

28. Quoted in Stuart Crainer, "Doing the right thing," *Director,* October 1988.

Chapter 10

1. Tom Peters, *Liberation Management,* New York: Knopf, 1992.

2. Kevin Barham & Claudia Heimer, *ABB: The Dancing Giant,* London: FT/Pitman, 1998.

3. Barham & Heimer, *ABB: The Dancing Giant.*

4. Barham & Heimer, *ABB: The Dancing Giant.*

5. Richard Pascale, *Managing on the Edge,* New York: Simon & Schuster, 1990.

6. Jerry Porras & James Collins, *Built to Last,* New York: Century, 1997.

7. Elfun Society History, www.elfun.org, accessed May 1, 1999.

8. D. Hambrick & G.D.S. Fukotoni, "The seasons of a CEO's tenure," *Academy of Management Review,* 1991, *16*(4).

9. Richard Pascale, *Managing on the Edge,* New York: Simon & Schuster, 1990.

10. Pascale, *Managing on the Edge.*

11. Pascale, *Managing on the Edge.*

12. Albert Vicere & Robert Fulmer, *Leadership By Design,* Boston: Harvard Business School Press, 1998.

13. General Electric Annual General Meeting, 1990.

14. Janet Lowe, *Jack Welch Speaks,* New York: Wiley, 1998.

15. John Byrne, "How Jack Welch runs GE," *BusinessWeek,* June 8, 1998.

16. Lowe, *Jack Welch Speaks.*

17. Max Ways, "Tomorrow's management: A more adventurous life in a free-form corporation," *Fortune,* July 1966.
18. Author interview. See Thomas Stewart, *Intellectual Capital,* London: Brealey, 1997.

Chapter 11

1. Peter Senge, *The Fifth Discipline,* New York: Doubleday, 1990.
2. Chris Argyris, "Teaching smart people how to learn," *Harvard Business Review,* May-June 1991.
3. Argyris, "Teaching smart people how to learn."
4. Quoted in K. Napuk, "Live and learn," *Scottish Business Insider,* January 1994.
5. Peter Senge, "A growing wave of interest and openness," Applewood Internet site, 1997.
6. Author interview.
7. Author interview.
8. Author interview.
9. Arie De Geus, *The Living Company,* Boston: Harvard Business School Press, 1997.
10. Author interview.
11. Author interview.

The Author

Stuart Crainer is the editor of *The Financial Times Handbook of Management*. He is also the author of *The Tom Peters Phenomenon* (the biography of the management guru), *The Ultimate Business Library, Key Management Ideas*, and a number of other books. His work appears in the *Financial Times* and leading business magazines, including *Business Life, Human Resources, Across the Board*, and *Strategy & Business*.

Crainer is cofounder of the media content, concepts, and consulting firm Suntop Media.

Name Index

Subject Index

Booz·Allen & Hamilton

Booz·Allen & Hamilton is one of the world's leading international management and technology consulting firms, providing services in strategy, systems, operations, and technology to clients in more than seventy-five countries around the globe.

Founded in 1914, Booz·Allen & Hamilton pioneered the business of management consulting. Today, Booz·Allen has more than nine thousand employees in one hundred offices on six continents with sales exceeding $1.6 billion. Its client base comprises a majority of the world's largest industrial and service corporations, as well as major institutions and government bodies around the world, including most U.S. federal departments and agencies.

Booz·Allen is a private corporation organized into two major business sectors: the Worldwide Commercial Business (WCB) and the Worldwide Technology Business (WTB). WCB clients are primarily major international corporations; WTB generally serves governmental clients both in the United States and abroad.

Booz·Allen helps senior management solve complex problems through its expertise in more than two dozen industries as well as information technology, operations management, and strategic leadership.

Consistent with its position as a business thought leader, Booz·Allen publishes the award-winning quarterly journal, *Strategy & Business,* which reports on the latest developments in global management techniques, competitive tactics, and strategic thinking.

For more information, please visit Booz·Allen's Website at www.bah.com or contact the company at:

Booz·Allen & Hamilton
101 Park Ave.
New York, NY 10178
(212) 697–1900

This *Strategy & Business* book is an excellent business relationship-building tool. By giving this book to your clients, partners, and prospects, you can contribute to their knowledge in a business world where staying current is the only lasting competitive edge. Receive substantial quantity discounts when you place bulk orders. Let us personalize the books with your message.

For quantity discounts and customized orders, contact:

Bernadette Walter
Corporate Sales Manager
Jossey-Bass Publishers
350 Sansome Street
San Francisco, CA 94104–1342
phone: (415) 782–3122
fax: (415) 433–0499
e-mail: bwalter@jbp.com

MORE STRATEGY & BUSINESS BOOKS FROM BOOZ•ALLEN & HAMILTON

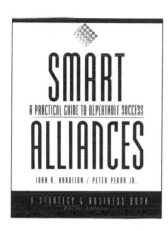

SMART ALLIANCES
A Practical Guide to Repeatable Success
John R. Harbison, Peter Pekar Jr.
Hardcover   208 pages
ISBN 0-7879-4326-6 $35.00

BALANCED SOURCING
Cooperation and Competition in Supplier Relationships
Timothy M. Laseter
Hardcover   288 pages
ISBN 0-7879-4443-2 $40.00

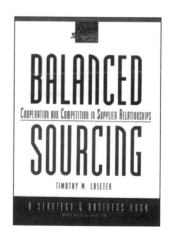

More Strategy & Business Books
from Booz·Allen & Hamilton

THOUGHT LEADERS
Insights on the Future of Business
Joel Kurtzman, Editor
Hardcover   192 pages
ISBN 0-7879-3903-X $27.00

CHANNEL CHAMPIONS
**How Leading Companies Build New
Strategies to Serve Customers**
Steven Wheeler, Evan Hirsh
Hardcover   256 pages
ISBN 0-7879-5034-3 $35.00

AVAILABLE IN BOOKSTORES OR CALL 800.956.7739